HF
1755
.T29

Terrill, Tom E.

The tariff, po-
litics, and Ameri-
can foreign policy,
1874-1901

DATE DUE

DEC 0 3 '91			
3 '92			
NOV 17 '92			
MAY 1 6 2003			

The Tariff, Politics, and American Foreign Policy 1874-1901

The Tariff, Politics, and American Foreign Policy 1874-1901

Tom E. Terrill

CONTRIBUTIONS IN AMERICAN HISTORY
NUMBER 31

GREENWOOD PRESS
WESTPORT, CONNECTICUT ● LONDON, ENGLAND

Library of Congress Cataloging in Publication Data

Terrill, Tom E
    The tariff, politics, and American foreign policy.

    (Contributions in American history, no. 31)
    Bibliography: p.
    1. Tariff—United States—History. 2. United
States—Commercial policy—History. 3. United
States—Foreign economic relations—History.
I. Title.
HF1755.T29   382.7'0973   72-140921
ISBN 0-8371-5819-2

Library of Congress Catalog Card Number: 72-140921
ISBN: 0-8371-5819-2

First published in 1973

Greenwood Press, a division of Williamhouse-Regency Inc.
51 Riverside Avenue, Westport, Connecticut 06880

Manufactured in the United States of America

To Sarah

Contents

Acknowledgments

"If anyone says 'tariff' to you," an exasperated editor advised in 1894, "shoot him on the spot." Such advice probably would strike a responsive note among those who had a part in the development of this book. My family and friends have had remarkable patience. Or they were poor shots.

Initially, William Appleman Williams guided this study. His ability to ask good questions and to grasp strengths and weaknesses in an argument amazed me. His intolerance for inferior work provided a needed incentive. Walter LaFeber generously lent timely encouragement and his knowledge of source materials. Stanley I. Kutler performed his editorial task with skill and grace. Herbert R. Ferleger's gift of his research files gave me important leads. On several occasions Robert D. Ochs gave support in ways available only to departmental chairmen. Brian O'Farrell, Richard A. Rempel, Thomas J. McCormick, J. Rogers Hollingsworth, Robert M. Weir, and Edward P. Crapol read parts or all of the manuscript. Crapol helpfully shared his research notes, and he and Weir gave attentive, critical hearings.

Libraries and librarians, of course, had a crucial part. I am especially indebted to the staff of the Library of Congress, the Wisconsin State Historical Society library staff, in particular Miss Ruth Davis and Miss Josephine L. Harper, and to the University of South Carolina library staff, especially Mrs. Mary E. Goolsby and Mrs. Davy-Jo Ridge. Mrs. Lila Lisle Green of the Iowa State Department of History and Archives graciously answered requests for aid. The librarians of Hiram College also lent valuable assistance.

Important financial support came from the Committee on Research and Productive Scholarship of the University of South Carolina, the American Philosophical Society, and the University of Wisconsin. Mrs. Diane Bell, Mrs. Florence Keister, Mrs. Linda Henderson, and Mrs. Frances Blanton typed the manuscript.

As for the debt to Sarah, my wife—the dedication speaks for itself.

The Tariff, Politics, and American Foreign Policy 1874-1901

Introduction

The Gilded Age is most popularly characterized as the period in U.S. history when the great bridges and factories of America were built, and, depending on the point of view, the heroes (or villains) of the age were Andrew Carnegie and John D. Rockefeller who developed (or destroyed) the environment. Politicians stood by passively or actively connived. They orated endlessly and meaninglessly, often about the tariff.

The politicians and the politics of the Gilded Age deserve better. So does the tariff, one of the dominant issues of national politics in that era. Historians have treated the tariff much as one treats an unwanted member of the family. The sheer volume of tariff rhetoric spewed forth by politicians and editors has been sufficient to discourage historians. Yet the tariff rhetoric and legislation of the late nineteenth century contain critical insights into the era. Both help make sense of the political context, and show how American political leaders dealt with that political context and with some of the ramifications of the dynamic economic growth of the Gilded Age. Both clarify the political leaders' basic assump-

3

tions, many of which antedated the Civil War and prevailed into the twentieth century. Finally, they document the emergence in the 1880s of a crucial consensus about America's place in the world and the need to expand foreign trade.

The prime focus of this study is on the professional political leaders of the two major parties. The Gilded Age presented those leaders with an unusual problem they urgently needed to resolve. Not until after World War II did the two major parties vie for power on as equal terms as they did from 1874 to 1896. Six presidential elections brought six different White House occupants and four changes of party. The Republicans usually controlled the Senate, the Democrats the House.

Actually, this balance of power was part of a larger political era that Walter Dean Burnham has called the "Civil War system." The Republicans dominated most of the northern states and the Democrats, the southern and border states. This system evolved from the emergence of new voting patterns and the collapse of the Democratic party in the 1850s, the sectional struggle, and the Civil War. The vicissitudes of the Civil War and Reconstruction gave the Republicans a commanding position from 1860 to 1874. Democratic fortunes improved dramatically in the 1874 congressional election, when for the first time since 1859 the Democrats gained control of the House of Representatives.[1] For some twenty years after 1874, the Democrats enjoyed political parity with the Republicans nationally. The table on page 5—giving aggregate figures based on results in presidential, congressional, and gubernatorial elections from 1874 to 1892—illustrates that equipoise lasted until the 1890s.[2]

The timing of the 1870's revival of the Democratic party can be largely explained by contemporary events. When the depression struck in 1873, the Republicans were in power. At the same time southern Republicanism declined with the rapid fall of Reconstruction governments in the South in the early 1870s. But these events do not explain the strength of the residual support for the Democrats in the North or the configuration of that northern support. Partisan loyalties of northern voters followed ethnic and religious,

| Office | Percentages Held by | | |
	Democrats	Republicans	Other
Presidential electors	50.6	48.3	1.1
U.S. Senators	47.5	51.0	1.5
U.S. Representatives	55.9	41.7	2.4
Governors	48.9	49.5	1.6

not economic, lines. In the northern states most Catholics supported the Democratic party. The converse was true of Protestants, although Protestants who had migrated to the Midwest from southern and border regions usually voted for Democrats. Irish-Americans usually voted for Democrats. But as contemporary politicians knew, they could be very unpredictable.[3] For instance, part of the political magnetism of the Republican James G. Blaine came from his popularity with the Irish. Americans of English origins favored the GOP, while German-Americans split their vote. These patterns of political allegiance and voting behavior reflected the political realignment that had occurred in the 1850s and that remained remarkably durable into the 1890s. Not until the wrenching depression of the 1890s did this change. This political configuration was a prime reason for the political equipoise of the Gilded Age.[4]

Urban political machines reinforced these alignments. The machines and their bosses helped immigrants to adjust to American life. Votes and partisan loyalty (to the machine, not necessarily the national parties) were exchanged for aid in adapting to a new environment and, in many cases, for an opportunity to begin the ascent on the social ladder. By the late nineteenth century, Irish and east European immigrants, especially the Irish who came in the 1840s and 1850s, began to make their presence felt politically in northern cities like New York, Philadelphia, Chicago, and Boston. These groups usually supported Democrats and were a significant factor in the successes the Democrats enjoyed in New York, Illinois, and even in Massachusetts where in 1890 a Democrat won the gubernatorial race for the first time since the Civil War.

Voter turnout figures from the Gilded Age indicate that elections involved far more than the political fate of candidates. Not even in the 1930s did the United States have as high a voter turnout as it did in the late nineteenth century.[5] Undoubtedly, the abundance of job opportunities through patronage and the thorough local and state level organizations that could be found in many areas helped account for the heavy turnout. The closeness of electoral results put a premium upon getting out the vote. Before civil service reforms cut deeply into patronage, politicians could offer a large number of concrete rewards to those responsible for mobilizing the vote. Money for votes and a partisan press aided these efforts. So did the fact that elections provided a major source of mass entertainment for Americans in the Gilded Age. Yet, neither patronage, organization, a partisan press, money for votes, nor even the dearth of entertainment explain the very large votes of this era. Certainly, they cannot account for the ethnic, religious configuration of the vote.

On election day, the voter could affirm who he was and where he stood in the community. In the America of the Gilded Age that community was his neighborhood, his village, or his farm and the adjoining farms. There his national origin and religious affiliation assumed great importance. The ethnic, religious configuration of voting behavior and the heavy voter turnouts of the Gilded Age confirm these assertions. Establishing who you were and where you stood in the community suited the crucial needs of a people undergoing the rapid economic growth and dislocation that occurred during this period. No wonder people clung to ethnic and religious affiliations and party loyalties, or that they found solace in sentimental novels and in Horatio Alger stories that promised success and were couched in familiar symbols.[6] The traditional, simplistic theology of the popular missionary to the cities, Dwight L. Moody ("God is love. . . . But if you do not accept His love, . . . do not think that God will receive harlots and drunkards, and sinners, unredeemed, into His Kingdom."[7]), offered assurance and security. So did the Victorian Gothic architecture of the era: built solidly, furnished in solid oak, designed to demonstrate its owner's solidity in a fluctuating world, and styled after a bygone and supposedly more solid time.

From 1873 to 1900 the American economy burgeoned. Yet during thirteen of those twenty-seven years the economy fell into serious recession or severe depression. Cities, railroads, industries, and the population, including the massive emigration of European peasants, grew rapidly. An industrial, urban society displaced rural and village America. Promising farms turned to dust. New groups, in particular the professionals and the managers, forged to the front.[8] The Jeffersonian ideal of a land of family farms and the presumed homogeneity of Jacksonian America disappeared, not to be recaptured by the single tax scheme of Henry George or any other attempt to preserve the small landholder as the keystone of the Republic. Americans enjoyed significant increases in real personal income during the Gilded Age, but many believed that disparities in wealth and income had widened alarmingly. The labor strife that seemed to be symptomatic of a discordant society caused grave concern. In 1877, a strike disrupted much of the national railway system. Labor stoppages increased markedly in the mid-1880s and 1890s,[9] highlighted by the Haymarket Massacre of 1886 and the Pullman strike of 1894.

The tariff issue fitted the times and the needs of the national political leaders neatly. Both parties used the tariff as a device to appeal for social harmony and to break the national political equipoise. The choice of the tariff also fitted the history and tendencies of the parties. Historically, the Republicans had supported high tariffs, though they were not unanimous on the issue. Conversely, the Democrats had favored low tariffs; yet in the 1870s and 1880s they had a strong protectionist faction. The strength of that faction explains why the Democrats did not take a firm stance on tariff reduction until 1887. Ideological tendencies were important, too. Republican leaders favored an activist government and policies that encouraged industrialization. The opposite tendencies of Democratic leaders reflected their states' rights tradition and the greater preponderance of agrarian elements in that party.

But the Democrats cannot be dismissed as merely antiquated agrarians whose imagination was paralyzed by their admiration for Thomas Jefferson. A significant number of important Democratic leaders favored industrialization and were keenly attuned to many of its consequences. Both parties also contained elements of all the principal economic groups: manufacturers, merchants, bankers, lawyers, farmers, and workingmen. Very probably, most manufacturers were Republicans. But, as will be seen later, Republican politicians were hardly the cat's-paw of an omnipotent, monolithic Big Business. Both parties had their share of the "respectable" people. Not until the major political realignment that occurred during the depression of the 1890s and the 1896 presidential election did this arrangement change significantly.

The decision of the political leaders to focus on the tariff also came about through a reductionist process of logic. Their selection had to fall within the range of legitimate political alternatives in the Gilded Age. Also, a number of nineteenth-century issues had been resolved, though some only temporarily. The Homestead Act of 1862 had fulfilled the promise, and something of the reality, of cheap land for family farms. The expansion of slavery had been ended, and by the mid-1870s American blacks were being abandoned with little more than a paper ballot for protection against southern whites and the boll weevil. A system of national banks had been created through the Banking Act of 1863. A federally subsidized transcontinental railway had been built. The questions of how to fund the federal debt incurred as a result of the Civil War, on what basis to stabilize the currency in circulation, and on what monetary standard would the United States base its currency were settled by January 1875. But monetary issues remained unsettled, as indicated in the Greenbacker campaign of the late 1870s and the struggles with the silverites.[10] The modest concessions to silverites in the 1878 Bland-Allison Act and the 1890 Sherman Silver Purchase Act failed to appease the silverites. In 1893 the Democrats virtually destroyed their party in the successful but bitter fight to repeal the latter act. Three years later silverites, led by William Jennings Bryan, captured the Democracy and forced a climatic conflict in the 1896 presidential election. Until then neither party had made currency or the monetary standard a national issue because it was too divisive.

Other issues were either too divisive, or they lacked the broad appeal necessary for breaking the political equipoise. The Republicans found that Civil War and Reconstruction memories had lost their voter appeal. Romanticizing the bloody conflict was left to another generation. Land reform, railway regulation, or immigration restriction were inadequate for building wider coalitions. The temperance issue had to be avoided, for it disrupted the ethnic, religious followings of both parties. For similar reasons any real or apparent assault upon parochial schools had to be avoided. Failure to handle the temperance or school issues adroitly could bring a swift response from the electorate. In 1889 and 1890, when Iowa Republicans supported temperance legislation and when Illinois and Wisconsin Republicans passed laws that appeared to harm parochial schools and the Germanic culture of some of their constituents, they suffered unprecedented defeats at the polls.[11] Finally, attention could easily be focused on the tariff. It was the largest revenue source for the overflowing national treasury.

Neither a sober citizenry, the sanctity of public schools, or Americanizing the populace was the prime object of the professional politicians. The object was to get elected; issues were secondary. In this the politicians followed the established patterns of major parties in American history. The national political leaders of the Gilded Age focused on the tariff, an issue that was less divisive than other issues and one that potentially had a broad voter appeal. Politicians shaped their tariff rhetoric and legislation to achieve their primary object. Such a position allowed each party to identify itself clearly with a national issue that might give them the national cohesion necessary to counter the centrifugal forces of sectionalism, ethnic and religious differences, dynamic but uneven economic change, or perspectives limited by the boundaries of a neighborhood or small community.[12]

Political leaders claimed that their tariff policy (either protection or tariff reduction) promised national cohesion because their policy offered something to Americans in every economic and geographical category. The social harmony that supposedly once existed could be restored. Moreover, their programs, they assured the voters, would sustain and increase the rate of American economic growth while minimizing economic dislocation. In other words they promised prosperity and social harmony without fundamentally altering the nation politically or economically. Such hopes accorded with the prevalent assumption that in spite of current distress man was marching boldly and rapidly along the road to progress, that the "people of plenty" were by definition happy people. There would be no need to change private enterprise capitalism (which was presumed to be of divine origin or to derive from the laws of nature). Along with the viability of the tariff issue, such assumptions indicate that despite the serious discord present in late nineteenth-century America, there were no irresolvable ideological divisions among the majority of Americans.

The march toward prosperity did not halt at the national borders. Both protectionists and tariff reductionists* assumed this, although partisan rhetoric obscured the emergence of this crucial consensus. Increasingly concerned about the boom-bust pattern that dislocated the American economy in the Gilded Age, prominent Republicans and Democrats concluded by the mid-1880s that the United States urgently needed to expand its foreign trade in order to have continuous prosperity. Like many of their contemporaries, these politicians assumed that such economic expansion was natural. Important leaders and factions in both parties then linked the tariff to an enlarged foreign market. In 1882, the Democrats presented an elaborate defense of tariff reduction as a means to obtain trade

---

* A word about the use of the term tariff reductionist: Supporters of low tariffs have often been inaccurately referred to as tariff reformers. Lower tariffs were not necessarily in the interest of the majority of Americans, nor were those supporting lower tariffs necessarily motivated by a serious concern for the majority's welfare. Not all those who favored lower import duties could be called free traders. Hence, the term tariff reductionist—hopefully a neutral and more accurate term.

expansion, and the Republicans soon countered with protection and reciprocal trade agreements. Thus, before these ideas were more generally accepted in the 1890s, important political leaders (and some agrarian groups) had developed a rationale for American trade expansion.[13]

Tariff rhetoric could take flight to distant shores and return again to meet the latest political development or to respond to the outrage of the discontented. Tariff rhetoric had a remarkably pliable quality—no doubt one of its most useful assets for the politicians. In accordance with their primary object of winning elections, the politicians shaped their tariff arguments to build greater coalitions. Hence, the Republicans assured the workingmen, whose vote was very unpredictable,[14] that high tariffs protected them against imported products produced by European "pauper labor." In an effort to reverse their losses in the South, Republican leaders promised that their protectionist policy would facilitate southern industrialization. Democrats also skillfully handled tariff rhetoric to suit the occasion. In the 1880s, they intensified their claims that lower tariffs would ease the flow of agricultural exports. This argument, aimed at the midwestern and Plains states' farmers (most of whom were Republicans), coincided with the farmers' acute awareness of their dependence on large foreign sales. Economic events aided the Democrats. After 1886 as profits and hopes declined and disappeared, these farmers became increasingly cool toward the Republicans. When in 1889 and 1890 the Republican-controlled legislatures in Illinois and Wisconsin passed legislation believed to be harmful to parochial schools and the Germanic culture of many in those states, the Democrats there told the voters that it was to be expected. Just as Republicans had interfered in the "natural" workings of the economy with their high tariffs, now they had interfered in the personal lives of citizens.[15] Hopefully, all that tariff talk might smother the silverites. The national Democratic party, led by Grover Cleveland, had little else to offer.

Probably no one will ever know if the vast outpourings of speeches, editorials, pamphlets, and books on the tariff swayed a large number of voters or had a significant impact on the outcome of elections. Groups that shared an economic interest, such as midwestern wool growers, did have strong feelings about the tariff, at least about some duties. But how these groups acted on election day cannot be known, for available research materials and methods are inadequate.[16] Political leaders, however, believed that their tariff positions had wide voter appeal and were critical factors in many elections. Tariff stands may have been the decisive factor for a small percentage of voters—no small matter considering the closeness of many elections in these years.

Other fundamental assumptions of the political leaders are evident in the tariff rhetoric and legislation of the Gilded Age. Protectionists accepted the premise of the "American system": it was legitimate for the government to encourage economic growth by subsidizing private enterprise.[17] So much for the laissez-faire myth. Tariff reductionists perceptively asserted that through such intervention the government disproportionately rewarded its more advantaged constituents. Such policy issues, along with other issues raised during the tariff debates, did not end with the close of the nineteenth century: they remain critical issues today.

The tariff reached a climax as an issue in the 1890s. Republicans emerged from the political upheaval of that decade as the dominant party, and protection became the fixed policy. William McKinley, whose name was synonymous with protection, went to the White House in 1897. That same year a Republican-controlled Congress passed the Dingley Tariff Act. Not until 1909 did Congress enact a new general tariff, the Payne-Aldrich Tariff Act. Once freed from his preoccupation with the Spanish-American War and its ramifications, McKinley turned his attention to the expansion of American overseas trade through reciprocal trade agreements. But in 1901 an assassin's bullet ended his efforts.

That McKinley was so committed to reciprocity was fundamentally ironic. He had long defended protection as the way to make America economically independent. Yet, like many of his contemporaries, he came to define American prosperity in terms of foreign economic expansion and an interdependent world economy. Such a course was probably unavoidable, but that does not cancel the irony. Its tragic result was that in the twentieth century the United States would often pursue a foreign economic and political policy that led her to oppose revolutionary change in the world.

The ideological, political, and foreign policy facets of the tariff issue in the latter part of the nineteenth century in the United States provide the focal points of this study. Some facets of the tariff, such as interest groups and their relationship to Congress, the presidents, or specific tariff measures, receive little attention. In addition, no attempt has been made to determine the actual economic impact of the tariff on the American economy in the late nineteenth century. Rather, the focus is on the political and economic effects that American leaders *thought* the tariff had.

1

Politicians
in Search of an Issue

In 1874, the Republicans lost badly in the congressional elections.[1]
For some twenty years after that, the GOP and the Democrats
fought on virtually equal terms. To assure its own hegemony each
party sought broader bases of voter support. In 1874, probably
few political leaders could have expressed or would have thought
to express their problems of long-term political survival so concisely. Yet, in the 1870s, they began to turn to the tariff as the
primary issue in their efforts to construct wider, more stable coalitions. Eventually, the tariff became one of the central political
issues for the remainder of the nineteenth century. At the same
time, American foreign policy began to take shape along lines
which later became familiar. Only later, in the 1880s, did that
policy became closely tied to tariff policies and debates.

Things of a more immediate nature, however, confronted
American political leaders in 1874. Reconstruction was coming
to its dreary, inglorious conclusion. The scars of the recent bitter

congressional fight over specie resumption remained. Most important, the economy had entered the second year of a severe depression.

The central event of the 1870s was the depression of 1873-1877. More serious than the depression of the 1880s and less than that of the 1890s, the economic decline of the 1870s was one of the longest in American history. Most observers declared that the cause was merely the result of the dislocations of the Civil War. Adjustment was their only prescription; nothing fundamentally ailed the American economy.[2] Rising industrial production despite falling prices, frenetic, if sporadic, railroad construction, and steady migration of settlers to a supposedly inviting West buttressed their assumptions. While the wholesale price index fell from 135 in 1870 to 110 in 1876 and to 90 in 1879 and rose only to 100 in 1880, the industrial index climbed from 25 to 42, steel production multiplied 18 times, and railroad mileage increased from 60,301 to 93,262 miles in the ten years after 1870. For every four Americans in 1870, there were five in 1880. Most of these lived on farms, whose acreage had expanded from 407,723,000 to 536,064,000 acres in spite or because of declining agricultural prices.[3] Clearly, such growth softened the shock of the 1870s' depression and the 1877 strike.

Fortunately, other events in the decade provided distractions to cushion the effects of the depression. In addition to the depression, the end of Reconstruction, and the Chicago Fire of 1872, there were the 1877 railway strike, the scandals of the Grant administration and of Boss Tweed and Tammany Hall, the Reverend Mr. Henry Ward Beecher's trial for adultery, the Granger movement, the extended battle over Greenbacks and the resumption of specie payments, the centennial celebration in 1876 including the Centennial Exposition of that year, and the presidential election which did not end until the Compromise of 1877.

The frontier also may have comforted Americans against economic distress. The lure of the West and the self-employed farmer persisted. At least enough attraction remained to prompt the House to hold hearings in 1878 on a bill to subsidize the settlement of unemployed urbanites on western public lands,[4] but interest in the measure lapsed as the economy recovered in 1878 and 1879. Much more importantly, rising exports of western wheat were major factors in the economic recovery. The significance of the increase was noted by American leaders, including President Rutherford B. Hayes. Their views found cogent expression in a *Bradstreet's* editorial written several years after the depression of the 1870s and when the nation was in the midst of yet another economic crisis. The editor saw an urgent need "to develop and emphasize the importance of the agriculture of the United States in relation to its export trade." Agriculture had been "much the most important . . . in maintaining the commercial prosperity of the United States during the recent past." If the United States was to maintain its "commercial prosperity," it had to find markets abroad "for its surplus agricultural products."[5]

This analysis approximated one that David A. Wells, the influential popular economist, had made by the early 1870s. The former special commissioner of revenue believed that the American economy was fundamentally awry. Wells concluded that the economy had a basic flaw that would prevent sustained growth and would lead to frequent, very serious economic malfunctions. He did, however, assume that periodic economic fluctuations were natural, and he allowed for the presumed salutary effects of the recovery from the dislocations of the Civil War and of the resumption of specie payments. Claiming he saw a fundamental shift in the economy in the 1870s, Wells asserted that agricultural and industrial production would always considerably exceed domestic demand. With his imagination restricted by classical economics, the solutions he proposed depended primarily on a larger foreign trade. Wells consistently linked his diagnosis and prescription to tariff policy. High tariffs, he said, restricted the American marketplace; low tariffs would broaden that market by easing the exchange of goods and products and by reducing the cost of manufacturing through cheaper imported raw materials.[6] Eventually, the Democratic party, in part influenced by Wells, made similar connections in its appeal for a low tariff policy.

In the 1870s, some congressmen concurred with Wells, although their analyses lacked his sophistication and usually stressed agricultural and commercial, not industrial, interests. Representatives Henry R. Harris (Georgia) and Horatio G. Burchard (Illinois) were exceptions. Using examples drawn from cotton farming and textiles, Harris argued that the tariff had overstimulated American agriculture and industry. Thus, agricultural and industrial production exceeded consumption and was "a dead weight" on the whole economy. Larger foreign markets would ease the burden of the surplus and, by keeping more Americans employed, would lead to an increased home demand, which had slackened during the depression.[7]

Republican Congressman Burchard did not hesitate to attack the tariff policies of his own party which he linked to the depression of the 1870s. His remarks are of particular interest because the tariff debates of the 1880s and 1890s had a very similar emphasis. American industry, the Illinois congressman told the House in 1878, already had the advantages of "the superior intelligence of our labor, the inventive genius and managing tact and skill of our people in applying and using labor-saving machinery and less expensive processes." "Give American manufacturers raw materials free . . . [and] they can place their goods upon our [own] markets at prices that will defy foreign competition and chase the goods of their foreign rivals across the Atlantic." Ignoring the rise of European protectionism in the 1870s, Burchard deprecated a policy of "exclusion and restrictions." The "nation is of age. It and its industries are no longer infants." It "is our interest to follow in the pathway of other nations," and Congress should make the "future policy" of the United States "wider commerce [and] foreign markets for her manufacturers as well as her surplus agricultural products."[8]

Most exhortations of the trade expansionists, however, in the 1870s were not related to tariff reduction. In 1874 Senator William Windom of Minnesota, who had a direct economic interest in the vital industries (wheat production and processing) of his home state, chaired a special Senate committee that investigated how to improve rivers in the Mississippi Valley. The committee delivered a report which defended such improvements, especially for the Mississippi River, as providing a competitive alternative to the railroads and a means of easier access to vital foreign markets for agricultural products. Windom reiterated the ideas of the committee in 1878, when he told the Senate that only waterways could provide the cheaper freight rates which would allow American wheat to compete effectively for the European market, particularly the British market. *"The farmers of the interior of this continent are therefore wholly dependent upon the water routes for a sale of their surplus grain."*[9]

Windom also defended his proposals as legitimate governmental subsidization of private enterprise and as a public works method for providing employment to relieve a depression. While he favored economy in government spending, he decried "the bastard thing which demagogues" misleadingly called economical government. "True economy," he asserted in the spirit of Hamiltonianism and Republicanism, "consists in the development of resources, and the increase of wealth by honest, judicious, and careful application of means to that end; but the 'economy' of the demagogue is the mere pretense of saving money in order to gain votes."[10]

Windom's subsidization ideas found support both in and out of Congress. In 1878 Senator Samuel B. Maxey of Texas, for example, called for shipping subsidies and improving Galveston harbor so that wheat and flour could be more easily moved from Texas, Iowa, Kansas, and Nebraska to foreign markets. In particular, he wanted to exchange flour for Brazilian coffee, and he was willing to back reciprocity treaties with Latin America.[11] Maxey's focus southward reflected not only his Texas background but also an assumption that Latin America promised great opportunities for American economic expansion. Many American leaders shared this assumption and acted upon it in the late nineteenth century.

Prompted, in part, by the depression, Congress took several significant steps southward and westward in the 1870s. In spite of its dismal experiences with federal shipping subsidies, the Senate in 1878 approved a subsidy supported by the Hayes Administration for a New York-Rio de Janiero line operated by John Roach, Philadelphia shipbuilder. But the House defeated the measure by a vote of 159-89.[12] The 1876 goodwill tour of Brazilian Emperor Dom Pedro to the United States and to the Centennial Exposition, and the small but established American flour trade with Brazil, may have combined with reactions to the 1870s' depression to overcome the misgivings of the Senate, but not those of the House. Eventually, however, Congress did appropriate money in the 1880s to improve Galveston harbor. When the work was completed in 1891, President Benjamin Harrison went to Galveston to laud it as a major port for an expanded United States-Latin American trade.[13]

Congress was less hesitant with respect to Hawaii where the United States presumably had vital interests. Both the House and the Senate accepted the 1875 Hawaiian reciprocity treaty that had been negotiated by the Grant Administration.[14] The House debate on the treaty demonstrated considerable sophistication among American leaders. The report of the House Ways and Means Committee showed that the proponents (the majority) and the opponents of the agreement shared assumptions about America's position and interests in the Pacific and about Hawaii's relationship to these interests. "The Pacific Ocean," asserted Congressman Fernando Wood for the majority, "is an American ocean, destined to hold a far higher place in the future of the world than the Atlantic. It is the future great highway between ourselves and the hundreds of millions of Asiatics who look to us for commerce, civilization, and Christianity."[15]

The minority accepted this assessment, even adding an Hawaiian corollary to the Monroe Doctrine. They joined the majority in stating that no European power "should be permitted to obtain the sovereignty of the islands, or to gain such influence in them as to menace our security." A European-controlled Hawaiian naval base could, they believed, threaten the Pacific coast of the United States. But they expressed much greater concern about the security of American shipping in the Pacific and

open sea lanes to the Far East. The economic development of
Hawaii by Americans and the chances of expanded trade between
the United States and Hawaii mildly interested them, but visions
of Hawaii as a "foot-hold" for American commerce in the Pacific
aroused great interest.[16]

Thus, the Ways and Means Committee agreed on strategy, but
not on tactics. Fearing a possible British takeover because Hawaii
could not "maintain [its] autonomy," the majority argued for
acceptance of the reciprocity treaty, a move which they presumed
would be the first step toward the annexation of Hawaii by the
United States. The minority shared this presumption, but they
strongly opposed annexation unless Hawaii was clearly threatened
by a European power. Carefully coached by David Wells, Congressman William R. Morrison developed a perceptive, sophisticated case against establishing a formal American empire in the
Hawaiian Islands: such an empire would require expensive occupa-
tion forces and civil services, the United States would be obliged
to defend an outpost two thousand miles from its borders, and
certain interest groups would gain from the treaty arrangements
at the expense of others. Morrison dismissed the British threat.
The United States, he claimed, held Canada as a hostage against
British incursions upon the vital interests of the United States.
Rather, Morrison urged an approach that had the overtones of the
later Open Door policy. American commercial interests could be
best served by the "neutrality of the commercial nations" with
respect to Hawaii, by keeping Pearl Harbor open to the "Pacific
commerce of the world," and by "an open but firm diplomacy,
which claims only equal but no exclusive rights."[17] Despite their
perception of the nature and consequences of formal empires, however, the minority jeopardized their own position because they
accepted the grand design in the Pacific that the majority
advocated. Both the majority and the minority were expansionists.
To categorize them as imperialists versus anti-imperialists is to
obscure their vital, shared assumptions.

The Hayes Administration, inaugurated in 1877, followed this
expansionist impulse. It sponsored the 1878 treaty with Samoa,

and it reiterated the American determination to dominate any isthmian canal constructed across Central America. The administration also investigated the possibilities of reciprocal trade agreements with Latin America and with France; supported those interested in reviving the American commercial marine; instructed American diplomats to search vigorously for new markets for exports; and took steps to make the Consular Service more responsive to the needs of American foreign commerce. These efforts reflected the beliefs of Secretary of State William M. Evarts and President Hayes. In his first annual message, the president told Congress: "The long commercial depression in the United States has directed attention to the subject of the possible increase of our foreign trade and the methods for its development, not only with Europe but with other countries, and especially with the states and sovereignties of the Western Hemisphere."[18]

Although no implicit first step toward annexation was consciously intended when it ratified the Samoan treaty, the American government vaguely agreed to defend the islands if they were confronted by foreign encroachment. In return, the United States received a non-exclusive right to construct a fueling station at Pago Pago and to enjoy the advantages of a free port there.[19] Scarcely conceived of as a beachhead for expanded trade with the Samoans, this excellent harbor was envisioned as a valuable port for an enlarged Pacific trade. Earlier Americans had had dreams of American merchant keels dominating the Pacific, and now the Congress of the 1870s was at least partially prepared to turn those dreams into reality.

President Hayes and Congress also bestirred themselves when a French company, headed by Ferdinand de Lesseps, proposed to build a canal across what is now Panama. President Hayes was blunt. The "policy of this country is a canal under American control." Then he elaborated:

The United States cannot consent to the surrender of its control to any European power or to any combination of European powers. If existing treaties between the United States and other nations or if the rights of sovereignty or property of other nations stand in the way of this policy—a contingency which is not apprehended—suitable steps should be taken by just and liberal negotiations to promote and establish the American policy.

Congress emphatically concurred.[20] When the de Lesseps' project failed dismally, the United States was able to defer acting upon these sentiments. But the American government remained highly sensitive about a Central American isthmian canal.

Encouraged by the State Department, numerous congressional proposals for reciprocal trade agreements with Latin America, as well as Canada and France, were made in the 1870s. Mexico received special attention. Clearly aware that investors would shy away from unstable foreign markets, dictator Porfirio Diaz worked to give Mexico political stability and attempted to pacify the northern parts of Mexico which bordered on the United States. Congress applauded Diaz and hailed American investments in Mexican mines, ranches, and especially, railroads that linked Mexico and the United States.[21]

The interest in reciprocity was intense enough to cause serious concern to rigid protectionists who viewed it as a threat to the tariff wall. William D. Kelley attacked reciprocal agreements as an infringement of the congressional right to establish tax policies. Joseph Wharton sought reassurance from the State Department, which was then engaged in attempts (that ultimately proved abortive) to negotiate reciprocity agreements with Latin America in the late 1870s. Secretary of State Evarts assured him that the department would not risk the protected position of American industry. Evarts even suggested that the United States really wanted to extend her tariff wall around Latin America in the form of a customs union similar to the German *zollverein*.[22] This American scheme was not a new idea (it had been espoused by Stephen Douglas in the 1850s)[23], but in the 1800s the scheme received greater attention and support.

The oratory and actions of the politicians reflected a widely shared interest in exports in the United States. For instance, in 1875 the National Grange Executive Committee began working with the Mississippi Valley Trading Company in an effort to expand agricultural exports and to redirect transportation routes used for farm exports. They hoped to divert these shipments from northeastern to southern ports. This diversion, they hoped, would also enhance their political and economic position vis-à-vis the Northeast.[24] In 1877 the Wisconsin legislature petitioned Congress for a railroad land grant for northern Wisconsin to obtain "a more direct transit to the Atlantic seaboard and European ports."[25] The national convention of the Grange, meeting that same year, asked Congress to "deepen and improve the channels of the Gulf ports, and establish a more perfect system of postal and reciprocal treaties of commerce with the Republic of Mexico and the Central and South American States."[26]

At the instigation of the Pittsburgh chamber of commerce, the Export Trade Convention met in Washington in February 1878. When it issued its call for the convention, the Pittsburgh chamber declared it "essential to the business prosperity of this country that an enlarged export market should be secured for our over productions [*sic*] of manufactured goods." The actions of the convention delegates reflected the tone of the invitation. They passed resolutions urging the removal of "any discriminating charges against the exports" of the United States, construction of a modern merchant fleet, with federal subsidies if necessary, and the creation of a department of commerce in the federal government. Several delegates then presented the resolutions to President Hayes, whose response was friendly but vague. With the exception of shipping subsidies, whose value it questioned, the National Board of Trade concurred.[27] An eminent business journal, *Bradstreet's*, cogently expressed these ideas when it editorialized in 1879: "The rapid rate at which we are increasing our productions demands that we should lay a firm hold on every new outlet that is within our grasp." Earlier, the influential *Iron Age* had argued a similar case.[28]

No group in the 1870s, however, pressed for trade expansion

as persistently and intensely as did groups in the 1880s and, especially, the 1890s. No crisis mentality developed nor did adequate political or economic institutions exist in the 1870s to make economic expansion urgent national business. By its nature, the depression of the 1870s lacked the immediate impact of subsequent slumps. Moreover, the nature of Washington politics hindered the development of an integrated trade expansion program. Underorganized, divided by partisanship, and preoccupied with local concerns, the politicos wandered more than they led. No American leader—certainly not President Hayes—had the leverage of a Bismarck who led Germany to a new tariff policy in 1879.[29] James Blaine as secretary of state finally achieved something of an integrated expansionist strategy in the early 1890s. But Blaine had the advantages of a better organized Congress, his considerable manipulative skills, a growing interest in exports among several industrial groups, and mounting agrarian discontent loudly vocalized by the Populists. In the 1870s business and other interest groups were hardly better organized than Congress. Large-scale corporate structures were only just being built, and there were few coordinated, skilled lobbies. By the 1890s much of this had changed.

Thus, rhetoric exceeded action. But the principal ideas of trade expansion in the 1880s and 1890s—reciprocity, a *zollverein* with Latin America, and tariff reduction, along with American control of a Central American isthmian canal, construction of a modern merchant fleet, and drawbacks (refunds) on customs duties—were articulated in the 1870s. Pointing toward the future, President Hayes told Congress in his last annual message (1880) that the "prosperous energies of our domestic industries and their immense production of the subjects of foreign commerce invite, and even require, an active development of the wishes and interests of our people in that direction."[30]

Other patterns emerged from the political rhetoric of the 1870s. Increasingly, the two parties divided sharply over the tariff—a reflection of the changed political realities of the decade. The flush times of Republicanism in 1872, when President Grant won reelection by a landslide margin, were gone when the Democrats scored major gains in the 1874 congressional election. American voters had used a congressional election to express their disenchantment with the Grand Old Party, which was severely burdened by a major depression, a fourteen-year reign as the dominant party, serious intraparty feuds, the inept and corrupt Grant Administration, and an abortive attempt to reconstruct the defeated Confederacy. The jerry-built Republican coalition, erected in the crisis of sectionalism and civil war, collapsed under the weight of these burdens.

The collapse ushered in a political era, unusual in the United States, in which no major party had national dominance. In the twenty years following the administration of Ulysses S. Grant, the White House had six different occupants—one as the result of an assassination. Four times in those twenty years a new president also meant a change of party. Generally, the Democrats controlled the House, and the Republicans the Senate. Hardly had one election ended before preparations for the next began. Thus politicians had to find the basis for broader coalitions. Republican and Democratic leaders eventually chose the tariff as a major means of becoming the dominant party.

The Republicans seized the initiative in seeking political dominance. Protectionism, which had been politically expedient in the 1860s,[31] now became party dogma. Although after 1874 the GOP politicos hardly pursued the most direct route to protectionism, they increasingly identified themselves with high tariffs. By the election of 1880 protectionism virtually equalled Republicanism. The Democrats later assumed an opposite position. The Republican choice was both natural and forced upon them. The GOP, which included champions of industrialization and the spiritual heirs of Hamilton and Clay among its strongest factions, naturally took up protectionism. More likely than Democrats to represent industrial areas, freer from Civil War ghosts, and less concerned about the niceties of states' rights and constitutional liberalism, the Grand Old Party could respond more positively to the needs of industry. By the mid-1870s time and events had tarnished the Republicans' Civil War image as the party of national unity and loyalty, and voters had wearied of the GOP's use of "bloody shirt" rhetoric to appeal to patriotism and Civil War memories. The party then shifted to stress the second of its basic elements—the promotion of industrial America and its corollary, protectionism. During the election of 1880, as during that of 1860, political necessity led the Republicans to reaffirm the truth of the protectionist gospel.

Political necessity had forced the Republicans to embrace protectionism in 1860. GOP leaders had understood that appeals to defend the Union were not enough to insure victory at the polls. They had also sensed that their abolitionist image disquieted northern voters whose distaste for the South did not include an eagerness to free black men. Thus, in their national convention of 1860, the Republicans combined their Free Soil tradition with rising industrial ambitions. Over the protests of some, they adopted a high tariff plank in their platform to attract urgently needed electoral votes from the industrial East, particularly Pennsylvania. In so doing party strategists demonstrated a clear awareness that railroads had linked the farms of the Midwest with eastern industry and the eastern laborer. During the 1860s the Republican Congress enacted legislation that reflected these relatively new economic patterns and that was based upon an anticipated northern coalition of farmers, laborers, and manufacturers. The passage of the Morrill Tariff, the Homestead Act, and the Morrill Act for land grants by agricultural and technical colleges logically followed. Confronted by a resurgent Democratic party and an unhappy electorate in the 1870s, the Republicans fell back upon their 1860 strategy to construct an even stronger coalition that was more suited for the intensive political warfare of the late nineteenth century.

Accordingly, the GOP aimed its tariff rhetoric at a broad spectrum of group interests. High tariffs, workingmen were told, assured high wages in American industry and shielded American labor against the products of "pauper" European labor. Similarly, security against European industry within the national market was promised to the industrialists. And, according to the "home market thesis," increased industrialization and urbanization assured farmers an expanded domestic market and less dependence upon export sales. Such appeals might lack logical consistency (for example, high wages might deter industrialization), but if these groups found protectionism appealing, the Republicans could develop a larger political following and achieve national political ascendancy. Protectionism, moreover, had a nationalistic appeal that was anti-European, especially anti-British, in orientation. Thus, protectionism allowed the Republican party to reaffirm its claims as the party of national unity.

Political events before the 1874 election had indicated a growing GOP commitment to high tariffs. Protectionism had begun to be equated with party loyalty in the 1860s and the early 1870s. The politically shrewd had fallen into line. Deviants had received summary treatment. Thus, the Republican Congress in 1870 dispensed with the services of David Wells, then United States special commissioner of revenue, after he deserted protectionism for lower tariffs. In 1865 Wells had so distinguished himself as one of the three-member United States Revenue Commission that Congress created a position for him, commissioning him to produce a thorough study of the whole American economy. As special commissioner, he openly attacked high tariffs in his 1868 and 1869 *Reports* and advocated gradual reduction. Congressional favor evaporated. The protectionist phalanx led by Representative William Kelley of Pennsylvania terminated the special commissioner's office amid unfounded charges that Wells had been plied with British money.[32] Wells later returned to plague the Republicans as a major spokesman for tariff reduction and advisor to the low tariff forces of the Democratic party.

The 1872 presidential election decimated tariff reductionist forces within the Republican party. These forces had joined other anti-Grant people to form the Liberal Republican party, an ephemeral coalition of political opportunists, protectionists and tariff reductionists, and idealists concerned about corruption, federal tax policies, civil service reform, and the inabilities of President Grant. To the chagrin of the low tariff contingent at the Cincinnati convention, the product of this admixture was the presidental nomination of Horace Greeley, an adamant protectionist. The dispirited Democratic party failed to nominate a candidate of its own and endorsed Greeley.[33] Thus, the party with a strong southern wing and with many southern supporters tied itself to the editor of the *New York Tribune*, a man with an abolitionist history.

The volatile editor was no match for a war hero president in full command of the Republican party machinery. Astute Republican politicians with low tariff leanings, like the ambitious James A. Garfield, dutifully supported Grant. Grant crushed Greeley in the election, and the liberal Republican movement was shattered. Some Liberal Republicans drifted back into the regular party, others went into political retirement, and a few, like David Wells, joined the Democratic party. "The Democracy," Garfield told his closest political ally prematurely, "are stunned, perhaps killed by their last defeat, and there seems to be no limit to the power of the dominant party."[34]

Not only did the Democrats survive the 1872 election disaster, but as the 1874 election results clearly demonstrated they showed remarkable recuperative powers. A reinvigorated Democratic party challenged the Republicans for national leadership on virtually equal terms during the next two decades. Moreover, even before the 1880s, when tariff reduction became part of the Democratic party orthodoxy, the Republicans discovered that the tariff issue had not conveniently died with the demise of the Liberal Republicans.

Democratic leaders in the House grasped tariff reduction in 1875-1876 as a way to embarrass the Republicans and to enhance the stature of their party in preparation for the 1876 presidential election. While pleading with David Wells to help the Ways and Means Committee revise the tariff, Speaker Michael C. Kerr acknowledged his political motives: "It will be vain for them (the Democrats on the committee) this session to attempt very radical and sweeping changes, but they must give an intelligent earnest [*sic*] of true tariff reform, and put the country in possession of our general purpose, and put upon the (Republican) Senate the duty of rejection or concurrence.''[35] Encouraged by a group of New York importers and fortified by their generous contributions for his personal expenses, Wells went to Washington and helped draft the Morrison Bill of 1876. Wells and the sponsor of the bill, Congressman William R. Morrison of Illinois, thus began a decade of collaboration on tariff reduction. During this time Wells gained increasing influence among the Democrats.[36]

Their initial labors, however, were thwarted by the House, and the Republican Senate did not have to face "the duty of rejection or concurrence." House Republicans joined with protectionist Democrats, led by the formidable Samuel J. Randall of Pennsylvania, to defeat the measure.[37] Apparently not persuaded by Speaker Kerr's political tactics, many congressional Democrats preferred to avoid a firm stand on tariff reduction that would divide the party and possibly alienate voters in the pivotal Northeast. This consideration and other grave concerns—the Greenback issue and the fear that a depressed economy would be further disrupted by tariff revision—carried great weight in an election year. Congressman Morrison, however, stubbornly viewed his 1876 defeat as merely a temporary setback in a moral crusade on behalf of the common man, especially the farmer. Somewhat ineptly but persistently, he battled for tariff reduction until he left Congress in 1886.

In 1878 the Democrats introduced another bill to lower import duties. The Wood Bill (named for Fernando Wood, the New York Democrat and chairman of the House Ways and Means Committee) was a more determined attempt to alter the tariff than the Morrison Bill, and was taken more seriously by its opponents. Workingmen in Pennsylvania demonstrated "spontaneously" against the bill. The American Iron and Steel Association, the National Association of Wool Manufacturers, and the National Wool Growers' Association lobbied against the measure as an attack upon the sacred principles of protectionism. A number of businessmen sent adverse petitions. The majority of these expressed concern that tariff revision might disturb an economy only just recovering from a depression, or fears that revenue losses might endanger resumption of specie payments.[38]

Two of the Republicans' strongest protectionist champions, William Kelley and William McKinley, engaged Wood and his House supporters. But the tempest subsided abruptly. After a brief debate, the House eliminated the enacting clause of the Wood Bill by a 134-121 vote. Significantly, twenty-three Democrats opposed the measure, and only four Republicans favored it.[39] The cool reception to the bill in the House must have been anticipated. Certainly, the well-organized protectionist Democrats had had no change of heart since the defeat of the Morrison Bill, and the House must have known that even if it passed the Wood Bill neither the Republican Senate nor the White House would approve it. Economic distress, agrarian discontent, and economic principles may have motivated the Democratic tariff reductionists, but political motives were surely present. The bill allowed the reductionists to jibe the GOP and portray the Republicans as the party of high taxes—but the reductionists did so at the risk of party harmony.

Tariff agitation did not die with the Morrison and Wood Bills. In 1879 and again in 1880, congressmen filled the hopper with tariff bills. There were fifty such proposals by February 1880, most of which, except for another general reduction bill by Morrison, dealt only with individual commodities. All this labor brought two results. Quinine was put on the free list in 1879,[40] and the likelihood increased that Congress would develop legislation to create a commission to study the tariff and make recommendations for revision of customs duties schedules.

The immediate stimulus for such a commission in 1879 was a bill sponsored by Senator William W. Eaton, a Democrat and protectionist from Connecticut. He claimed he wanted a more objective study of the tariff than could be provided by Congress.[41] Actually, more mundane considerations motivated him. He and William H. Barnum, protectionist manufacturer and Connecticut Democratic boss, no doubt wanted to prevent tariff reduction or aligning the Democrats with lower tariffs. Making an objective study, seeking the counsel of wise businessmen, and getting politics out of business were clichés that gave the tariff commission idea a veneer of respectability. Many supporters, perhaps including Eaton, believed that the commission promised a more rational approach to sound tariff legislation, and that tariff revision was necessary. Whatever Eaton's motives may have been, he was undoubtedly aware that many in Congress and business thought that the administration of the tariff and the duty schedules needed revision. Not only had the tariffs been written in haste in the 1860s and early 1870s, but the rapid industrial change of the United States since then had made some of the tariff provisions obsolete. Some in Congress also sincerely wanted expert advice on the increasingly complex tariff matter. The proposed commission promised this advice. Moreover, businessmen who frantically sought predictability and stability in postbellum America welcomed the commission as a preventive against annual tariff agitation in Congress.[42]

Political considerations, of course, were not neglected. Simply to block attempts to revise the tariff was politically unwise on the eve of the 1880 presidential election. The commission scheme gave the appearance of doing something, while not doing anything or, at least, postponing action. Some Democrats attacked the measure as a ruse to avoid tariff reduction, and the Republicans lent credence to the Democrats' charge. Even two of the leading rigid protectionists, Joseph Wharton and Daniel J. Morrell, presidents respectively of two of the strongest protectionist pressure groups, the Industrial League and the Iron and Steel Association, backed the Eaton Bill.[43] Although the Eaton Bill was not passed in 1879, the Republicans were willing to accept the ideas of the bill. But since they were then becoming increasingly committed to protectionism, it is doubtful that they intended the commission to be either objective or non-political. Later, when the 1882 report of the Tariff Commission, created by the Republican Congress elected in 1880, raised a storm, the Republicans discovered the dangers of political expediency.

Beginning in the 1870s certain axioms evolved in the course of tariff history in the late nineteenth century. The first axiom was that tariff revision formed a counterpart to the currency issue. Frequently, when debate on the currency issue was at its peak, tariff revision was temporarily set aside. Until the partial resolution of the money controversy in the 1870s, the tariff took a subordinate place. This was repeated in the 1893 gold standard struggle that was fought before the Wilson-Gorman Tariff Act was passed in 1894. That struggle undermined the efforts of the second Cleveland Administration to reduce import duties significantly. The battle of the standards again eclipsed the tariff as the central issue in the 1896 presidential election. Conversely, when the money issue was dormant, the tariff issue assumed new life, as in the 1880s and in 1890. But occasionally, as will be seen, they were actively related.

Second, the political uses of the tariff were infinite. Both major parties employed the tariff issue to unify an increasingly discordant society and to construct broader political coalitions to break the political equipoise. Following the Republican lead, but taking a different course on the tariff, the Democrats attempted to appeal to a larger political following by stressing lower tariffs. New England manufacturers, to cite one example, developed an increasing interest in cheaper raw materials and foreign markets after 1880. As this interest heightened, they turned their attention to the Democratic party's low tariff arguments. This may have helped the Democrats make some significant inroads in such Republican strongholds as Massachusetts in the late 1880s and early 1890s. But when the national Democratic party veered away from the control of the Cleveland Democrats and from the single gold standard, waves of panic in New England destroyed these inroads.[44]

By emphasizing the tariff issue, both parties tried to avoid more divisive or less attractive issues such as currency, civil service reform, and temperance. This emphasis also gave the parties some basis for distinguishing themselves from each other and for mobilizing the party faithful. Tariff positions became the litmus paper test for political affiliation, while intraparty divisions over the tariff were forgotten for the sake of party unity. Astute politicians, like William McKinley and Nelson P. Aldrich, built their political careers on their knowledge of and positions on the tariff.

The tariff divisions between the Republicans and the Democrats, however, were more than sham distinctions. Government subsidization of economic development and the evolution of an industrial America generally harmonized with the Republican frame of mind. Limited government and a grave suspicion of an industrialized, urbanized economy better suited the Jeffersonian mentality of the Democracy. These inclinations reflected basic political realities, too. Republican congressmen and leaders were more likely to be from industrial areas than their Democratic counterparts.

Not all Democrats viewed the world with agrarian, commercial, and anti-industrial biases. A significant minority of Democrats, perhaps best represented by men like Congressman Abram S. Hewitt of New York, an industrialist, were keenly sensitive to the needs of industry.[45] These Democrats added a very important dimension to the arguments for lower taxes on imports. They linked their tariff position to the changing industrial needs, real or imagined, of an American economy which eventually developed a keen interest in an expanded market beyond American shores. In the process, the Democrats established clear ties between the tariff issue and American foreign policy. Thus, well before the overproduction mania of the 1890s, major Democratic leaders called for a tariff policy that they claimed was more in keeping with the requirements of an industrial nation. They were hardly mossbacks of political economy. Eventually, the Republicans, supposedly the more forward-looking party, followed the Democratic lead, and accepted these connections between tariffs and diplomacy.

In the 1870s most Democratic congressmen made a more simplistic connection between foreign trade expansion and the tariff. Tariff barriers interfered with the international flow of products upon which many Americans were dependent. This interference affected the commodity-producing farmer most adversely because, as the Democrats correctly asserted, he had to export a high percentage of his production. Manufactured goods also allegedly suffered, but manufacturers exported much less than the farmers and did not yet have an urgent need for expanded foreign trade.[46]

The Democrats reduced their trade theories to one misleading quantitative theory: since foreign trade is essentially barter, countries tend to trade in similar amounts.[47] Thus, it followed that the United States as the largest consumer of Brazilian coffee exported a large quantity of goods and products to Brazil. Wrong. The United States had a very unfavorable balance of trade with Brazil. Britain brought most of the Brazilian coffee to the United States as part of its Britain-Latin America-United States-Britain triangular trade. And, in the process, the shipping profits also flowed back to Liverpool and London. Still, the Democrats were right in a generalized sense: tariffs often did, and do, impede the flow of world trade.

Later, as in 1882, the Democrats developed a more sophisticated formula which connected tariff reduction, rapid technological change, and recurrent depressions. David Wells played a major role in devising this formula, as did Abram Hewitt and Edward Atkinson, Massachusetts businessman and political gadfly.[48] The persistence of the Democrats and the pressures of the economic slump of the 1880s forced the Republicans to respond with something more positive than the "home market" cant. As early as 1878, William McKinley suggested that the American manufacturer was not yet prepared to compete aggressively for foreign markets but would one day.[49] Many Republicans concluded in the 1880s that that day had come. In 1878, however, the Democrats' attempts to connect tariff reduction with foreign trade were oversimplified, and despite the brief, intense interest in trade expansion in the 1870s, their efforts to connect tariff reduction with foreign trade lacked broad appeal.

The tariff involved more than broad frames of mind or approaches to American diplomacy. Senator John Sherman, veteran of Ohio's political quicksands, observed axiomatically in 1895 that the tariff was also a district issue. Congressmen and senators abided by a prime dictum of political survival: please the constituents and the pressure groups in your district even at the expense of consistency. Hence, Delaware's Senator Thomas Bayard, a leading low tariff advocate and darling of the Mugwumps and free traders, dutifully kept a watchful eye out for Du Pont interests.[50] Tariff reductionists in Kentucky attacked the tariff as government largesse dispensed to industrial plutocrats at the expense of common man. Yet, the same men often adopted a very protective attitude toward the bourbon and tobacco industries.

A final axiom about tariff revision was that tariffs were easier to modify than overhaul. Formidable obstacles prevented any attempt to alter import duty schedules significantly. Once raised, the tariff wall was virtually indestructible. As more and increasingly sophisticated machinery was developed to produce a wider range of products, the tariff schedules became longer and longer, a fact demonstrating the difficulties of defining goods and materials as to kind and quality. Importers and manufacturers told a series of congressional committees that the systems of import duties often failed to keep pace with industrial trends. Given the rate of industrial change in the late nineteenth century, this was not surprising. In any event, strategically placed congressmen and senators had a field day as brokers for their own and others' constituents. Sharp partisan divisions further complicated the process.

The tariff combatants comprised large numbers of lobbyists, publicists, editors, biased government statisticians, and citizens eager to exert influence in Washington. While lobbying lacked the sophistication found in the twentieth century, the National Wool Growers' Association, the National Association of Wool Manufacturers, the Industrial League, and the American Iron and Steel Association were hardly amateurs. Individual manufacturers, such as iron magnate Joseph Wharton and sugar refiner Henry O. Havemeyer, found willing allies in Congress. The *New York Evening Post* and the *Louisville Courier-Journal* were two of the outstanding journals for the low tariffs: others, like the *New York Tribune* and the *Philadelphia Press*, were adamant defenders of protectionism. Both sides had their philosophers: Henry C. Carey for protectionism and David Wells, as apostate from the Carey School, for the low tariff. Each side also had its advocates in academe. Convinced that the young were being misled by free traders like William Graham Sumner of Yale and Arthur L. Perry of Williams, Joseph Wharton endowed a business school at the University of Pennsylvania as a protectionist citadel. Delegates of concerned farmers and worried representatives of organized labor made frequent appearances in Washington. Another participant in the tariff controversy was the ubiquitous Edward Atkinson, once a Boston textile company executive and later an important insurance entrepreneur. An incredibly prolific writer of letters, articles, and books, Atkinson tried to guide Congress toward a moderate program of tariff reduction. He worked tirelessly to bridge the gap between militant tariff reductionists and nervous New England industrialists who inclined toward lower import duties but who feared Democratic low tariff forces who might go too far. "Other issues come and go," a weary contemporary journalist sighed, "but the tariff issue goes on forever."[51]

During the 1870s, the basic outlines for trade expansionism and tariff agitation in the 1880s were laid. The new president, James Garfield, took office in 1881 and immediately selected James Blaine as his secretary of state. More than domestic political considerations were involved. Blaine's appointment indicated the Garfield Administration's determination to pursue the foreign trade policies of the 1870s more vigorously. The Republican commitment to an "impartial" tariff commission and the growing power of the tariff reductionists among the Democrats clearly showed that the tariff was a live issue. The events of the 1870s, strongly stimulated by a depression and the results of the 1874 election, were therefore portents of the future.

2

Division and Consensus: Tariff Policies and Market Expansion

As the 1880s succeeded the 1870s, the emerging partisan divisions over the tariff became much clearer. The 1880 presidential election, the foreign policy of the James Garfield Administration, the creation and labors of the Tariff Commission of 1882, the Mongrel Tariff of 1883, and the reciprocal trade agreements program of the Chester A. Arthur Administration provided ample opportunities for a clarification of these divisions. Coincidentally, the tariff reductionist forces in the Democratic party found needed direction and cohesion, particularly from Congressman John G. Carlisle of Kentucky. A collision course was set, although the collision did not occur until President Grover Cleveland's annual message in 1887.

The outline of this course appeared clearly in the 1880 presidential campaign, when unlike the presidential election of 1876, the tariff became a major national issue. Initially, however, neither the candidates nor the parties took a sharply focused tariff position in 1880. James Garfield, who emerged as a compromise dark horse nominee from a deadlocked Republican convention, was a recent convert to strong protectionism. In his letter of acceptance, he, like the Republican party platform, emphasized the "bloody shirt" and only alluded to protectionism as a defense of the wages of American labor.[1] Following the dictates of tradition, he avoided public appearances during the campaign and waited for the office to seek him. But behind the scenes Garfield assumed the major responsibility for campaign organization. He carefully instructed Republican speakers in early August to limit their oratory to "the solid South and to the business interests of the country." In late September after the Republicans had lost Maine for the first time in years, Garfield clarified these vague terms for John Sherman. Garfield wanted Republican campaigners to emphasize "the Tariff question which so deeply affects the interests of the manufacturers and laborers. The argument of the 'Solid South' is well enough in [sic] its way and might not so be overlooked[,] but we should also press those questions which lie close to the homes and interests of our people."[2]

Garfield's instructions reflected both a timely political response to public attitudes and a seemingly profound shift of priorities. How the Republican leadership came to its decision to emphasize the tariff issue is unclear. The continuing collapse of southern Republicanism and the Democratic victories in the 1878 congressional elections had indicated that President Hayes' policies had failed to stem the revival of the Democratic party. Yet, even if it had wanted to, the Republican leadership lacked the necessary public support to return to the aggressive tactics of the early Reconstruction years. Senator John A. Logan told John Sherman in July 1879 that the "bloody shirt can no longer win hegemony for the Republican party. We must find and use issues which are more applicable to the needs of the voters." James Blaine, an intuitive political genius, may have been the catalyst in 1880. Rebounding from the surprise defeat of the GOP in Maine, Blaine reportedly told the Republican National Committee in mid-September "to fold up the bloody shirt and lay it away. [Something Blaine actually never did.] It's of no use to us. You want to shift the main issue to protection. Those foolish five words of the Democratic platform, 'A tariff for revenue only,' give you the chance.''[3]

Whatever its origins, the shift in campaign emphases obviously indicated that Republican leaders believed voters were more concerned about their own welfare than that of black men or about other Civil War and Reconstruction issues. Accordingly, Republicans stressed their commitment to protective tariffs and altered the focus of their attack on the Democrats. The GOP tried to link tariff reduction to economic distress and the Democrats to tariff reduction; voters then would equate a Democratic victory with economic distress. Such a strategy became standard with the Republicans in 1880 and remained so for many years.

The shift of priorities by the GOP was only superficially profound. Despite its idealistic elements, the party had always been primarily the party of the Union. To most Republicans concern for American blacks was secondary. Thus, the Republican emphasis on protectionism merely represented a different way to continue its nationalistic claim to be the party of the Union. Through its appeal to a ''harmony of interests,'' protectionism promised to achieve a union through economic means rather than military and political methods, and to perpetuate that union through an era of disruptive change.

Republicans on the stump followed Garfield's instructions, and they received unwitting assistance from the Democrats. As they had done in their 1876 platform, the Democrats took a clearly ambiguous position in favor of ''a tariff for revenue only.''[4] But unlike what they had done in the 1876 campaign, the Republicans attacked the apparently safe Democratic tariff plank. In view of the mounting surplus in the Treasury, the Republicans could claim that the Democrats favored sharply decreased import duties. Blaine, the GOP's most able stump speaker, waved the ''bloody shirt'' liberally, praised his party for defending the financial morality and stability of the country, and wrung his hands over the prospects of the laborer left defenseless by Democratic free tradism.[5] The Republicans persisted in their tariff assault until the election ended.

Yet, probably no particular national issues figured decisively in the 1880 result. The ethnic and religious affiliations of the voters explain more about the result. Moreover, Garfield, as the nominee of the party in power, had the advantages of glowing prosperity following the depression of the 1870s and the generally respectable record of the Hayes Administration. In addition, Garfield was aided by northern fears of unreconstructed Democrats, a stronger party organization than the Democrats had, and his personal assets: poor boy-made-good, Civil War veteran, extensive political experience, and a pious image. Though touched by several of the major political scandals of the 1870s, he had miraculously escaped with hardly a blemish.[6] General Winfield Scott Hancock, the aged warrior the Democrats had nominated, had an heroic posture, but he failed to stir passionate loyalty; his nomination appeared to be the desperate ploy of the victory-starved Democrats, who would have chosen Samuel Tilden if he had been well. But many GOP politicians thought their high tariff posture had won the election. Such an assumption buttressed their protectionist inclinations.

The 1880 election results meant that for the first time since 1874, the Republicans controlled the White House, the House, and with the support of Senator William Mahone, a Readjuster from Virginia, the Senate by one vote. (The Democrats, however, recaptured the House two years later in the 1882 congressional elections.)[7] Also, the new Garfield Administration was not encumbered, as its predecessors had been, by Reconstruction, an economic slump, or the stigma and bitterness which had been left by the 1876 presidential election and the Compromise of 1877. The administration was increasingly willing to leave the South to its own devices, and could therefore think about charting new courses under the leadership of a relatively young president with extensive political experience.[8] Garfield's assassination in 1881 aborted these bright prospects, but not before some of the course had been plotted.

After his election, Garfield acted decisively to assert party leadership over the Republican bosses, like Roscoe Conkling, and to unify and bring distinction to the GOP by developing a bold foreign policy. Though at times suspicious of Blaine's mercurial personality and his propensity to indulge in political manipulations, Garfield respected his secretary of state and gave him wide latitude in foreign policy. Both men thought in expansive terms about the American economy, and both sensed the domestic political uses of diplomacy. "I believe with you as President, and I in your full confidence," Blaine told Garfield when he accepted the State Department appointment, "I could do much to build up the party as the result of a strong and wise policy."[9] In his inaugural, President Garfield told his audience: "Our manufactures are rapidly making us industrially independent, and are opening to capital and labor new and profitable fields of employment. Their steady and healthy growth should still be matured. Our facilities for transportation should be promoted by the continued improvement of our harbors and great interior waterways and by the increase of our tonnage on the ocean." Moreover, he continued, the "development of the world's commerce has led to an urgent demand for shortening the great sea voyage around Cape Horn by constructing ship canals or railways across the isthmus which unites the continents." This "subject," he assured his listeners, "is one which will immediately engage the attention of the Government with a view to a thorough protection to American interests."[10]

By May 1881 Garfield and Blaine resolved to develop a strategy for overseas economic expansion based on reciprocal trade agreements, an approach that had been revived in the 1870s. When as a part of the Republican intraparty power struggle Roscoe Conkling dramatically resigned from the Senate that same month, the Garfield Administration was confident that its expansionist foreign policy had sufficient popular appeal to heal the party rift. "Do not be alarmed," the president assured an anxious A. L. Conger, a leading figure in Republican circles. "We shall develop a policy [reciprocity agreements with Latin America] during my administration which will make the Republican party more popular with the

people of the country than it has been since the day of its birth.''
In June, Secretary of State Blaine initiated discussions for a reciprocal trade treaty between Mexico and the United States.[11]

Blaine acted with a confidence based on the security of strong
presidential support and his awareness that the president and he
agreed on the future direction of American foreign policy. He was
one of the first major Republican party leaders to argue that the
American economy must have greater markets beyond its borders
in order to maintain prosperity. As early as 1878, Blaine became
a strong supporter for a federal subsidy to John Roach's proposed
New York-Rio de Janeiro shipping line.[12] In a sense, Blaine was
a heretic because he publicly and repeatedly rejected the protectionist idea of a self-sufficient economy surrounded by the walls
of the protective tariff. In doing so, he placed himself dangerously
close to the arch-enemy, the Democrats and the tariff reductionists,
many of whom increasingly attacked protective tariffs as a barrier
to an urgently needed expansion of American exports.

Unlike many Republicans, Blaine accepted this Democratic
challenge. He integrated pragmatic politics and his personal ambitions with reciprocity treaties, nationalism, an analysis of the needs
of the American economy, a concern for maintaining the gold
standard by achieving a better balance-of-payments position, and
the traditional areas of the national interests of the United States
(Latin America and the Pacific). He visualized the United States as
the dominant world power of the future. Yet, his visions had less
sweeping aspects. Blaine had strong presidential aspirations; he
wanted to insure Republican dominance; and he hoped to imitate
one of his heroes, William H. Seward, who as secretary of state
had developed a grand design for foreign economic expansion.

As a nationalist, Blaine welcomed an American challenge to
the economic hegemony of England. At the same time, he was
keenly aware that Anglophobia appealed to Irish-Americans, who
traditionally voted Democratic. On the stump he twisted the British
Lion's tail with special skill. He also wanted to reduce American
gold exports which, he thought, aggravated American monetary
problems and resulted from the British-controlled triangular trade.

A reciprocal trade program offered an opportunity to amend the tariff without significantly altering its protectionist nature, and if it became a successful and popular program, it might help unify the deeply divided GOP and aid him politically. Finally, protectionism combined with reciprocity, he believed, would appeal to the industrial dreams of the South. He hoped this would lure the South into Republican ranks, something other policies had failed to achieve.[13]

Blaine's expansionism ran counter to the ideas held by other prominent Republicans in the 1880s. William McKinley, Joseph G. Cannon, Thomas B. Reed, Justin S. Morrill, and William Kelley, among others, contended either that the American economy was virtually self-sufficient or that the need for foreign markets would develop only in the distant future. Reed concisely and brilliantly expressed the self-sufficiency argument on the floor of Congress in February 1883. "The great sophism of Bastiat is that he always argues about what would be the effect if the city of Paris were cut off from the rest of the world. It would be . . . preposterous to ask Paris to supply all its own wants. . . . But when he and his imitators persist in reasoning by analogy from Paris to a great country like this with everything in it, he and they palm off worse sophisms than he ever pretended to expose."[14]

That most of the opposition to Blaine came from Congress, including Republicans, was symptomatic of late nineteenth-century American politics. From the 1870s into the twentieth century, the various administrations in office were consistently in advance of most congressmen and senators on foreign policy, and they found persistent, strong congressional opposition to their foreign policies and actions. Even when intraparty feuds were quieted, an interparty battle was a real possibility because seldom did either party control Congress and the presidency at the same time. More than merely the result of political and personal power struggles, however, the conflict reflected the "separation of powers" and other institutional realities. The executive branch had the initiative in foreign policy. Despite its organizational weaknesses, the executive was smaller and better organized and, hence, freer to innovate than Congress. Moreover, since the executive served a broader constituency than Congress, its thinking was usually more national in scope. The presidents of the Gilded Age, however, often lacked the political leverage to lead Congress.

But such congressional opposition obscured the extent to which late nineteenth-century American leaders shared fundamental assumptions about American foreign policy. They might disagree about an individual reciprocity treaty, such as the treaty with Hawaii, but not about fundamentals such as the preeminent interests of the United States in Hawaii. The financing of the Central American isthmian canal was debatable, but who should control that canal was beyond doubt. Opinion differed over the value of reciprocity treaties with Latin America, but not over the rightfulness of American predominance in the Western Hemisphere.

Blaine simply ignored congressional opposition and used the relative freedom of the State Department to initiate programs built upon his analysis and assumptions. He made a significant beginning in realizing his grand strategy, especially in light of the tragic disruptions of the Garfield Administration and the early days of the succeeding Arthur Administration. Patronage problems and Garfield's conflict with Conkling, in which Blaine was deeply involved, preoccupied the president and the secretary of state. The murderous assault on Garfield in July 1881, then his prolonged lingering, and finally his death in September left national politics and decision-making in limbo for nearly three months. Arthur slowly assumed the reigns of power. Though he was not likely to retain Blaine, one of his bitterest foes, in the State Department, he did not announce his replacement by Frederick T. Frelinghuysen until late November.

Blaine moved precipitously as secretary of state, especially after he realized that President Arthur would soon remove him. While he remained passive toward Europe, he focused his attention on the Pacific, particularly Hawaii, and Latin America. Worried about the possibility of increased British interest in Hawaii, he warned the Hawaiian government that the United States firmly opposed any attempt by "any of the great European powers" to encroach upon Hawaiian independence. (He also applied this "no transfer" principle to Cuba.) He disingenuously claimed that American policy was not "selfishly intrusive." The United States adhered to its traditional policy of circumscribing the alternatives open to the Hawaiians. Thus, the United States limited the independence it was supposedly defending. "Hawaii," he explained, "although, much farther from the Californian coast than is Cuba from the Floridian Peninsula, holds in the western sea much the same position as Cuba in the Atlantic. It is the key to the maritime dominion of the Pacific States, as Cuba is the key to Gulf trade . . . under no circumstances can the United States permit any change in the territorial control of either which would cut it adrift from the American system, whereto they both indispensably belong." Nor could Hawaii "be joined to the Asiatic system." If Hawaii lost its independence, it had to join "the American system, to which they belong by the operation of natural laws, and must belong by the operation of political necessity."[15]

Latin America received Blaine's greatest attention and effort. Overly eager to breathe new life into the Monroe Doctrine, to reduce British power in Latin America, and to act as peacemaker, Blaine tried unsuccessfully to exert American influence in the War of the Pacific. He initiated correspondence with Great Britain either to revise or to abrogate the Clayton-Bulwer Treaty, so that he could help secure American dominance over any isthmian canal in Central America. He also opened negotiations with Mexico for a reciprocity treaty. With similar motives and with an eye to furthering American economic expansion in Latin America, Blaine proposed that a Pan-American conference meet in 1882. Though innovative, his proposal lacked precise planning.[16]

A grave concern underlay Blaine's foreign policy. John Roach, who, with Blaine's support, had tried to get a government subsidy for a steamship line between the United States and Brazil in 1879, told of an 1881 conversation between the secretary and himself. According to the Philadelphia shipbuilder, the secretary had asked: "will not the time come when the great question will be in this country, overproduction?" Then, he continued, the "inventive genius of our people [will produce] . . . such wonderful results that unless some outlet is made for our surplus manufacturing industries, which are growing more rapidly than the products of the soil, will not the question come up, 'What are we going to do with this surplus?' '' Blaine added, ''Well, that has been my South American policy; we can expect to sell our agricultural products in those countries of Europe where they cannot raise their own bread, but can we dispose of any of our manufactured articles there, where they have cheaper labor and can more than supply their own wants?'' The ''only policy'' Blaine foresaw was a drive ''to build up trade in manufactured articles with those countries where we have the advantage in distance.'' Blaine assumed, according to Roach, that Latin America would want American surplus production for the ''next hundred years'' and ''that those countries are so peculiarly situated that we should have the advantage . . . in trading with them.''[17]

When Garfield's successor, Chester Arthur, reversed himself and withdrew his support from the Pan-American meeting, Blaine was furious. He attacked the president and his new secretary of state in a scathing public letter in which he revealed something of contemporary politics and his personal involvement in and the motives of his foreign policy. Arthur's reversal and Blaine's response became part of the continuing Stalwart-Half-Breed factional dispute in the Republican party and foreshadowed the struggle for the 1884 GOP presidential nomination. Blaine charged that Arthur's action was an expression of timidity in foreign affairs, an affront to the Latin American nations which had been invited, and an effort to smear him politically. ''The foreign policy of President Garfield's Administration,'' he claimed, ''had two principal objects in view: first, to bring about peace and prevent future wars in North and South America; second, to cultivate such friendly, commercial relations with all American countries as would lead to a large increase in the export trade of the United States, by supplying those fabrics in which we are abundantly able to compete with the manufacturing nations of Europe.''[18]

At first glance, Blaine appears to have subordinated commerce to peace, and some observers have argued that economic expansion was a secondary theme in Blaine's thought.[19] But he made his position very explicit. "To obtain the second object the first must be accomplished . . . . Peace is essential to commerce, is the very life of honest trade."[20] He understood that stable, long-term trade expansion required international peace, and that a disharmonious Latin America provided the European powers, especially Great Britain, with an opportunity and an excuse to intervene in Latin America. He wanted the United States to create peaceful relationships in the Western Hemisphere and to dominate the hemisphere. He was not subordinating the central and vital role of economic expansion. Thus, Blaine defended a Pan-American· conference as preferable to a continuous pattern of "friendly intervention here and there." He argued further that the conference might have created an era of peace during which the "Southern continent, whose wealth . . . might have received new life."[21]

Blaine had always been keenly aware of economic interests. Throughout his political career he had a big business and industrial orientation. He frequently invested in railroads and manufacturing. During and after Reconstruction, he was more interested in the industrial growth of the United States than in transforming the South. He moved amiably and easily among a wide circle of intimates that included Andrew Carnegie, W. R. Grace, the shipping magnate and an early investor in Latin America, and Stephen B. Elkins, who along with his father-in-law, Henry G. Davis, strongly influenced the politics and controlled much of the wealth of West Virginia. His closest and most deeply devoted political supporters were W. W. Phelps, the wealthy New Jersey entrepreneur, and Whitelaw Reid, the millionaire owner and editor of the *New York Tribune*. The American delegation Blaine selected for the Pan-American conference (1889-1890) was dominated numerically by industrialists and big businessmen.[22]

Blaine completed his scornful attack upon the Arthur Administration with a glance to the past and with visions of a commercial empire. The United States had at one time been interested in a foreign policy "especially designed to extend our influence in the Western Hemisphere" and in the "expansion of our commercial dominion." Lamentably, American commerce and interest in Latin America had declined. Then, taking direct aim at President Arthur and the new Secretary of State Frelinghuysen, Blaine concluded: "If the commercial empire that legitimately belongs to us is to be ours, we must not lie idle and witness its transfer to others."[23] Blaine's public airing of his grievances let him vent his bitter disappointment at the abrupt end of his State Department career and his bold plans.[24] But, in doing so, he further divided the already factionalized Republican party, he undoubtedly brought the Democrats considerable pleasure, and he placed himself very close to the thinking of the tariff reductionists.

In his attack upon the Arthur Administration, Blaine clearly sensed his proximity to the reductionists, and he tried to hedge against this. He agreed with the reductionists that the United States had an unfavorable balance of trade with Latin America. But he rejected the reductionist argument that the protective tariff so increased American production costs that American manufacturers could not compete with Europe in the world market. The United States, he claimed, could already compete with Europe in Latin America in a number of articles. These included "coarse cottons and cotton prints, boots and shoes, agricultural implements of all kinds, some household items, carriages, ordinary kerosenes, white lead, lead pipe" and other lead articles. Then, he struck at a particular weakness in the trade expansion analysis of the reductionists. "In the trade relations of the world it does not follow that mere ability to produce as cheaply as another nation insures a division of an established market, or indeed, any participation in it." Rather, he contended, it was necessary to have special trade relations.[25] Implicitly, the Pan-American conference would have created these special relations.

In spite of his hedging, Blaine's basic assumptions closely paralleled those of David A. Wells, the major American spokesman for free trade, a widely read economist, and a central figure in the Democratic party's alteration of its approach to connect tariff reduction with increasing American export trade. Both argued that American prosperity depended on the immediate expansion of American exports, and both emphasized industrial exports.

Wells might have charged Blaine with timidity. Where Blaine believed only a limited number of American industries were competitive with European industries in the early 1880s, Wells claimed that with cheaper raw materials most American manufacturers could arrive at that point immediately.

Whether they acknowledged it or not, Blaine, an ardent protectionist, and Wells and his Democratic friends who favored low tariffs had arrived at a common ground; only tactics—how to achieve the desired end—separated them. This tactical dispute became an intregal part in the tariff debates of the 1880s and 1890s. Few people at the time sensed this consensus or the sophistication of Blaine's and Wells' ideas.

Few people, then or since, grasped the complexities and subtleties of Blaine's political and diplomatic views. He relished bold moves; he occasionally amused himself, while he sat in his study, by spinning a world globe, and contemplating the destiny of that sphere.[26] He was generally hailed as the father of modern Pan-Americanism and was roundly condemned for his rash intrusion in the War of the Pacific, his extreme partisanship, his political "wheeling and dealing," and his clever, but often demagogic, oratory. He still defies clear analysis. Blaine embodied the Gilded Age—its glittering visions and its vulgarities, its strange blend of shrewdness, chicanery, and startling candor. Like his era, he attracted and repelled his contemporaries and subsequent generations. On five occasions he was seriously considered for the presidency. He received the nomination only once; then he lost the election. "The most popular and unpopular man in America," newspaperman Charles E. Russell wrote of him, "the most beloved and the most hated."[27] Undoubtedly, such sentiments and the usually cautious nature of his successor, Frelinghuysen, influenced Arthur when he decided to retreat from the proposed Pan-American conference.

The president abruptly changed course at the urging of Frelinghuysen and J. C. Bancroft Davis, who was Frelinghuysen's choice as assistant secretary of state. When Frelinghuysen entered the State Department, he asked Davis to review Blaine's Latin American policies thoroughly. Davis, who was already gravely suspicious of Blaine, advised an immediate retreat. He feared that Blaine's aggressive foreign policy, especially American intervention in the War of the Pacific, would lead to military involvement for the United States. Davis told his close friend, former Secretary of State Hamilton Fish, that "I convinced myself . . . that we were on the highway to war." Frelinghuysen agreed and persuaded the president. Domestic political considerations (anti-Blaine feelings) no doubt helped the Arthur Administration convince itself. So six weeks after he sent the invitations to the conference, the president awkwardly reversed himself. He claimed that Central and South America were too unsettled by border disputes and the War of the Pacific for a conference to meet in 1882; he said he had acted too hastily.[28] But Blaine's defeat was only temporary and superficial. Later, when it reverted to an aggressive diplomacy and encompassed Latin America, the Pacific, and even Africa, the Arthur Administration showed it accepted and acted upon the basic assumptions of Blaine's diplomacy. Blaine got another opportunity to implement his foreign policy when he returned to the State Department during the administration of Benjamin Harrison.

Throughout the remainder of 1882 and into 1883, the Arthur Administration shifted to a less vigorous foreign policy. But even as Frelinghuysen led a diplomatic retreat, he clearly indicated that his vision was not circumscribed by the continental limits. He did not, he assured Senator John F. Miller of California—a fellow Republican and a member of the Senate Foreign Relations Committee—oppose a conference per se, but he thought the 1882 meeting was premature "and might be very injurious." According to Blaine's proposal, the secretary elaborated, the United States would have the same number of votes that each of the countries represented at the conference would have. Then, the United States could not control the conference. "That Congress might see proper to vote that no inter-oceanic canal should be constructed that should belong to or be under the control of any one nation, but should be the property of all nations."[29]

Still, Frelinghuysen thought that "good has resulted from the Congress having been proposed. It has called directly the attention of our people to the importance of a defined South American policy." He wanted the president to develop and refine such a policy—a policy that was blatantly paternalistic. Once he had obtained Senate approval, then the president could present his program to the Latin Americans to determine "whether they approved or disapproved of the policy suggested and what modifications they have to ask of the United States," the leading power of the Western Hemisphere.[30] Clearly, Blaine's charge of timidity was inaccurate. The diplomatic maneuvers of the new Arthur Administration were awkward, but its thinking was hardly timid.

Personal considerations and domestic politics, as much as the calculations of international politics, influenced the foreign and domestic policies of the Arthur Administration. As early as mid-1882, the president knew that he had Bright's Disease and that his life would be shortened. Accordingly, he made little effort to secure his own re-election.[31] Arthur, however, probably wanted to secure a better place for himself in history—an understandable motive for a man whose spoilsman reputation overshadowed his skills as a political organizer. "He isn't 'Chet' Arthur any more," a New York associate remarked, "he's the President."[32] In addition, the Republican party needed positive achievements to present to an electorate that was less and less stirred by Civil War memories and not consistently Republican in its voting. And the Democratic party, resting upon a firm foundation in the form of the Solid South and strong support in the North, was a constant threat. These considerations help explain Arthur's strong, though unsuccessful, efforts to revive southern Republicanism, his support of civil service reforms and tariff revision, and his later vigorous foreign policy.[33]

In his first annual message in 1881, Arthur proposed a moderate tariff reduction to Congress. Others prodded Congress, too. Not only the Democrats but commercial and industrial groups and nonpartisan reformers as well had agitated for tariff modifications during the late 1870s. They continued their efforts in the early 1880s. The New York State Chamber of Commerce, while avoiding either a high or low tariff position, protested the import tax system as cumbersome and open to fraud. In November and December 1881 protectionist conventions met in Philadelphia, Chicago, and New York. Each called for some kind of tariff alteration. "I know," one Republican congressional leader told the House in March 1882, "of very few people in the United States who admit they have no complaint against some part of the details of the present tariff."[34]

These pressures, combined with economic factors and political considerations (e.g., a mounting surplus in the Treasury, discrepancies in the duties' schedules and difficulties in administrating tariffs which were dated, and a strong economy that was healthy enough to undergo the disruptions of tariff revision without great risk), fueled the Republican engine for action on a new tariff. That the GOP controlled Congress and the White House also was not overlooked; protectionism would supposedly be safe in the hands of its "friends."

To facilitate tariff revision, Arthur asked Congress to create a tariff commission composed of experts from outside Congress and appointed by the president. Such a commission would presumably be free from political pressures and could devise a sound tariff bill. A number of House and Senate Democrats disparaged the commission as a sham to avoid significant reductions of import duties, and as an unconstitutional move to transfer congressional authority to legislate taxes to a non-elective body. Most of the debates about creating the commission, however, involved a reiteration of low tariff versus protectionist arguments, and they had a sharply partisan nature as Democrats voiced the former set of views and Republicans the latter.[35]

Despite the heated debate, Congress passed legislation creating a tariff commission by comfortable margins that reflected some bipartisan support for the commission. That the Senate but not the House had passed a similar bill (the Eaton Bill) in the previous

Congress undoubtedly eased passage. Moreover, whatever their position on the tariff, most congressmen agreed that some sort of tariff revision was necessary and politically wise. They also would be happy to see the endless wrangling over the tariff at least temporarily removed from Congress. Some legislators, Senator Thomas F. Bayard of Delaware for example, supported the measure in hopes that the commission would be a representative group that would give needed expert advice. Bayard naively anticipated that the commission would include David Wells.[36] Considering Wells' reputation as a free trader, his past feuds with prominent Republicans, and his desertion of the GOP for the Democratic party, this was unrealistic.

When President Arthur selected the Tariff Commission of 1882, he ignored Wells and used his appointive powers to give protectionists control. Manufacturers dominated it, and they used it for their own interests. This ultimately endangered the Republican coalition that included groups whose interests did not necessarily coincide with those of the manufacturers. Led by their chairman, John L. Hayes, a strong protectionist and secretary of the National Association of Wool Manufacturers, the commissioners heard testimony during the summer of 1882. A few academicians, like William Graham Sumner of Yale, pleaded for free trade. E. P. Wheeler, representing eastern free traders, predicted a series of depressions if the United States did not find more foreign customers, and he urged tariff reduction in order to increase the exports of American goods.[37] Most of the witnesses, however, represented their own business interests, and they expressed alarm at suggestions of a general, marked tariff reduction. Their prime concern was with the domestic, not the foreign market.[38]

Surprisingly, the commission recommended moderate tariff reductions. Chairman Hayes, perhaps aware of the coming 1882 congressional elections, contended that public pressure made tariff revision mandatory. The commission reasoned that failure to compromise might jeopardize all of the high duties. Reflecting its bias for manufacturers, the commission recommended substantial reductions on raw materials, though not for the reasons that tariff reductionists would use. By so favoring manufacturers, the commission's report aroused the constituents of a number of congressmen and senators, in particular the wool growers of the Midwest.[39] Furthermore, it endangered the Republican coalition of producers and processors, and of northern farmers and manufacturers. Finally, the commission raised unanswerable questions concerning the definition of a raw material and at what point in its processing a raw material ceased to be a raw material. In view of these considerations, it was no surprise that all semblance of objectivity ended when President Arthur sent the report to Congress.

The Republicans in Congress ignored most of the report. They wrote and passed a tariff bill which maintained the coalition between producer and manufacturer. The Mongrel Tariff reduced a number of internal taxes and left import duties near their previous heights. One exception was the duty on raw wool, which was reduced. American wool producers protested vigorously, but without immediate effect.[40]

Congress moved with remarkable speed. The Democrats had regained control of the House in the congressional election of 1882, and men who favored a low tariff appeared to be in the ascendant. Congress received the report of the tariff commission in December 1882, only three months before the forty-seventh Congress ended, and in its haste passed a bill that contained confusing provisions. As a result, the Mongrel Tariff earned its name and only served to intensify the whole tariff controversy.[41]

During the debates over the creation of the tariff commission and the writing and voting on the Mongrel Tariff, the protectionists and the tariff reductionists refined their rhetoric. For the most part they relied on traditional arguments which they tailored to contemporary economic data or, sometimes, the reverse. They went back to these arguments time and again in the tariff debates during the rest of the 1880s and in the 1890s. The protectionist orthodoxy rested on the basic assumptions of economic nationalism and of the responsibility and right of the government to assist the economic development of the nation. Thus, they accepted Hamiltonianism and what Robert A. Lively has called "The American System." The tariff reductionists based their appeal on the presuppositions that protectionism disrupted a naturally harmonious domestic and international market, and that it operated as favoritism for certain economic interests.[42]

In advocating nationalism, the protectionists contended that national welfare was the first concern of a national government. They agreed that internationalism and world peace were laudable aspirations, but thought these were unrealistic dreams in a world divided into nation states, especially at a time when Europe was showing increasingly protectionist inclinations. They defined national welfare as rising standards of living and as national economic independence based upon a growing private enterprise economy. Only a balanced economy (a high level of industrial, commercial, and agricultural development), they argued, could guarantee true independence. They declared that a protective tariff was vital to this process. Republican Congressman John A. Kasson, one of the House leaders, declared he favored a protective system which would create "a sure foundation for the maintenance of national industries, without which no nation can be independent and without which no nation can make its people prosperous and happy."[43]

To this economic nationalism, the protectionists linked anti-European sentiments, particularly Anglophobia, an especially strong sentiment among Irish-Americans. Specifically, the protectionists claimed that high capital and wage costs, as well as the immaturity of American industries, prevented American manufacturers from competing on equal terms with their European counterparts, especially British manufacturers. Thus, they concluded, American industry needed a protective tariff to defend itself against Europe. Such arguments also had obvious appeal to European immigrants who had come to the United States to find a higher standard of living. Such arguments also revealed the attention the Republicans gave to the important ethnic vote.

The protectionists argued that the growth of American industry—which was enhanced by high tariffs—would benefit all

Americans, which in turn would promote social harmony. As industrial production increased, prices on manufactured goods would fall, which would benefit the consumer. The number of jobs would increase, and wages would remain high and even rise higher. As the number of well-paid wage earners rose, American farmers could sell a greater percentage of their crops in the domestic market, which was more reliable than the foreign market. The protectionists pointed out that the American farmer was threatened by an increasingly competitive world agricultural market. Some Republican leaders, such as Kelley and McKinley, demonstrated a genuine concern for workingmen,[44] many of whom had emigrated to this country to improve their standard of living. While these leaders were not sensitive enough to the threat of large American manufacturers to the small manufacturers, they were aware of the anxieties which European imports caused the smaller industrialists and the workers. Too, the protectionists understood that too many American farmers were dependent on an increasingly competitive world market.

Many of the protectionists also contended that greater exports of American manufactured goods were not an immediate concern. In 1883, Representative Joseph G. Cannon of Illinois expressed a typical view. After the United States had fully developed the continent, then ''we will have to look elsewhere in the world for a market.'' This, he claimed, would not occur for a long time.[45] Pointing to the coincidence of high tariffs and the rapid growth of American industry after 1865, the protectionists claimed that the protective tariff was the primary cause of this development. They claimed too much, but the syllogism had superficial validity and appeal. In addition, they raised fears that lower tariffs would undermine industrial development, cause lower wages and unemployment, and destroy the farmers' home market.

In reply to this barrage, the tariff reductionists deployed the mystical battalions of natural economic law, and offered the vision of an international order in which goods flowed smoothly from nation to nation and created an atmosphere of good relations. As national governments realized their true interests (when they discovered which products they were best suited to produce), they would tear away the barriers to the free exchange of goods.

The tariff reductionists also opposed protectionism on several specific grounds. They charged that the high tariffs unjustly raised the average American's cost of living. Clearly, they understood that government intervention in a private enterprise economy often favors some groups (usually the better organized and more aware) to the disadvantage of others. They claimed, for example, that the American laborer lived under the burden of unjust taxes and that these taxes did not guarantee high wages to him. With a rather sophisticated argument, tariff reductionists stated that measuring labor costs solely by hourly wages was misleading because the great technological changes—along with his own attitude—made the American worker more efficient than any other. Thus, in reality, industry had lower labor costs in America than in other industrialized countries, and the American workingman did not need a protective tariff. The tariff, the reductionists continued, fell as unmerited profits into the coffers of large corporations. Moreover, responding to the growing American fear of monopolies in the 1880s, the reductionists claimed that protectionism fostered trusts. After asserting that "the higher rate of wages [of American workers] means a higher productive power," Congressman Roger Q. Mills denied that protectionism either raised or sustained American wages. "What does it [protectionism] do?" he asked, "It enables you to make 'trusts,' combinations, and 'pools.' "[46]

The tariff reductionists declared that the prosperity of farming depended upon maintaining and raising the levels of farm exports. Ideally, they admitted, American farmers should sell all their products on the home market, but this would not be possible for many years. The farmer had to sell a large percentage of his produce abroad, and he thus operated in a market beyond the jurisdiction of American tariff laws. But he bought in a protected market where high tariffs increased his cost of living. Lower tariffs would help the farmer by allowing a freer flow of goods in the world market and by cutting the costs of his necessities. As lower tariffs stimulated industry, the farmer would have a stronger home market. Some, like Congressman Richard B. Bland, extended their case to contend that national prosperity depended upon a strong, flourishing agricultural sector.[47]

Thus, in their rhetoric and thinking, the tariff reductionists, like the protectionists, often reduced American agriculture to the simplistic image of "the farmer." The complexity of American agriculture and the divergent interests of farmers—such as those of the commodity farmer and the truck garden farmer who served the rapidly developing urban markets of the Midwest and the East —were obscured. Exports were of more immediate concern to commodity producers and livestock producers (the latter were usually ignored by the reductionists) than to other agrarians. Only when clear ties between exports and general prosperity were established did the export orientation of the low tariff congressmen apply to agriculture generally.

Increasingly in the 1880s, the Democrats gave particular emphasis to tariff reduction as a means to achieve overseas economic expansion. The Democrats had made this connection before 1880, but later they significantly altered their low tariff-expansionist argument by giving expansion major emphasis. Previously they had criticized high tariffs as simply barriers to the free flow of international trade in which, the farmer, because he exported a large percentage of his commodity production, had a particularly vital stake. As the index of industrial production rose in the 1880s, the Democrats shifted their concern to the industrial vote and the exports of manufactured goods, while they retained their argument about agricultural exports.[48] Influenced by David Wells, the Democrats gave increasing attention to the technology-overproduction-depression argument for free raw materials.

Like most tariff reductionists, Wells consistently censured high tariffs in the traditional way (as a hindrance to the free exchange of goods and products), but he developed and gave greater emphasis to a low tariff-trade expansion argument more suited to the rapid industrial and technological changes of Gilded Age America. As early as his 1868 *Report* as United States special commissioner of revenue, Wells had begun to develop a case in which he modified his laissez-faire philosophy to accommodate it to the transformation of the American economy.

Rapid industrial growth and technological change, Wells contended in innumerable speeches, articles, and books, brought many benefits and some serious consequences. New technology allowed vastly increased production, lower production costs and, hence, cheaper goods and lower labor costs, even though American wages remained stable and relatively high. But the greatly augmented industrial capacity had serious ramifications: this capacity exceeded domestic demand, which led to overproduction and depressions with dangerous domestic social consequences. As a devotée of laissez faire, Wells refused to consider a number of possible solutions—such as direct government action to expand domestic purchasing power—to the crisis he visualized. Instead, he sought relief in foreign markets. To enable the American manufacturer to further reduce his production costs in order to compete more effectively in the world market, he recommended duty-free raw materials. Given this advantage, Wells believed that American industry could capture markets in underdeveloped countries, particularly in the Western Hemisphere, that relied upon imports for manufactured goods and machinery.[49]

Wells' views carried great weight with Democratic tariff reductionists, and his importance increased as their power in the Democratic party increased. Wells worked closely with Congressman William Morrison, who chaired the Ways and Means Committee for several years in the 1880s. Wells also knew and advised other powerful Democrats, including Congressmen William M. Springer, Samuel S. Cox, John Carlisle, William C. P. Breckinridge, William L. Wilson and Abram Hewitt, Senators James B. Beck and Thomas F. Bayard, and Manton Marble, editor of the *New York World*. He also advised the administrations of Grover Cleveland, and his most intimate friend, Edward Atkinson, had great influence with the Cleveland Democrats.[50]

In spite of Wells' difficult personality and his reputation as a political extremist who demanded the immediate end to all import duties, the Democrats often, though discreetly, sought his counsel.

Congressional Democrats used his ideas and suggestions in writing the minority report on the Mongrel Tariff of 1883. In 1890, Wells either wrote or strongly influenced the minority report against the McKinley Tariff Bill. Then, in 1894, he was invited to counsel the Democratic leadership on the Wilson-Gorman Tariff.[51] Wells obviously had considerable insights into the functioning of the economy and a deeply respected knowledge of tariffs. In addition, circumstances helped open the Democratic leaders to his influence: economic crises in the 1880s and 1890s, the ascendancy of the Democratic tariff reductionists, the search by the Democrats for new issues in order to bury the Civil War past, and the need to make a positive record which would create a new party image and develop a broader coalition for the sake of self-perpetuation.

Congressman Abram Hewitt gave the most cogent presentation of Wells' analysis in March 1882. With considerable perception, Hewitt began by warning that economic recovery, which started in 1879, would end abruptly. He accurately assessed one of the prime factors in ending the depression of the 1870s: a great rise in agricultural exports in 1879, especially wheat. Hewitt admitted that by providing cheaper transportation railroads had helped the farmer. If the world production of wheat returned to earlier levels, however, prices would fall dangerously despite the advantages of cheaper domestic transportation. If this occurred, the whole American economy would collapse. Only a larger foreign market would sustain the recovery and only tariff reduction would allow for increased exports and prevent overproduction and economic collapse.[52]

Hewitt then moved to the main theme in his plea for lower import duties. He declared that *"access to the open markets of the world for our manufactured products is essential to the continuance of our prosperity."* He did not want the total overthrow of protectionism. He sought duty-free raw materials which would allow the American manufacturer—through lower costs—to charge less for his products and, thus, to compete successfully in international markets. Although he claimed that taxes were too high and that rigid protectionism favored monopolies, he subordinated these ideas to his main concern for exports and economic well-being.[53]

He warned that, *"If we shall fail to deal with this question now and at once, it is inevitable that we shall soon be relegated to the condition of suffering in which we found ourselves during the trying era between 1873 and 1879."* He foresaw "convulsions and revolutions," "sufferings and horrors." If these occurred, the "whole structure and genius of our government must be changed in order to meet the primary necessity . . . for preserving social order." To freshen the memories of his congressional colleagues, he recalled the rail strike of 1877 and the use of federal troops to restore domestic peace. If such events became a pattern, the federal government would undermine local authority and endanger individual liberty.[54]

Hewitt's views were not disinterested. He represented New York City with its great interest in international trade, and he was an eastern iron manufacturer who may have imported some raw materials, such as iron ore. Thus he may have had a personal stake in the tariff program that he proposed: Senator John Sherman accused him of as much. The quick-tempered Hewitt denied this, and claimed that he used only domestic iron ore. His proposal, he said, would actually cost his company some competitive advantage. Twice he demanded a public apology from Sherman; not surprisingly, none came. Sherman replied only in private correspondence, and then only vaguely.[55] Sherman may have had a point, but to dismiss Hewitt's remarks as merely the expression of self-interest was too simple and unfair. Hewitt's conception of society was broader than one based upon short-run calculations of his own profits and losses. He had firm convictions and expressed them without hesitation. He had very advanced views on labor. For example, he knew that labor suffered from periodic unemployment because of technological change, and he suggested that a private enterprise establish a fund which would aid working-men temporarily displaced by technological change.[56]

Hewitt's remarks were the result of shrewd thinking by the leaders of the Democratic party. Throughout the 1880s and into the 1890s they concentrated on protectionism. As Wells and Atkinson had suggested, tariff reduction on raw materials was the first step towards general tariff reduction.[57] By abstaining from a general assault on every protected article, the Democrats hoped to divide the protectionists, escape the free trade label, and achieve that first step. Not all Democrats liked these subtle tactics. Representative Frank H. Hurd of Ohio, for example, frequently gave frantic, free trade tirades.[58] Some Democratic leaders also knew that they could not propose any tariff revision that promised only to put raw materials on the free list. Any Democratic tariff had to offer some lower duties on manufactured goods, even if this offended manufacturers. Western and southern Democrats, as William Morrison told Wells, could not confront their agrarian constituents with such a tariff.[59] A Democratic tariff had to be a tariff that reflected a broad coalition.

Naturally, voter appeal strongly influenced the Republican and Democratic tariff arguments and strategy. In order to stay in office, they tried to reach a broad spectrum of economic interests. In addition to their concern for overseas economic expansion, therefore, the Democrats tailored their raw materials argument to appeal to a variety of interests. They assured the farmer and the laborer that free raw materials meant a lower cost of living. They used the idea to try to break the Republican coalition of producer and processer. For example, they particularly emphasized duty-free raw wool. In this case, they urged a program in the interest of the wool manufacturer and against the interest of the midwestern wool grower. Some manufacturers responded favorably to this proposal. To the charge that they were pursuing a contradictory course by promising the farmer a low cost of living while seeking to remove the tariff on wool, the Democrats claimed that only a few farmers relied on wool for a major source of their income. They went on to console the wool grower: if his sheep were worth less for wool production, at least his coat cost less.[60]

The Republicans, after their experience with the Tariff Commission of 1882 and the 1883 Tariff Act, fought against free raw materials because they knew the dangers of the appeal of free raw materials to the protectionist alliance. Senator John Sherman, whose Ohio constituents were furious about reduced duties on wool in the 1883 Tariff Act, candidly admitted that "the dogma of free raw materials is more dangerous to the protective policy than the opposition of free traders." Free raw materials had a definite appeal to some American industrialists. By cutting their costs, they could compete better with other American and European manufacturers in the domestic and foreign markets. New England ironmakers wanted to purchase duty-free coal from Nova Scotia in order to cope with the vigorous Pennsylvania ironmakers who had easier access to domestic sources of coal. Silver and lead smelters from Kansas clashed with western silver interests; the Kansas smelters claimed they needed duty-free silver and lead from Mexico if they were to survive. By the end of the 1880s, one eastern iron and steel factory used iron ore from Cuba, although it had to pay a large import duty on the ore.[61]

Still, the free raw materials argument failed to stir many leaders of American industry. Some manufacturers, in particular the Pennsylvania iron and steel manufacturers, wanted to maintain their comparative advantage of drawing cheap raw materials from nearby domestic sources. Other industrialists feared that free raw materials would immediately lead to free trade. Henry Saltonstall, a Massachusetts woolens maker and a friend of some of the leading tariff reductionists, expressed the feelings of the industry. Although his remarks were written in 1888, they apply more generally. He told W. C. P. Breckinridge, a member of the House Ways and Means Committee and a leader of the Democratic party, that most informed textile manufacturers wanted tariff revision, but they feared that the free traders "will go too far, and the reductions [will] be so sweeping as to seriously injure or kill them." Saltonstall explained that "we are afraid that if we do go for free Wool, the Wool Growers will go for free goods, and if they succeeded we would all be dead in a week."[62]

Saltonstall's ambivalence pointed to a basic dilemma of the Democratic tariff reductionists. Where could they begin without threatening many important interests? Manufacturers, for example, supported tariff reduction if it helped them, but they feared the Democrats would "go too far." Such fears were also reinforced by the manufacturers' general suspicion of the Democrats. Therefore, the protectionist, or a standpat, position had a great advantage over tariff reduction.

During the tariff debates of 1883, and again in 1884 and 1886, the Democrats repeatedly stressed the urgency for greater markets for American products and consistently linked this to tariff reduction. Representative Joseph Wheeler of Alabama declared in 1883, for example, that the protective tariffs destroyed American foreign trade and that to "have prosperity we must have foreign markets." The following year, Congressman James F. Clay of Kentucky told the House that the productive capacity of many American factories exceeded "the home demand and the small export demand." As a consequence, these factories ran on "three-quarters time and frequently on half time," and the whole economy was depressed. The protective tariff frustrated American foreign trade and thus brought on the depression of 1882-1885.[63] Neither Wheeler nor Clay specified which industries needed foreign markets.

The economic expansionist arguments of the tariff reductionists also provided an answer to the protectionist charge that a low tariff would favor Great Britain. The reductionists claimed that the United States was ready to—indeed had to—invade a world market dominated by the British. The protectionists had raised a new "bloody shirt" in attacking the low tariff as a pro-British policy. By using their economic expansionist theme, the reductionists attempted to take this "bloody shirt" away from the protectionists and to blunt the protectionists' appeal to Irish-American Anglophobia.

Because of their preoccupation with the tariff and their strong commitment to their technology-overproduction-depression analysis, Wells, Hewitt, and other supporters of this analysis ignored or neglected some of the serious hindrances to expanding American industrial exports. Most importantly, the majority of American manufacturers had only a casual interest in exports until the 1890s.[64] They lacked experience in, knowledge of, and effective organization and banking arrangements for foreign markets. Very few companies even had overseas representatives or designed their products to suit foreign consumers. The relatively poor communications system between the United States and many of the world markets aggravated the situation.

Though the United States had improved its consular service modestly during the Hayes Administration, it was still very inadequate. The pitiful state of the United States Navy hardly assured American businessmen of the forceful support necessary in the politically unstable parts of the world. The similar condition of the merchant marine, many businessmen and politicians incorrectly believed, barred an increased export trade. Actually, the particular flag of the carrier was a matter of indifference, but a stronger American merchant fleet could at least have earned the shipping fees and helped the American balance of payments. Even if all these things had been remedied, American products still faced other barriers: discriminatory tariffs, harbor duties, and customs house practices. Spain, for example, favored Spanish merchants in the Cuban trade. In response to American merchants' complaints, the United States government tried with some success in the 1880s and 1890s to put Spanish and American shipping on the same footing. (After the Spanish-American War, the United States secured the favored position once enjoyed by Spain.)

The protectionists occasionally noted these flaws, especially the weakness of the American merchant fleet, in the expansionist case of the tariff reductionists. With pride of parenthood, the Republicans claimed that the drawback system, which they enacted in 1861 and which allowed a 90-percent rebate of import duties paid on materials used in exported manufactures, virtually provided for the free raw materials the reductionists sought.[65] Although Democrats such as Hewitt supported drawbacks, most Democrats criticized the arrangement as too cumbersome and inadequate. Obviously willing to take part of the loaf and to work to get the rest, Hewitt favored drawbacks and tariff reduction.

But generally the protectionists denied that the United States had any immediate or great interest in foreign markets. Senator

Justin S. Morrill of Vermont took an extreme position: he contended that the day when national prosperity depended on international commerce had ended. "National wealth," he said, "must now and hereafter be mainly created by labor at home; and the home market is the only one of value over which any nation now has absolute control." More typically, Representatives Cannon and William McKinley assumed that until the United States had fully developed its domestic economy, it had little concern for foreign markets. When Congressman Roger Q. Mills linked tariff reduction to foreign trade, McKinley replied that the foreign market "is only mythical in the present condition of our country . . . . We cannot command a foreign market until we can control our own.[66]

Congressman William M. Springer, a prominent Illinois Democrat, expressed the Democratic challenge to the smug domestic market orientation of the majority of Republican congressional leaders when he told the House in 1882 that the real tariff issue was between those satisfied with the status quo and those wanting to open new markets. He claimed that

> the real issue presented to the country in this debate [on the Mongrel Tariff] has been greatly misunderstood or willfully misstated. It is not between free trade and protection. I know of no party in this country or in this House who proposes free trade as a remedy for existing tariff abuses. The issue is not one between the advocates of free trade and the advocates of protection. On the contrary, the issue is between those who desire an immediate revision of the tariff and the reduction of its excessive and prohibitory duties, and especially the removal of those burdens which are causing factories, mills, and workshops to be closed for the want of a market for their products, and depriving thousands of laborers all over the country of employment, producing strikes, lockouts, and low wages; and those who desire to postpone tariff revision indefinitely and thus preserve existing taxes, fearing

a change might result in depriving a few favored interests of the advantages they now have.[67]

While some Republicans were ready to wall off the American economy from the rest of the world, others took up the Democratic challenge of economic expansion. These Republicans tacitly accepted the technology-overproduction-depression thesis of Wells, and they, too, defined domestic prosperity in terms of overseas economic expansion. Secretary of State Blaine, supported by President Garfield, had based his bold foreign policy on such an analysis. The Arthur Administration also accepted the assumptions of the overseas expansionists. After a brief tactical retreat from Blaine's assertive diplomacy, Arthur and Frelinghuysen acted with surprising boldness. Stimulated by the depression of 1882-1885, by a resurgent Democratic party that regained control of the House in the 1882 elections and at the same time found a new national leader in Grover Cleveland, newly elected governor of New York, and, perhaps, by the remarks of Congressman Hewitt and other Democrats, President Arthur and Secretary Frelinghuysen sought increased foreign trade through a series of reciprocity treaties and by seizing the diplomatic initiative in several areas in which the United States had vital interests.

Beneath the heated rhetoric of intra- and interparty conflicts, a crucial consensus about the American economy and its future was emerging by the middle of the 1880s.

3

In Search of Markets: The Foreign Policy of the Arthur Administration

The Democrats regained control of the House as a result of the 1882 congressional elections. Consequently, the Arthur Administration and the Democrats worked on separate but parallel stages during the last two years of Arthur's term. Each reacted to the depression of the 1880s, attempted to improve the fortunes of their parties, and sought their own version of tariff reduction.

Before the forty-seventh Congress ended in March 1883, it enacted two pieces of legislation which placed two needed credits on the Arthur Administration ledger: the Pendleton Act for civil service reform and the Mongrel Tariff. Despite the apt label of the latter, at least the Republicans had done something, though very little, in the way of tariff legislation. But with the House in Democratic hands and the Senate still Republican, the prospects for more legislative achievements were dim indeed. President Arthur turned logically to foreign policy where he could outflank the Democrats.

Prior to the 1882 campaign, the president had pressed Congress to take steps to build a modern navy, and had opened negotiations for a reciprocal trade convention with Mexico. As early as his first annual message, Arthur declared, "We must be ready to defend our harbors against aggression; to protect, by the distribution of our ships of war over the highways of commerce, the varied interests of our foreign trade and the persons and property of our citizens abroad; to maintain everywhere the honor of our flag."[1] Congress appropriated funds in 1882 and 1883 to build five new steel cruisers and a dispatch boat and to complete four monitors already under construction—a major step toward creating a modern American navy.[2] But only the fact of a resurgent Democratic party, his need to achieve a positive record, and the economic slump of the 1880s roused the president and his cautious secretary of state, Frelinghuysen, to vigorous action.

The ascendant Democratic tariff reductionists coincidentally reopened the tariff struggle during the forty-eighth Congress. Stimulated by rising political aspirations and the depression of the 1880s, which they believed tariff reduction could alleviate through lower domestic prices and greater exports, the reductionists moved to control the House and isolate the protectionists in the Democratic ranks. They pushed Pennsylvania's Samuel Randall, the leading Democratic protectionist in the House, aside and elected John Carlisle of Kentucky as Speaker. William Morrison became chairman of the Ways and Means Committee. Under his leadership, the committee held another set of tariff hearings in 1884 and reported a strong reductionist bill. But the Morrison Bill of 1884 fell victim in the House to a combination of Democratic protectionists, led by Randall, and Republicans. The Democrats' preoccupation with the 1884 presidential election also helped defeat the measure. Thus, the full commitment of the Democrats to low tariffs awaited another day, when a forceful president made them a matter of party loyalty.

The 1882-1885 depression set the framework for much of what the House Democrats attempted during the forty-eighth Congress and, especially, for the foreign policy of the Arthur Administration. Concern for national honor and defense had its place in the thinking of the administration. So did its awareness that, as one of Arthur's close advisers remarked, "A great party can't be carried along on negation."[3] But the depression shaped the nationalism and the political aspirations of the administration. "One of the gravest problems which appeal to the wisdom of Congress," Arthur told Congress in December 1884 in the outstanding address of his presidency, "is the ascertainment of the most effective means for increasing our foreign trade and thus relieving the depression under which our industries are now languishing."[4] The administration sent the same Congress the Frelinghuysen-Zavala Treaty which would assure United States control of any isthmian canal constructed in Nicaragua, the convention of the Berlin West Africa Conference in which the United States had participated, and reciprocal trade agreements signed with the Dominican Republic and with Spain for the Spanish West Indies. The Mexican reciprocity treaty had passed in the Senate in March 1883 and now (because of a provision added by the Senate) waited for House action. Secretary Frelinghuysen had also urged Congress to revise the consular service thoroughly in order to facilitate trade expansion.[5]

Ironically, this vigorous response to the depression took place despite the relatively mild nature of the economic slump. Unemployment, according to the conservative estimate of the United States commissioner of labor, involved at its worst only 1 million workers (7-1/2 percent of the labor force).[6] Other economic indicators—wholesale price indices, gross national product figures, railroad mileage—also showed that the economy had slowed down considerably but had not collapsed.[7]

But the timing of the 1880s' depression gave it a peculiar psychological impact. It followed within four years the long, severe crisis of 1873-1879 and occurred in a decade in which Americans became acutely aware of the social tensions of industrialization and urbanization. Moreover, no one could anticipate that the depression would be briefer and milder than its predecessor. A short, sharp bank panic in May 1884 heightened anxieties and pointed to a repetition of the 1870s. But the mood of the country was quiet; the violence of 1877 was not repeated.[8]

The quiet obscured a deep sense of urgency. Because of the rapid social change of the 1880s, this disquiet would have existed even without a depression. Economic malaise merely complicated matters. Industrialization and urbanization of the United States proceeded at an increasing rate. The wave of immigrants became a tidal wave, with a growing percentage of southern and eastern Europeans. Modern large-scale industrialization threatened the Jacksonian dream of self-employment, although some Americans clung desperately to the self-made man myth. Others turned to science, the new final authority, which was transformed into a social philosophy, Social Darwinism. Americans could then have it either way: they were where they were because of their personal deeds or misdeeds, or because nature had put them in their place. Not surprisingly, labor unrest pervaded during the 1880s, and radicals of various stripes alarmed the nation. Henry George, the single-tax reformer, attracted growing attention because of his fervent attacks upon the inequities in the distribution of wealth and income.[9] Americans who thought George either a radical or an ignorant demagogue were terrified by his appeal. But profound changes in attitudes and ideas occurred. Elements in the Protestant and Catholic churches, for instance, rekindled their concern for man as a social being, and the Social Gospel movement, which has had an immense impact since, was born.[10] A group of young economists, led by Richard T. Ely, began to challenge the verities of classical economics. They called for the inductive study of economics instead of the deductive method of classical economics, and asserted that, contrary to classical economics, ethics and economics were interrelated.[11] There was, as Samuel Reznek has written of the 1880s, "a proliferation of new attitudes, new principles, and particularly new policies, demanding and defining a more active role for the state and government in business."[12]

President Arthur and his advisers assumed that government had a responsibility to mitigate the depression of 1882-1885 and to ease the domestic tensions. They evolved their own analysis of the causes of and remedies for the depression and based their policies on this analysis. First, they believed that American farms and factories were producing more than the country could consume. Increased exports, they argued, were necessary to relieve the saturated American market.[13] Second, they asserted, as David Wells and Abram Hewitt had done earlier, that greatly increased agricultural exports could not be anticipated. Such gains had played an important role in the economy in the past, but the administration did not think that the exports of crude agricultural products would continue to increase. Some people even expected them to decline.

In the past, Secretary of State Frelinghuysen told Congress on March 20, 1884, the United States had a ready market for its surplus agricultural production and petroleum because of European demand and favorable conditions for production in the United States. He noted that "conditions of international demand and supply are undergoing radical changes which the near future will intensify." European efforts to increase the supply of these crude products had "resulted in awakening competition for the supply even of those products which we have heretofore controlled." One consequence he pointed to was European restrictions on American pork exported to Europe. The United States must prepare, the secretary argued, to meet the competition, and he urgently recommended a complete revision of the American consular service in order to do this.[14] Frelinghuysen's analysis of the situation, and the subsequent actions of the Arthur Administration, suggest that it had concluded that the traditional pattern of trade between the United States and other industrialized countries was undergoing a profound change. Thus, the administration focused its attention on countries which had little or no industrial development.

Frelinghuysen's lengthy analysis of agricultural exports was generally accurate, at least in the aggregate sense. The amount of crude foodstuffs exports rose in 1879 and 1880, then declined sharply. (The per unit value, however, did not drop quite as rapidly as the quantity of exports did.) Using 1913 as an index

of 100, the Commerce Department recorded the following quantitative decline for crude agricultural exports:[15]

1879	148.5
1880	162.3
1881	117.7
1882	81.4
1883	82.7
1884	77.2
1885	70.9

The index did not again reach 100 until 1891.[16] The large decline
in 1882 can only partly be explained by the poor American harvest
of 1881 and the revived crop production in Europe. American
agricultural exports were confronted by mounting obstacles.
Several European countries—Germany, Russia, Turkey, Italy, and
Switzerland—had raised high tariff barriers against American farm
products.[17] Other retaliatory measures increased difficulties. Using
the dubious charge that American pork was peculiarly dangerous
to health, several European countries had virtually closed off the
significant American exports of pork.[18] In addition, growing
agricultural exports from India, Egypt, Argentina, Russia, and
Australia threatened the position of American wheat farmers and
cotton growers. The State Department warned in May 1882 of a
"remarkable increase" of cotton and wheat exports from Bombay.
In August, it took notice of a large growth of wheat shipments
from northern India which passed through the Suez Canal.[19]

Other government officials recognized this new challenge to
American agricultural exports. Commissioner of Labor, Carroll D.
Wright, in his first annual report, which was devoted to depressions in the United States, related the impact of the Suez Canal
and the consequent cheaper transportation costs on the rapid
development of commercial farming in India. The major crop,
Wright pointed out in 1886, was wheat. He concluded that the
"direct result of that Indian development has been an increase in
the imports of Indian wheat by Western Europe and a decrease

in the imports of American grain." The decline in farm exports had caused "fear" and "apprehension" and reduced "the consuming power of one-half our population."[20] Many congressmen made similar analyses.[21]

"The heavy decline of the export of wheat from our country," commented *The Banker's Magazine* (New York) in April 1884, "is a grave matter." The English were turning from the United States to India for their wheat; the consequent loss of trade was having an adverse effect on the American gold supply.[22] Evidently, the magazine related these events to a fear that the battle of the monetary standards might be resumed. A month later, the same magazine reported a "great decline" in American wheat prices because, it believed, of increasing competition from Argentine, Russian, Indian, and Australian grain. A "commercial revolution" had occurred, and "this country has been very suddenly and very rudely awakened from the dream of basing its foreign trade upon the supposed power of retaining the markets of the world for breadstuffs against all competition, and of selling at good prices all it had the capacity of producing." But, the editor assured his readers, there were hopeful signs in the growing home market and the American genius for finding new entrepreneurial outlets in the United States.[23]

Other Americans, particularly President Arthur and Secretary Frelinghuysen, were not so calm. They made their first move in August 1882, when they opened negotiations with Mexico for a reciprocity treaty.[24] The administration was not blazing a new trail. Prior to 1880, such agreements had been negotiated with Hawaii, Mexico, Canada, and the German *zollverein*. Only the first was still in force. The agreements with Mexico and the German *zollverein* never received congressional approval, and the agreement with Canada had been allowed to lapse. During the 1870s, as American investments in Mexican railroads, mines, and ranches increased, Congress demonstrated renewed interest in a reciprocal trade agreement with Mexico.[25] Such a treaty would assure a more stable setting for American trade and investment in Mexico and would give American products a competitive advantage over comparable European products.

From this modest beginning, Arthur and Frelinghuysen initiated reciprocity negotiations involving the Spanish West Indies, the British West Indies, El Salvador, Colombia, and the Dominican Republic. They also supported congressional efforts to extend the Hawaiian treaty.[26] These negotiations and reciprocal trade agreements, they claimed, were excellent devices to "gain control of those markets for our fields and factories." No doubt they were aware that reciprocal trade agreements might result in reduced revenues and thus reduce the embarrassing Treasury surplus and blunt the demands for sweeping tariff reduction. At the same time, the administration sent the newly created Central and South American Commission to Latin America to examine ways to expand American trade there. The commission was told to concentrate on the possibilities for reciprocal trade agreements.[27] Then, having switched from a bearish to a bullish mood, the administration plunged into Africa and grasped at an American-dominated isthmian canal in Nicaragua.

The administration integrated its trade expansion program with such a canal. After failing to win British agreement to abrogate the Clayton-Bulwer Treaty,[28] Frelinghuysen tried to outflank the English. The result was the Frelinghuysen-Zavala Treaty of December 1884. For the right to the land on which to build the canal, the United States would have assumed a virtual protectorate over Nicaragua.[29] This involved a clear violation of the Clayton-Bulwer Treaty, but that did not seem to deter Frelinghuysen or Arthur. "The negotiation of this treaty," the president explained, "was entered upon under a conviction that it was imperatively demanded by the present and future political and material interests of the United States." The administration then announced that the reciprocity treaty with the Dominican Republic was intimately linked to the canal treaty. Arthur and Frelinghuysen believed that the treaty would increase American trade with the Dominican Republic. As this happened, an American colony would develop at Samana Bay which would "become the great coaling station of the European world's new highway of commerce, via Nicaragua, to the Pacific."[30] A majority of the Senate was also convinced that urgency rendered the Clayton-Bulwer Treaty invalid, that strained relations with Great Britain were not too high a price to pay for the gains of the new treaty. The necessary two-thirds of the Senate did not support the administration, but a majority did (32-23).[31]

Arthur and Frelinghuysen pursued new customers for American products as far as Korea, the Middle East, and Africa. Madagascar was under heavy pressure from French imperialists. To ease this pressure and support American merchants who had an active trade in Madagascar, the United States granted diplomatic recognition to the government of Madagascar in 1883.[32] Then, in 1884, the Arthur Administration went much deeper into Africa. In an unprecedented move, it granted diplomatic recognition to the flag of the International Association of the Congo which later evolved into the Independent State of the Congo. This curious step lent needed international respectability to an organization led by the unscrupulous, ambitious King Leopold II of Belgium, a regal Jim Fisk. The American government, however, did not question Leopold's sincerity or methods. Leopold had promised that the Congo would be an area of free trade if it were controlled by the International Association. The United States also hoped the Association would be able to stop Portugal's attempts, supported by Great Britian, to take over the mouth of the Congo River. When Leopold received diplomatic support from the French, the stage was set for a serious power struggle over the Congo.

The German Prime Minister, Otto von Bismarck, acted quickly to move the conflict over the Congo and other European disputes involving Africa to the conference table. The United States received an invitation to the Berlin West Africa Conference which met from November 1884 to February 1885. Arthur and Freling-huysen hesitated. They feared they might involve the United States in something that had the hint of an entangling alliance with

Europe. Finally, the United States sent a delegation. Thus, the Arthur Administration, following its analysis of the depression of the 1880s, found itself involved in a European diplomatic conference on the future of Africa. But by the end of the conference, fears about entangling alliances and adverse criticism in the United States caused the administration to waver. Consequently, it did not submit the convention from the Berlin meeting until their last day in office. President Grover Cleveland later removed the agreement from the Senate and never resubmitted it.[33]

The reciprocity negotiations led to treaties with Mexico, Spain, and the Dominican Republic, but not with England. The American interpretation of the most-favored-nation clause in existing treaty arrangements prevented agreement with the English. The Arthur Administration insisted upon conditional most-favored-nation clauses in its reciprocal treaties to avoid a general assault on the American tariff wall. For example, if Great Britain had a commercial treaty, including a most-favored-nation clause, with Spain covering the Spanish West Indies, the British could insist that they had an equal share in the benefits of a reciprocity treaty between the United States and Spain. Thus, Great Britain could breach the American tariff wall with a flanking maneuver. Arthur and Frelinghuysen wanted to prevent this by using conditional most-favored-nation clauses. The British, who were more concerned with principle and general policy than with the interests of the British West Indies, "entirely and emphatically dissent[ed]" from the American interpretation of these clauses.[34] These differences were not resolved during the Arthur Administration.

Of the agreements negotiated, the administration and Congress thought the Mexican and Spanish treaties were the most important. Proximity and existing economic relationships made Mexico and Cuba (the central concern of the Spanish agreement) logical targets for economic expansion. By 1883, Mexican-American commerce reached $28 million, and Americans were investing in Mexican mines, ranches, and railways, which were to be connected to American railways. By the same year, Cuban trade with the United

States amounted to $81 million while Spain's Cuban trade was less than $13 million. Cuban sugar plantations and iron mines also attracted some investment from the United States.[35]

Physical nearness and close economic ties should have made Canada part of Arthur's reciprocal trade agreements program. But staunch Republican voters—some manufacturers and farmers and their economic associates in the western states and states bordering on Canada—vigorously opposed Canadian reciprocity. Protectionists of all stripes also feared that Canadian reciprocity would be a major breach in the tariff wall, allowing Great Britain to flood the American market by way of Canada. Canadian reciprocity was understandably popular with Democratic tariff reductionists.[36]

Though neither the Mexican nor the Spanish treaty ever went into effect,[37] each revealed significant developments in the tactics of American economic expansion. The arguments for and against the treaties were repeated in future debates over reciprocity programs. The Arthur Administration discovered that reciprocal trade agreements, like tariff legislation in general, had to pass through a hazardous course of politics and special interests. The administrations of presidents Benjamin Harrison and William McKinley, both of which developed reciprocal trade programs, subsequently profited from the experiences of Arthur and Frelinghuysen.

The provisions of the Mexican and Spanish reciprocity agreements revealed the tactics of the Arthur Administration's Latin American trade strategy and reflected the administration's analysis that the United States should work to increase exports of manufactured goods in exchange for non-manufactured products. Almost all of the Mexican products which could enter the United States duty-free were agricultural. These included beef, barley, coffee, fresh fruits, raw hides (without wool), hemp, sugar, and non-manufactured leaf tobacco. The free list for American products emphasized manufactured goods: rolling stock, locomotives, engines, machinery, sewing machines, steel bars for mines, crude petroleum, and some farm products. Significantly, the treaty provided for the elimination of Mexican interstate taxes on American products, a concession no other foreign country would enjoy.[38]

Confident that most American provisions and agricultural products were competitive in Cuba, even under the pre-treaty burdens, the United States concentrated in its Spanish negotiations on obtaining "favoring duties" that "our manufactures . . . need" in Cuba. The treaty reflected this concentration.[39] The State Department, however, carefully pointed to the large tariff reductions on American wheat and wheat flour shipped to Cuba and Puerto Rico as evidence of its attention to the interests of American farmers.[40] The United States substantially reduced or eliminated duties on Cuban and Puerto Rican products, primarily agricultural. The majority of the Spanish concessions were on manufactured products, including a reduction from $4.70 to $1.65 a barrel on American flour and a 50-percent reduction on cotton textiles. Spain also removed discriminatory flag duties and clarified a number of legal questions about the security of American holdings in Cuba.[41]

John W. Foster, who negotiated the treaty as the United States minister to Spain, deliberately and cleverly used Cuban economic dependence on the United States to pry a favorable treaty from the reluctant, suspicious Spanish. The treaty, Foster congratulated himself, "will be annexing Cuba in the most desirable way."[42] Thus, while the Spanish expended their limited treasury and manpower to govern the "Pearl of the Antilles," the United States could expand its exports to meet a depression crisis and to secure an increasingly dominant position in Cuba—trade plus the Monroe Doctrine.

Defenders of the reciprocity program built their case upon the basic assumption that America produced more than it could consume. This overproduction was not an occasional phenomenon; it was occurring with increasing frequency and it was precipitating depressions. The depression of the 1880s, according to this argument, pointedly illustrated the overproduction analysis. Expanded exports, secured through reciprocity, promised to alleviate or even to eliminate overproduction and, possibly, depressions. All of this was to be effected without altering the basic nature of the American economy or the protective tariff, while depriving the Democratic tariff reductionists of one of their primary arguments (tariff reduction to facilitate economic expansion), and appeasing the spirit of American nationalism through an invigorated Monroe Doctrine.

American leaders assumed that Latin Americans, as fellow citizens of the Western Hemisphere, eagerly awaited reciprocal agreements and American entrepreneurs and products. Pressure through trade retaliation could persuade the reluctant. Economic aggressiveness could give substance to the Monroe Doctrine, too long a mere piece of paper, and challenge European, especially English, economic dominance south of the Rio Grande.[43] Economic expansion to the south also fit one of the basic assumptions of Adam Smith, which most Americans of the nineteenth century accepted: industrialized countries can very profitably exchange manufactured goods for raw materials. Reciprocity was typical of the nineteenth-century American mind that liked the "Big Scheme"—such as inflation as an economic cureall—and was presented in an overly optimistic fashion.

Congressional opponents of Arthur's reciprocal trade program had a more mundane view of things. Seemingly not alarmed by the depression of the 1880s and unattracted by visions of a Latin American commercial empire, they looked first to serving the interests of their constituents. They raised a variety of objections to reciprocity treaties. When President Arthur presented the Mexican treaty for ratification in February 1883, Senate opponents mounted a strong attack. Only after the administration reconciled itself to a potentially crippling amendment requiring the House to pass legislation to implement the treaty did the Senate concur by a very narrow margin—41 to 20—in March 1884. The vote did not follow party lines closely: 25 Republicans and 16 Democrats supported Arthur against 10 Republicans and 10 Democrats. Apparently, the interests of constituents outweighed party affiliation. Senators from tobacco-growing and sugar-producing states feared a heavy influx of Mexican tobacco and sugar. Therefore, some senators from Virginia, South Carolina, North Carolina, Maryland, Kentucky, Pennsylvania, Connecticut, and Rhode Island opposed the treaty. The one exception was Democratic

Senator James B. Beck of Kentucky who supported the administration.[44]

During the debate on the Mexican agreement, the opposition, led by Senator Justin Morrill of Vermont, objected that too much revenue would be lost, that the United States would receive too little for its concessions, and that the president had invaded the constitutional prerogative of Congress to enact revenue legislation. Countries which were not party to the reciprocity treaties could claim the benefits of these agreements through "most-favored-nation" clauses in prior treaties. As Morrill pointed out, most nations claimed that there were no exceptions to these clauses.[45] The Arthur Administration tried to meet this criticism by putting conditional clauses in its reciprocity treaties.[46]

Rigid protectionists thought that reciprocity was an opening wedge for free trade. Tariff reductionists interpreted reciprocity as an attempt to evade significant tariff reduction. There were exceptions to the latter: David Wells, New York Democratic Congressmen Abram Hewitt and Perry Belmont, and Senator John Tyler Morgan, Alabama's exuberant expansionist. Morrill also worried that reciprocity would lead to a revival of the Canadian reciprocal trade agreement, and he believed the Mexican treaty was the work of American railway interests in Mexico.[47] Former President Grant, an active promoter of American railroads in Mexico and a business associate of Collis P. Huntington and Jay Gould, had served on the commission which arranged the treaty. Grant later became a publicist for his own handiwork when he publicly and energetically urged acceptance of the Mexican treaty.[48]

The enigmatic Wharton Barker, prominent Philadelphia Republican, sometime editor (*The American*), and metals manufacturer, was the first to develop an elaborate case against, and an alternative to, reciprocity treaties. Reciprocal agreements were piecemeal attempts at overseas economic expansion, and their negotiation unnecessarily aggravated relations between countries. Such treaties, if negotiated and put into effect in a serial fashion over a number of years, might destroy the most effective lever of the

United States—the domestic sugar market—against Latin America. Barker wanted to keep the duty on sugar, and then, offer to reduce the duty selectively in order to obtain concessions from Latin American countries that shipped sugar to the United States. The Central and South American Commission came to similar conclusions. Barker advocated a commercial *zollverein*, like the German customs union, to embrace North America, Central America, and the Caribbean. (He was vague about South America.)[49]

Barker aired his case in 1883 and 1884 in *The American* and in letters to several important American leaders: Blaine, Congressman Randall, Senator Morrill, Secretary of the Navy William E. Chandler, President-elect Grover Cleveland, and his uncle, Joseph Wharton, and Henry C. Lea, two of Pennsylvania's largest metals manufacturers and leaders of powerful protectionist lobbies. The limitations of available evidence preclude accurately determining the weight of his influence. Blaine did commit himself publicly to a commercial *zollverein* embracing the United States and Latin America during the 1884 presidential election, and that commitment occurred after corresponding and talking with Barker.[50] Whether this was more than a coincidence cannot be said. However, Barker was probably the first to argue openly for manipulating the American sugar tariff to secure trade advantages. When Blaine returned to the State Department under President Harrison, he and the president relied heavily on varying import duties on sugar in order to get better terms on foreign trade.

A scheme very much like Barker's emerged from a different quarter in May 1884. Consciously using the German *zollverein* as a model, Richard W. Townshend, an Illinois Democrat, presented a resolution in the House for an American customs union. He claimed his resolution envisioned "the establishment of a customs union . . . as against all other countries and the establishment of free trade" in the Western Hemisphere, except Canada. Such a proposal would please "protected manufacturers as well as . . . the advocates of free trade in this country, for while it establishes the same freedom of trade with these countries that now exists among our own States, great advantage would flow to our manufacturers in having an exclusive market." Happily, American manufacturers would not need to worry about competition from within this vast free trade zone because Latin Americans lacked the industry to compete with them. Once the Latin American market was secure, "then the danger of overproduction would pass away."[51]

But when Arthur's reciprocity program was considered by the forty-eighth Congress, tobacco-growers, sugar-producers, the Cigar-Makers Union, and hypersensitive representatives of protected industries like Joseph Wharton, John L. Hayes of the National Association of Wool Manufacturers, and James M. Swank of the American Iron and Steel Association, arrayed themselves against the reciprocity treaties. The latter group viewed any lowering of the tariff as a break in a vitally needed dike. Tobacco-growers and the Cigar-Makers Union feared that the treaties might lead to greatly increased tobacco imports, especially from Cuba and Mexico. Sugar-growers were alarmed about Cuban sugar.[52] Proponents of the treaty included ex-President Grant, Matias Romero, the enthusiastic Mexican Minister to the United States, and Porfirio Diaz, the Mexican strongman, who made a timely tour of the United States and its commercial bodies in 1883.[53]

If special interests hampered congressional approval of the treaties, political considerations were probably an insurmountable barrier. By the second session of the forty-eighth Congress, the Democrats were planning for their imminent return to the White House and a greater share of the patronage. Most Democrats were also very reluctant to pass any legislation that could be credited to the Republicans, or to commit President-elect Cleveland to a new course in foreign policy.[54] Moreover, most Democrats wanted no part of a trade expansion program that did not include general tariff reduction.

President Arthur received little consideration from the opposition. He got little more from his own badly divided Republican party. Continuing Republican factional disputes and Arthur's failure to support Blaine in the 1884 presidential campaign merely increased party disharmony. Blaine blamed Arthur for his defeat.

This bitterness, coupled with Arthur's reversal of policy on the Pan-American meeting and his replacement of Blaine in the State Department, widened the already deep division between the two men. During the campaign of 1884, Blaine had discussed his customs union plan, and he had explicitly supported the Mexican treaty. Although the president's program closely paralleled his ideas about the urgent need for American trade expansion, Blaine, in December 1884, rallied his congressional allies against Arthur.[55]

Arthur's and Frelinghuysen's atrocious timing was an additional obstacle to a positive reception of their trade expansion program. On the eve of the inauguration of a new president of a different party, a lame duck administration presented a lame duck Senate with the Spanish agreement, extension of the Hawaiian reciprocity treaty, a reciprocity treaty with the Dominican Republic, and the Frelinghuysen-Zavala Treaty. In addition, the Mexican agreement was waiting for House action. This excessive burden was added to the normally heavy workload that accompanies the last session of a Congress. At the same time, the administration was actively engaged in exploring opportunities for reciprocity treaties with Colombia, Guatemala, El Salvador, and Venezuela, and had official representatives at the Berlin West Africa Conference.[56]

More than a few congressmen must have shared the feeling of the *Commercial and Financial Chronicle* when it asked in a thoughtful, perceptive editorial:

What kind of a government do our people wish for in the future? This is a practical question that seems to be suggested by propositions that are now before the Senate for discussion, and by events that are at present transpiring. It is quite possible that a partial or absolute change is desirable. We may have pursued a peace-loving, non-interfering, humdrum sort of existence long enough, and a more brilliant course may be preferable now, involving contact with European politics, colonial settlement in other parts of the world, the defense of canals built in foreign countries, a large navy and army, permanently heavy taxes—in a word, an establishment as much like the old country governments as it is possible to develop on American soil.[57]

No large, well-financed pressure group supporting Arthur and Frelinghuysen emerged. In the mid-1880s interest in foreign markets was limited and sporadic. Preservation of the American market had far greater priority than extending the market. Arthur's program, with its strain on credibility and its extreme boldness, probably discouraged support from pressure groups and the public. The press was distinctly cool. "The fact of overproduction in every line of manufactures," the *New York Times* noted in November 1884, "is generally admitted, and the fact that our manufacturers are practically shut up in our home market is not disputed." But a month later the *Times* laconically complained that Secretary Frelinghuysen was guilty of poor planning in submitting so many new treaties to the short session of Congress in 1884. The *New York Tribune* followed the vacillations of the temperamental Blaine. It initially approved of the Mexican treaty as "the most important convention negotiated by the United States government in many years." The editors worried about overproduction and "that the markets for American products are too narrow; that the avenues of commerce all over the world have been seized by rival nations." But in December 1884, the *Tribune* opposed the Spanish agreement and, instead, gave some support to a *zollverein*, a "Union of American Powers"—excluding any European powers —"for the promotion and defense of American interests."[58]

The *Commercial and Financial Chronicle* claimed that lack of investment and slow movement of money—not overproduction—were the primary causes of the depression of the 1880s. The *Chronicle* did not support Arthur's trade expansion program.[59] Nor did *Bradstreet's*.[60] *Banker's Magazine* was erratic; it smugly told its readers in December 1884, "We need not be very much concerned in the country concerning the extension of our trade." A month later it said: "In this particular juncture, when prices are low and declining, when a large surplus exists in every branch of trade, when mills are idle and when poor prospects before them, this question of opening up new markets is one of pressing importance which should not be overlooked, notwithstanding the shortness of the [congressional] session." The magazine remained very cool toward the reciprocity treaties because of the uncertainty caused by the most-favored-nation principle. It did not discuss the Frelinghuysen-Zavala Treaty. It did support government subsidies to revive the American merchant marine, and it praised the 1884 annual report of Secretary of the Treasury Hugh McCulloch.[61]

McCulloch had warned that "the manufacturing industry of the United States . . . [was] in dire distress from a plethora of manufactured goods." Because manufacturing was "so essential . . . to the welfare of the whole country," the nation must deal with "[t]he all-important question" of expanding exports of manufactured goods. McCulloch directed the attention of Congress to Latin America as a potential market. In an odd move by a member of a Republican administration, he urged that Congress provide for free raw materials to improve the competitive position of the United States in the world market.[62]

Arthur and Frelinghuysen refused to give up what was already a lost cause. The president used his last annual message (December 1884) to warn Congress that ascertaining "the most effective means for increasing our foreign trade and thus relieving the depression" was "one of the gravest problems which appeal to the wisdom of Congress." The "main conditions of the problem," he explained, were that the United States had an inventive and mechanically gifted people, an ample supply of most raw materials, "a system of productive establishments more than sufficient to supply our own demands," a well-paid labor force with a high standard of living, and a system of taxation "yielding a revenue which is in excess of the present needs of the Government." This led to overproduction, which he admitted was a "complex" problem that could not be solved by any "single measure of innovation or reform." But he stressed overseas economic expansion and gave special attention to the "countries of the American continent and the adjacent islands [which] are for the United States the natural marts of supply and demand."[63]

To accomplish this expansion, Arthur offered a detailed elaborate program which greatly resembled a customs union plan:

1. A series of reciprocity treaties should be negotiated, and they should include a provision that "the benefits of such exchange . . . [would] apply only to goods carried under the flag of the parties to the contract." These treaties should include the removal of tonnage duties and imports.

2. The consular service should be placed on a salaried basis.

3. Congress should enact legislation which would "favor the construction and maintenance of a steam carrying marine under the flag of the United States."

4. A uniform currency for the Western Hemisphere which "would require a monetary union" should be established.[64] Thus, as Frelinghuysen had done in his instructions to the Central and South American Commission, and in one of the clauses of the reciprocity treaty with Santo Domingo, the president also appealed to the American silver bloc.[65]

Frelinghuysen cooperated with Senator John F. Miller, chairman of the Foreign Relations Committee, to get Senate approval of the Spanish treaty and, hopefully, with the exception of the Berlin West Africa Conference, congressional assent to his entire expansionist program. In a public letter of December 26, 1884, the secretary defended the trade treaties and the canal agreement as integral parts of an economic expansion program for the United States in Latin America, and as a remedy for domestic overproduction and the depression of the 1880s. Privately, he assured Senator Miller that the Spanish treaty was not to be considered the first step toward American annexation of Cuba. The treaty did, however, give the United States closer commercial ties which "confers upon us and upon them all benefits which would result from annexation were that possible." The Spanish treaty was part of "a series of international engagements" that, including pending trade agreements and the Frelinghuysen-Zavala Treaty, in "bringing the most distant parts of our country into closer relations, opens the markets of the West coast of South America to our trade and gives us at our doors a customer able to absorb a large portion of those articles which we produce in return for products which we cannot profitably raise."[66]

In January 1885, when Senator Morrill vigorously attacked the reciprocity agreements, Frelinghuysen's lengthy reply was the principal rejoinder of the defenders of the treaties.[67] At the same time, the *National Republican*, a pro-administration organ, wrote a series of editorials defending the administration's trade program as the solution to the depression. The Central and South American Commission, appointed by Arthur in the summer of 1884, dispatched a timely, preliminary report that claimed that the Latin American governments were very receptive to the idea of reciprocal trade agreements.[68]

Congress was unmoved. The Senate did not act on the Spanish treaty before the next president, Grover Cleveland, withdrew it from consideration. The Mexican treaty lapsed when no positive action was taken on the enabling legislation. Other efforts at reciprocity, except for the Hawaiian treaty which was renewed during the Cleveland Administration, died with these treaties. So did the Frelinghuysen-Zavala Treaty and American interest in the Berlin West Africa Conference.

Why had Arthur and Frelinghuysen fought for their program against such impossible odds? Tentative answers must suffice. Arthur clearly had a personal stake beyond the usual desire of a president to make his mark. He had entered the presidency under a cloud—by way of a political bargain and an assassin's bullet. John Foster, who had expended much effort and time to secure the Spanish treaty, was one member of the administration who felt it should receive its due.[69] Arthur's Bright's Disease may have been a factor, perhaps impairing his judgment. Frelinghuysen was also very seriously ill.[70] Neither had much to lose in an unsuccessful political battle. Their illnesses also help explain their poor timing. Both Arthur and Frelinghuysen firmly believed that their program could provide the primary solution to a domestic crisis. They also knew that many other American leaders, in and out of Congress, shared the broad assumptions, if not the specifics, of their expansionist strategy. To their credit, Arthur and Frelinghuysen believed that the federal government had some responsibility—though a very limited one—for economic recovery. Moreover, they had greatly refined the Republican policy of uniting reciprocity and protection with overseas expansion.

But for the time being the initiative had passed to the Democrats and the tariff reductionists after Cleveland won the 1884 presidential election.

4

Tariff Wars
Among the Democrats

Grover Cleveland became the twenty-second president of the United States in March 1885, the first Democrat to win the presidency since James Buchanan in 1856. The riches of federal patronage were transferred to Democratic hands; little else seemed changed. The Republicans retained control of the Senate where they added five new members. The Democrats kept their majority in the House, although they lost fourteen seats in the 1884 election.[1] Thus, the now familiar political equipoise of the Gilded Age remained.

In order to break the equilibrium and contain restive Democratic silverites, Democratic leaders increasingly stressed tariff reduction. This policy fitted their domestic political assumptions and needs and also suited their view that the United States had to expand abroad economically. Democratic tariff reductionists therefore pressed their continuing conflict with both Republican and Democratic protectionists.

Cleveland initially followed the lead of the reductionists in this struggle. Characteristically, he hesitated, and only in late 1886 did he take the lead. In 1887 he dramatically made low tariffs part of the Democratic orthodoxy in his annual message. Afterward came the near political annihilation of the protectionist Democrats, the "Great Tariff Debate" of 1888, and the first presidential campaign (1888) in which the tariff was the dominant issue.

In foreign policy, Cleveland and his Secretary of State, Thomas Bayard, accepted the broad outlines of the diplomacy of the Arthur Administration, though they rejected some of its tactics. Cleveland and Bayard moved cautiously during the first two years of their tenure, and their first diplomatic moves were negative. They did not resubmit the Frelinghuysen-Zavala Treaty to the Senate. In March 1885 they withdrew the agreement negotiated at the Berlin West Africa Conference. The president told Congress that he objected to the two treaties on the grounds that they violated the American tradition of avoiding entangling alliances.[2] Since the Arthur Administration itself had had grave doubts about the wisdom of its Congo policy, Cleveland's action on the West African Conference was not a complete reversal of policy. While Cleveland and Bayard were not prepared to go as far as the Frelinghuysen-Zavala treaty, they did temporarily increase the number of American troops in northern Columbia (to 1300) in order to protect American property and to keep the transit open during a crisis there in April 1885.[3] This move reflected the assumptions of at least three previous administrations (Hayes, Garfield, and Arthur). The United States intended to dominate any transoceanic canal in Central America.

The Cleveland Administration had grave reservations about overseas military intervention. In a long personal letter to his friend David Wells, Secretary of State Bayard expressed genuine fear that intervention might lead to overseas territorial expansion. Such an empire meant "the death knell of the Republic of our Fathers." A "career of territorial aggrandizement and personal and national ambitions" would have been launched and would be sustained by popular "visions of conquest," "vast expenditures" by Congress, and a colonial bureaucracy subject to partisan political whim. But Bayard refused to follow a non-interventionist logic—the United States had to be predominant in the Western Hemisphere. Sensing his own dilemma, he told Wells that: "I cannot throw into this letter in any decent shape my feelings and views in respect of the unhappy communities that lie to the South of our borders or the Island groups (that hang dead-ripe for plucking) off our Southern coast but it seems to me that logically we must soon be forced to decide upon the measure of our responsibilities as a nation and the line of action which necessity may compel us to adopt."[4] Despite his fears, Bayard could not bring himself to accept a non-interventionist policy in the Western Hemisphere. His was a self-created dilemma, one that would haunt American leaders for years to come.

At the same time, the Cleveland Administration reversed other elements of the Arthur-Frelinghuysen foreign policy. Cleveland recalled the reciprocity treaties pending with the Dominican Republic and Spain for Cuba and Puerto Rico. The administration showed no interest in the drafts of similar treaties with El Salvador and Colombia, and no efforts were made to renew reciprocity negotiations with Great Britain for the British West Indies. The president never fully explained these actions. He was willing to support such treaties if they did not threaten general tariff reduction. Accordingly, he favored reciprocity agreements with Canada, Mexico, and Hawaii. The Democrats probably feared that the Spanish treaty would lead to greatly increased imports of duty-free sugar. The consequent loss of revenue could significantly reduce the Treasury surplus and undermine a major rationale for general tariff reduction. The Spanish treaty, Cleveland knew, also faced stiff resistance in Congress, particularly from representatives of sugar and tobacco producing states, many of which were Democratic strongholds.

The Spanish treaty died, but the administration's concern to keep Cuba close to the American sphere remained. This concern received high priority. The administration acted promptly to secure the relaxation of Spanish restrictions against American shipping to Cuban (and Puerto Rican) ports. Convinced that the United

States minister to Spain would be a position of "more importance than any other Foreign Mission," Cleveland ignored partisan loyalty and prevailed upon John Foster, an experienced diplomat but a prominent Republican, to return to Spain for such negotiations. Foster accepted the assignment, even though he doubted that the Spanish would comply with the request. He was right; his mission failed. The Spanish government was preoccupied with a cholera epidemic, and it was also offended by the American refusal to ratify the reciprocity agreement. Jabez L. M. Curry, Foster's successor, was, however, able to get Spain to end its discrimination—at least *de jure* if not *de facto*—against American trade in the Spanish West Indies. The Spanish removed consular tonnage duties on imports into the Antilles and reduced passport fees in 1886. "Lying close at our doors, and finding here their main markets of supply and demand," the president explained, "the welfare of Cuba and Puerto Rico and their production and trade are scarcely less important to us than to Spain. Their commercial and financial movements are so naturally a part of our system that no obstacle to fuller and freer intercourse should be permitted to exist."[5]

Cleveland's assessment of the importance of Cuba was not mere rhetoric. Privately and more bluntly, Secretary Bayard expressed the administration's view that "it is an accepted fact in any American mind that *whenever* the Island leaves the possession of Spain it will fall into the hands of the United States—we quietly abide the event." He and the president nervously noted the death of the King of Spain in 1885, an event that could "lead to important results as to the welfare of Cuba and Puerto Rico." The State Department requested a report on the Cuban situation in the event of a "diplomatic or military contest between the United States and Spain." Ramon O. Williams, the United States consul general in Havana, wrote a lengthy and perceptive analysis. He reviewed the Cuban economy, the attitudes of the Cubans, and the state of the Spanish navy and army in Cuba. The island, he summarized, depended upon the United States economically because of its large exports of sugar to this country. He noted prophetically that if commercial relations between the two countries were disrupted, "the Government of Cuba would be instantly stricken . . . with economic paralysis." Spain would lose its power in Cuba and, would itself suffer severe economic decline because Cuba was the "pivotal point" of the Spanish commercial system. In the event of a Spanish-American war, the Cuban people would side with the United States. Spanish military forces in Cuba, Williams concluded, were weak, and the Spanish navy had the additional problem of relying upon outside sources for its coal. He was also concerned that Germany had colonial aspirations in Cuba.[6]

The Cleveland Administration extended its preemptive colonialism to two other insular outposts of the "American system": Samoa and Hawaii. In its efforts to maintain its foothold in Samoa, the United States ventured to the brink of war with Germany in 1888.[7] Hawaii received even more consistent attention. Bayard reminded the Hawaiian government that the United States would not allow any other power to dominate the islands, but he assured the Hawaiian minister to the United States, H. A. P. Carter, that the United States was anxious to "strengthen the autonomy" of Hawaii.[8] In this particular, the secretary was not completely candid. Bayard anticipated the annexation of Hawaii by the United States in a fairly short time.[9]

To insure American preeminence in Hawaii, Cleveland and Bayard renewed Frelinghuysen's efforts to prevent the lapsing of the reciprocity treaty between the two countries. The secretary, however, was reluctant to support the new treaty because it contained an amendment which secured Pearl Harbor for the United States. Why he had qualms about this and yet calmly anticipated American annexation of Hawaii in a few years was something he never explained. He may have believed that Hawaii would eventually ask for annexation, that by contrast the Pearl Harbor amendment looked like the United States had imposed its will upon Hawaii. In any event, he changed his mind, although neither he nor the president was happy with the Pearl Harbor amendment. Undoubtedly, Bayard's changed attitudes reflected his reaction to newspaper reports that Hawaii was negotiating a large loan from the British government. The Hawaiians quickly denied the reports. Bayard solicitously told Carter that such an agreement could undermine Hawaiian sovereignty. But Bayard quickly revealed the limits of his concern. Any such treaty with Great Britain, he warned, infringed upon "the preferred rights of the United States under their agreement with Hawaii in the treaty of 1875." He thereafter urged the immediate ratification of a new reciprocal trade agreement including the Pearl Harbor amendment in order to assure American predominance over Hawaii.[10] Hawaiian independence was good, if it was the right kind of independence. "As a result of the reciprocity treaty of 1875," the administration assured Congress in December 1886, when it urged acceptance of the new treaty, "those islands, on the highway of Oriental and Australian traffic, are virtually an outpost of American commerce and a stepping-stone to the growing trade of the Pacific." While most of the Polynesian Islands had been seized by European powers, "the Hawaiian Islands are left almost alone in the enjoyment of their autonomy, which it is important for us should be preserved."[11]

So prompted, the Senate ratified a new reciprocal agreement in 1887 by a vote of 43 to 11. The administration was supported by 22 Democrats and 21 Republicans, and was opposed by 2 Democrats and 9 Republicans. Senator John T. Morgan, Democrat from Alabama, and Senator George F. Edmunds, Republican from Vermont, led the proponents.[12] Leaders of both major parties thus reaffirmed American intentions to maintain predominance over the Hawaiian Islands. Future debates about the relationship between Hawaii and the United States concerned means, not ends.

There was no such harmony about reciprocal trade agreements with Canada or Mexico. Cleveland and Bayard sought, without success, to revive reciprocity with Canada and to obtain the enabling legislation for the Mexican reciprocity treaty of 1883. The administration rationalized its inconsistency about Canada and Mexico by claiming that "a common border line," which was difficult to defend and was an open invitation to customs violations, made reciprocal agreements "expedient."[13] Once again, various interest groups which felt threatened by reciprocity treaties with either Canada oȑ Mexico formed effective lobbies, and a congressional coalition remained immune to Cleveland's appeals. This resistance was based on the familiar combination of constitutional objections, the protection of constituent interests, the rigid protectionists' fear of any opening in the tariff wall, and the Republicans' determination to minimize positive achievements by a Democratic administration. Since the Republicans controlled the Senate, they were well-placed to frustrate the administration.

Although the Cleveland Administration supported some reciprocity treaties, it "believed that commercial policies including freer mutual exchange of products can be most advantageously arranged by independent but cooperative legislation."[14] Cleveland and Bayard worked to improve and rationalize the Consular Service, which was "not equal to the demands" put upon it by the "growth of this nation."[15] The administration asked that the Consular Service be reorganized on a salaried basis, and that provisions be made for periodic inspections of the consuls. It pointed to the *Consular Reports* as providing important information on world trade and economic developments.[16] In a similar vein, the State Department negotiated a series of parcel-post conventions with Barbados, the Bahamas, British Honduras, and Mexico, and sought comparable arrangements in South America and the rest of Central America.[17] Cleveland also gave tacit support to the calling of the first International Conference of American States (1889-1890), a policy of both presidents Garfield and Arthur.[18]

The Cleveland Administration eventually placed its greatest emphasis on overseas economic expansion through general tariff reduction. Such a reduction, the president told Congress in his 1887 annual message, would make our manufacturers more competitive "in foreign markets." "Thus our people might have the opportunity of extending their sales beyond the limits of home consumption, saving them from the depression, interruption in business, and loss caused by a glutted domestic market and affording their employees more certain and steady labor, with its resulting quiet and contentment.''[19] This policy of tariff reduction also harmonized with the political philosophy of the Cleveland Democrats, reflected the increasing power of Democratic tariff reductionists, and met some of the domestic political needs of the Democratic party. Thus, they could identify with a position on a major issue that distinguished them from the Republican party and could avoid more divisive issues, such as currency.

But the Democrats' sharp division with the Republicans obscured the fundamental consensus among American leaders about American foreign policy and the relationship of the tariff to that policy. Even before Cleveland's election, leaders of both parties had concluded that economic expansion was necessary and could be obtained by manipulation of the tariff.

Not, however, until December 1887 did President Cleveland commit himself and his party irrevocably to a general decrease of customs duties. When he did, Cleveland joined forces with some veterans of numerous tariff battles. The Democratic tariff reductionists had dueled protectionists in both parties since the 1870s, and the conflict had intensified in the 1880s. In 1883 the protectionists had the upper hand when the Mongrel Tariff was passed. Later that year, the Democratic tariff reductionists began an attack on Congressman Randall and his protectionist following among congressional Democrats. In June 1884 the tariff reductionists narrowly lost on a vote on a low tariff bill. They and the Democratic protectionists then struck an awkward compromise on the tariff during the 1884 national Democratic convention which met in July. The truce ended in 1885. Finally, in 1886, Cleveland terminated his policy of neutrality and joined the tariff reductionists.

The first sign of Randall's declining political fortunes came after the Democrats returned to power in the House after the 1882 congressional election. They did not reelect Randall as Speaker. Instead, after a bitter fight between the Randallites and the tariff reductionists, John Carlisle of Kentucky was selected.[20] Carlisle did not, however, immediately employ his new powers to rout Randall. He reappointed Randall to a position he had held previously, the powerful chairmanship of the House Appropriations Committee, but he put the Ways and Means Committee in the hands of tariff reductionists. William Morrison, the irrepressible low tariff Democrat, took over the chair of the Ways and Means Committee and called for new tariff hearings in 1884.[21] A number of manufacturers, merchants, farmers, politicians, free traders, and at least one group of labor spokesmen appeared before the committee.

Testifying in the midst of a depression, the witnesses transformed the committee room into a wailing wall. Almost to a man, they defended the high tariff as a necessary defense against foreign manufactures and a device to maintain the high level of American wages. Most of the witnesses freely acknowledged that their businesses and the whole economy were in a deep slump. The views of Joseph Wharton were representative; he drew a picture of an industry on the edge of catastrophe. "The whole business is in as precarious a condition as it can well be. We have squeezed our labor as far as we can do so with prudence, and in every way we are 'on the ragged edge.' "[22]

Like Wharton, most witnesses represented narrow economic interests. The Arnold Constable Company, a leading dry goods house, claimed that the import duty on fine cottons hurt the consumer. The company denied that its imports of fine cottons undermined the American manufacture of the product. The well-organized wool growers were the only farm spokesmen. David Harpeter, president of the Ohio Wool-Growers and Sheep-Breeders Association, argued that a protective tariff on raw wool was necessary if the American wool growers were to survive foreign competition. "I am not," he modestly assured the committee, "what is known as a high protectionist. I only want such a tariff as will enable us to raise sufficient wool to supply the wants of our great and good country."[23] Thomas Williams, leader of an ironworkers delegation from Youngstown, Ohio, told the committee that American wages and working conditions were far better than those he had known in England. English labor suffered, he believed, because of the English free trade policy. The Morrison Tariff, if passed, would reduce the American laborer to the level of the English laborer. He was recorded as saying that: "As an American citizen he objected to that. He did not believe that the workingman of America should be compelled to compete with the pauper labor, or the comparatively pauper labor, of England or of any part of Europe."[24]

Only the free trade spokesman demanded comprehensive tariff reduction. R. R. Bowker, book publisher and a member of the New York Free Trade Club and the Brooklyn Revenue Reform Club, attacked protectionism as discriminatory and harmful. He wanted gradual reduction, beginning with raw materials. Such a policy would enhance the purchasing power of the American consumer, and cheaper raw materials would accelerate the "demand for labor in a growing export trade." Thus, there would be "more work, steadier work, probably better wages." But Bowker, a close associate of David Wells, privately acknowledged that neither the New York Free Trade Club nor the Brooklyn Revenue Reform Club represented large industrialists. Most of the members were professionals, particularly lawyers; a few members were small industrialists.[25]

Ignoring the general protectionist consensus of the hearings and the more moderate proposals of Democrats like Congressman Abram Hewitt,[26] Representative Morrison introduced a new tariff bill in 1884 which proposed an across-the-board reduction of 20 percent. This tactic—reminiscent of the Republican tariff strategy of 1872—suggested that Morrison and his supporters were well aware that 1884 was an election year. The 20-percent blanket cut had a suspiciously arbitrary character, but it offered at least two significant advantages. Morrison and his committee proposed a simple, short route to achieve a substantial modification of the tariff. Endless haggling over customs duties with a complex array of interest groups could be avoided. A 20-percent reduction had dramatic appeal and could be easily explained to the voters. Morrison also called for adding a number of major items, including iron ore, copper, lead, nickel, coal tar, coal, lumber, and wool, to the free list. Again Morrison explicitly linked the tariff to increased foreign trade.[27] After a repetition of old arguments, debate ended, and the House killed the measure. On a motion by Ohio Democrat George Converse, the House struck the enacting clause by a vote of 159 to 155 and killed the bill. Forty-one Democrats joined 118 Republicans. Randall led the Democratic protectionist forces. These included twelve from Pennsylvania, ten from Ohio, six from New York, four from California, three from New Jersey, and one each from Connecticut, Illinois, Louisiana, Maryland, Virginia, and West Virginia.[28] The Randallites had prevailed.

Shortly after the defeat of the Morrison Bill of 1884, the national parties met in convention. The Democrats temporarily set aside their tariff divisions for the sake of party harmony. The tariff plank of the platform was a verbose straddle. After noting the rising surplus in the Treasury, the Democrats promised to reduce taxes without injuring "any domestic industry" and "without depriving American labor of the ability to compete successfully with foreign labor."[29] They did not want to repeat their 1880 "tariff for revenue only" mistake. Georgia's Senator Joseph E. Brown put Democratic feeling in his usually blunt terms: "I saw enough of the effect then, 1880, in Connecticut and New Jersey and Indiana and probably in other States to convince me that you will never carry them again on any such platform, and you will never succeed without them or part of them."[30]

After the tariff reductionists were blocked on the platform, Randall moved to further secure the position of the Democratic protectionists. He exchanged Pennsylvania's votes for a promise from Daniel Manning, prominent New York Democrat and later secretary of the Treasury, that Randall could control Pennsylvania patronage during the first Cleveland Administration. Boosted by these votes, Cleveland quickly got enough momentum to get the Democratic nomination. During the presidential campaign, Randall campaigned vigorously, especially in New York manufacturing centers, where he assured workingmen that the Democratic party was not a free trade party. For some time after Cleveland's election, Randall had considerable influence with the new president. Manning's cabinet appointment may have largely been Randall's doing.[31]

Whether the tariff issue affected the outcome of the 1884 election is impossible to determine. James G. Blaine, the Republican nominee, tried to focus the campaign on the tariff. Accordingly, the Republicans organized supposedly nonpartisan Tariff Clubs to distribute propaganda and provide speakers in behalf of protectionism. The GOP talked darkly of free trade, "pauper" labor, and English goods flooding the American market. Free traders, operating without the support or encouragement of the Democratic party, conducted a similar but smaller "educational" campaign that centered on New York and Massachusetts. But the depression, Blaine's public and Cleveland's private morality, Republican disunity, and the Reverend Dr. Burchard's famous phrase—rum, Romanism, and rebellion—probably were, if any issues were, more important.[32] The election of 1884 clarified neither the public's attitude toward the tariff nor that of the New Cleveland administration.

The mass party alignments and the political equipoise characteristic of the Gilded Age were reflected in the election returns. Cleveland led Blaine by only 68,214 votes out of 10,051,692 cast. He won in only four states outside the South and Border states: New York, New Jersey, Connecticut, and Indiana. Texas alone gave him more than a 130,000 vote margin.[33]

Ironically, Randall, leader of the Democratic protectionists, also secured a major victory from the election. Only two years after the Democratic tariff reductionists had defeated him in the speakership fight, Randall's political star ascended to new heights. For the first time in his long congressional career, his party controlled the executive. He was a principal broker for the patronage system, and he also continued to chair the critical House Appropriations Committee. Nevertheless, his fellow Democrats renewed their assault upon Randall during the first session of the forty-eighth Congress, which opened in December 1884.[34] The president did not interfere. Following the safe course of rigidly adhering to the separation-of-powers principle, Cleveland made no attempt to aid Randall.

Randall's congressional troubles quickly multiplied. Congressman Morrison reopened his favorite issue, the tariff, in late 1885. Morrison, perhaps a bit wiser after his experiences with his 1884 bill, reduced his demands. Probably in response to the concern of the southern Democrats to protect southern coal and iron, he reported a bill with a smaller number of items added to the free list and smaller reductions on other items. He added lumber, salt, wool, hemp, flax, and a few other minor items to the free list, and he asked for lower duties on cotton, sugar, pig iron, steel rails, and window glass. Given these cheaper raw materials, Morrison argued, American manufacturers could increase the foreign sales, "thus securing markets for the products of hands now idle for want of work to do." Congress should eliminate such barriers to trade "so that the country may continue to grow in wealth and prosperity."[35]

The prominent Democratic Congressman A. K. McClure told Cleveland in April 1886 that Morrison and Carlisle had an incidental goal: they wanted to use the bill to break Randall's power. McClure informed the president that the bill faced certain defeat, but Carlisle and Morrison "would be glad to have an issue with Randall as a preparatory step toward driving him out." McClure thought this would disrupt the Democratic party, "but I think that you can stop it." Cleveland ignored McClure's advice. By that time the president had committed himself to making tariff reduction the principal policy of his administration. Undoubtedly, the revival of the free silver movement in Congress—the 1886 "Silver Blizzard"—that chilled the Cleveland Democrats strongly influenced the president. The administration had worked unsuccessfully to secure an international bimetallic agreement that would have blunted the silverite movement.[36] The Cleveland Democrats desperately wanted to outflank the Democratic silverites in Congress, and tariff reduction provided the most viable means for doing so. Such a strategy necessarily involved an attack on Randall's power.

William McKinley, William Kelley's successor as the leading Republican spokesman for the tariff, led the House Republicans against the Morrison Bill in 1886. After reciting orthodox protectionism, he attacked the bill as directed against the interest of "the unorganized farmers of the country." He scored the Democrats for reducing the import duties on wool, hemp, and flax. With "cheap India wheat meeting us everywhere," the Democrats, he charged, wanted to block any attempt by the farmer to diversify. Thus, he charged, with a twist of the British Lion's tail, that the farmers "are to be the first victims of the British policy, through the agency of the American Congress."[37] The House never formally debated the Morrison Bill of 1886. The verbal shots of Morrison and McKinley were virtually the first and the last.

Morrison tried twice, without success, to get favorable action on his 1886 tariff bill. Cleveland tried, too. He dropped his reservations about intervening in legislative affairs and urged passage of the bill. Yet, House Democrats shied away from calling a caucus on the measure in order to make it an issue of party loyalty. Despite a mounting Treasury surplus and Cleveland's support of the measure, the House voted 157 to 140 in June 1886 not to debate a bill which promised to reduce government revenues. The Democratic protectionist ranks had shrunk to thirty-five, but Randall and his followers still held the balance of power in the House. The Democratic protectionists included representatives from Alabama, California, Illinois, Louisiana, Maryland, New York, Ohio, and Pennsylvania. The last undoubtedly reflected their industrial base, the sacred protectionist creed of Pennsylvania, and Randall's power. Concern for sugar interests and fear of the wrath of the wool growers probably swayed the Louisiana and Ohio congressmen, respectively. The Alabaman represented Birmingham, site of new, thriving coal and iron industries.[38] Similar interests may have influenced the Illinois, Maryland, and New York votes. Clearly, the president had suffered a defeat and a loss of prestige. The Republican press relished his embarrassment and asserted that he "had no influence whatever."[39]

Shortly after Cleveland's legislative reversal, Congress

adjourned for the 1886 elections. Public attention, as expressed by the press, focused on the New York mayoralty race. Abram Hewitt left Congress to save New York from Henry George. Other prominent tariff reductionists left Congress for less noble reasons. Morrison and Frank Hurd, Ohio's vociferous free trader, lost at the polls. Speaker Carlisle in Kentucky won a narrow victory. Hurd was probably a victim of congressional redistricting. Already endangered by the increasingly industrial nature of his constituency, Morrison was the target of a concerted national protectionist campaign that included liberal expenditures by the American Iron and Steel Association. Whatever the reasons for Carlisle's slim victory, his tariff stand was apparently immaterial.[40] But while some of the leading tariff reductionists fared poorly, so did the Democratic protectionists. Only seventeen of the thirty-five Democrats who voted with Randall in June survived, and low tariff Democrats made some inroads in solidly Republican Massachusetts. The Republican margin in the Senate fell from nine to two, and the Democratic margin in the House from forty-three to seventeen.[41] The voters thus displayed an independent spirit or acted on local issues. Moreover, and more important to politicians anxious to stay in office, something had to be done to break the political equilibrium of the 1880s.

Undaunted, the Democratic reductionists renewed the struggle when the forty-eighth Congress assembled for its second session in December 1886. They received open support from the president. Cleveland dwelt at length and bluntly on the tariff in his second annual message. Most of the arguments he used were not his, but the style was. In laborious rhetoric, he scorned the high tariff as a Civil War relic. Most industries had long since outgrown their need for congressional sustenance. The president emphasized the mounting Treasury surplus and decried "such . . . ruthless extortion." But he was no free trader. He favored gradual tariff reduction that would neither jeopardize the jobs of American labor nor disrupt American industry. Reductions should be directed toward lowering "the price of the necessaries of life" and "freer entrance" to raw materials for manufacturers. He also claimed that the consequent lower costs for the farmer would improve the competitive position of American agriculture in the world market. The president also spoke directly to the fears of a society undergoing great change and witnessing, apparently for the first time, the rapid growth in disparities in income and wealth. Not a few workingmen, said Cleveland, wondered if they got their "fair share of [the] advantages" of government. He went on to say: "There is also a suspicion abroad that the surplus of our revenues indicates abnormal and exceptional business profits, which, under the system which produces such surplus, increase without corresponding benefit to the people at large the vast accumulations of a few among our citizens, whose fortunes, rivaling the wealth of the most favored in antidemocratic nations, are not the natural growth of a steady, plain, and industrious republic."[42] Cleveland sensed that many Americans in the 1880s thought the times out of joint; yet, his solutions were pathetically inadequate.

Despite the president's remarks and his strong support of the Morrison Tariff Bill, the House again refused (154 to 149) to debate the measure and again the Democrats did not caucus on the bill. Randall and twenty-five other Democrats once more resisted Cleveland's heavy pressure and swung the balance against tariff reduction. The stage was thus set for a political collision between the Pennsylvanian and an embittered and humiliated president.[43]

Cleveland and the tariff reductionists thereafter systematically attacked Randall and the other Democratic protectionists. They refused to relieve the pressure of the Treasury surplus either by larger appropriations or by supporting reduction of internal taxes, or the duty on sugar, the major revenue producer among imports. Reversing a prior commitment, Cleveland ended Randall's control of Democratic patronage in Pennsylvania. He gave offices to Randall's old political enemies in Pennsylvania, including former Senator William Wallace and ex-Governor Robert E. Pattison, and he worked closely with two rising figures in Pennsylvania politics who were eager to displace Randall—William L. Scott and William M. Singerly. Both were tariff reductionists. Congressman

Scott was a wealthy and politically ambitious industrialist from Erie. Singerly, a self-admitted free trader, used his *Philadelphia Record* to assail Randall and to propagandize for tariff reduction.[44]

Only after this concerted effort did Randall's political power die. But he never compromised his tariff position, which he clung to by personal conviction and which was necessitated by the inflexible attitude of the district he represented. Thus, as the Democratic party moved toward tariff reduction as the essential party policy, Randall was trapped in a dilemma between party allegiance and loyalty to his convictions and his constituents. He chose the latter. Aided by his considerable skills, his acknowledged integrity, his reputation as a strong party leader over the years, and the persistence of protectionism among Democrats, the Pennsylvanian displayed exasperating strength against the tariff reductionists.

But Randall was fighting a losing battle. His home state was a major liability. Not only did it force successful politicians to defend high tariffs, but its solid Republicanism made it impossible for Pennsylvania Democrats to use its electoral vote as a political lever, except in national nominating conventions. By 1886, Cleveland did not need Randall's support or the Pennsylvania votes for renomination. In addition, it was widely believed, and was probably true, that the Republican legislature of Pennsylvania gerrymandered Randall's district to guarantee his reelection and the continuance of high tariffs. Undoubtedly, some Democrats willingly interpreted this as political collusion.[45] The Democratic leadership concluded that Randall was a serious liability and was expendable. In addition to the hostility of the tariff reductionists, poor health incapacitated him and his two most important political allies, Samuel Tilden and Secretary of the Treasury Manning. The former died in 1886, the latter in 1887.[46] Randall was completely routed when he lost control of the Democratic party in Pennsylvania in 1887-1888.

Cleveland and the reductionists maintained constant pressure during the remainder of the second session of the forty-eighth Congress (December 1886 to March 1887). Convinced of their own rightness and full of hope for the 1888 election, they blocked almost all attempts to reduce the Treasury surplus and relieve the economy of that strain. Cleveland maintained his parsimonious view of expenditures. For instance, after considerable thought, he dramatically vetoed the Dependent Pension Bill, a measure that slid through a Congress wary of the veteran vote and plied by the persistent lobby of the Grand Army of the Republic. Randall, by now the outcast, supported the unsuccessful effort to override the veto. At about the same time, he publicly probed an already irritated nerve—Cleveland's record on civil service reform.[47]

Speaker Carlisle prevented Randall from introducing legislation either to revise, but not significantly reduce, the tariff or to repeal internal taxes on tobacco and alcohol. The last would have eased the Treasury surplus and may even have caused a deficit, which, of course, higher customs duties could have covered. Although he risked the righteous indignation of the temperance movement, Randall had a well-conceived strategy. Many of the tariff reductionists came from Virginia, North Carolina, Kentucky, and Tennessee whose residents wanted these internal taxes repealed in order to increase tobacco sales or to produce whiskey without federal interference. Randall, however, was willing to let cities and states license distillers. He even claimed that a decentralized tax structure would weaken the power of the large distillers.[48] Carlisle's refusal to allow the House to consider Randall's bills prevented another major Democratic intraparty fight, kept the pressure on the surplus behind the reductionists' efforts, and may have hampered the expansion of home brew.

The Democratic leadership also turned a deaf ear to other schemes to relieve the surfeit of revenues—subsidies for merchant shipping, construction of a modern navy and improved coastal defenses, the Blair Education Bill, increased river and harbor improvement appropriations (particularly those for the Mississippi River), or the disbursal of excess funds to the state. By calling in government bonds in 1887, the administration did reduce the surplus by $98,741,600. But Congress adjourned in March 1887, leaving revenues to continue to exceed expenditures considerably.

The tariff reductionists were determined not to dissipate their advantage.[49]

In August, the Democratic intraparty struggle moved to the Pennsylvania State Democratic Convention which Randall had dominated for several years. Backed by Cleveland, Congressman William Scott worked energetically to control the convention. Newspapers followed the meeting like eager spectators at a boxing match. Randall had to make major concessions before the meeting ended. The Pennsylvania Democrats resolved that the government should quickly eliminate the Treasury surplus by a "wise and prudent reduction of internal taxation *and of duties on imports*." No Democratic state convention in Pennsylvania had taken such a step since Randall had come to power, and only the hand of the president kept Scott from trying to exact more from Randall.[50]

Then the top leaders among the Democratic tariff reductionists gathered at Oak View, Cleveland's summer residence in Washington, in early September to plan another campaign for lower customs duties. Their Oak View meetings led to the dramatic 1887 annual message, "The Great Tariff Debate," and the hotly contested election of 1888. In the warm days of late summer, however, one of the GOP's shrewdest politicians did not suspect what lay ahead. Concerned about the apathetic mood that pervaded national politics, Thomas Reed exclaimed: "If we don't meander forth and stir up something for ourselves in the next House, death on the palest of horses will be riding hard after us."[51]

The Democrats, if not the Republicans, were ready to "stir up something."

5

The 1887 Tariff Message

At the Oak View meetings of September 1887, the Cleveland Administration reaffirmed its commitment to general tariff reduction (a commitment that had clearly been made by December 1886) and developed a strategy to give substance to that pledge. The president had not only joined the tariff reductionists; he now led them. But he did so only after two years of wavering on the issue.

Inexperienced and naturally cautious, he at first avoided a firm stand on the chronically divisive issue. Initially, he occupied himself with efforts to establish the first Democratic administration in nearly a quarter of a century. Important leaders in the Democratic party had also warned against sweeping tariff reduction. One of these, of course, was Samuel Randall. Other Democratic protectionists, including Smith M. Weed, New York industrialist and an adviser to Cleveland, A. K. McClure, congressman and editor of the *Philadelphia Times,* and ex-Governor George Hoadly of Ohio, warned against making tariff reduction a major Democratic policy.[1] The fear of a divided party must have caused the president to vacillate on the issue.

H. H. Warner spoke for many Democratic businessmen when he told Cleveland in November 1884 that "The businessmen of the country are filled with grave apprehension for the future." They believed the Democratic party was a free trade party. The history of the party and its strong support of the (1884) Morrison Bill confirmed the belief. "Since the Election," Warner continued, "I notice a good many large manufacturers are shutting down. The apprehension of danger has turned to tangible fear." Businessmen interpreted even a slight reduction of the tariff on manufactured articles as a way to "discontinue business." High wages allegedly prevented them from competing with European manufacturers. To "bring labor down" to European standards would mean "Riot, and withdrawal of capital from manufacturing industries."[2]

But Cleveland's closest advisers had urged a tariff reductionist policy for several years. One of the most respected of these was Secretary of State Thomas Bayard, a vigorous supporter of lower customs duties and a close friend of David Wells. Secretary of the Treasury Daniel Manning and Manton Marble, his close adviser and former editor of the *New York World*, made an appeal in Manning's 1886 Treasury report for international bimetallism and tariff reduction. They linked tariff reduction to foreign market expansion. In doing so, they hoped to finesse the monetary crisis that threatened to divide the Democratic party and, at the same time, to attract the attention primarily of Congressman William Morrison of Illinois and secondarily of southern and western Democrats and voters. Finally, Manning and Marble emphasized free raw materials, particularly duty-free wool, in order to disrupt the crucial, but fragile, protectionist coalition of wool growers and manufacturers.[3]

Assistant Secretary of the Treasury Charles S. Fairchild, who succeeded Manning in late 1886, and Postmaster-General William H. Vilas, eventually Cleveland's closest friend in the Cabinet, concurred. Cleveland received urgent pleas for low tariffs from Morrison, Speaker John Carlisle, William Scott, Abram Hewitt, and Roger Q. Mills, who had replaced Morrison as chairman of the House Ways and Means Committee. Most of these advisers came from areas where agriculture was more important than industry; or, like Cleveland, they had firm connections with New York financial and mercantile circles. Thus, they had little direct interest in maintaining high tariffs. Moreover, most of them were strongly influenced by David Wells, the leading spokesman for tariff reduction, who advised the Cleveland Administration and congressional Democrats on tariff policy.[4]

Some industrialists also favored tariff reduction. Hewitt was particularly interested in duty-free raw materials. A number of agricultural implements makers adopted a similar position. Henry L. Lamb, manufacturer and member of the Massachusetts Reform Club, a tariff reductionist group, offered sage counsel: "it is good politics to push this tariff issue, that is *tax reduction,* relief of the people. The Republicans have taken an immobile and inflexible position . . . force the fighting on that position. . . . Give the people some issue besides spoils, offices, patronage." But Lamb was attentive to his own interests as well. The present tariff helped keep domestic iron prices at a high level. Thus, in his letter to Daniel Lamont, Cleveland's personal secretary, he continued: "the present price of iron is *stimulating* the development of Southern mines and furnaces to a point where our ironworkers in the North will be subject to a *domestic* competition more trying than foreign [competition]. This begins to be felt now." In addition to Cleveland's key advisers and some businessmen, a number of newspapers consistently demanded tariff reduction. Grass roots support for lower tariffs showed itself in the Republican state conventions of Minnesota, Iowa, and Nebraska and in the Democratic state conventions of Kentucky, Ohio, and Iowa that met in the spring and summer of 1887.[5]

Cleveland's philosophy of government, his self-image, and his personality were crucial factors in his decision to support general tariff reduction. A low tariff position fit his political philosophy, which was an approximation of laissez faire. With his tendency to moralize in thunderous tones and his self-portrait as a crusader, taking a bold stand appealed to him. Cleveland also believed that the public was burdened by excessive taxation and that, to compound the felony, these taxes favored one interest, primarily the manufacturers, against other interests. Such favoritism violated his political philosophy and his sense of justice. Cleveland turned to the low tariff for concrete political reasons as well. Such a policy appealed to certain interest groups, and it promised to give what he believed was a meaningful political issue to the public. Finally, he wanted to establish a political identity for the Democratic party that was separate from the Republican party, without falling under the domination of the resurgent silverite movement fueled by the rise of agrarian discontent in the late 1880s.

Cleveland's position was expressed cogently by Postmaster-General Vilas. Shortly after the defeat of the Morrison Tariff Bill in December 1886, Vilas defined tariff reduction as the "Cause" which, he believed, should be the "Commanding Center [?]" of political controversy. He wanted the two parties to divide over the tariff; "then the friends of the reform will be with the Democratic party and then it will be possible to touch the faith of a Democrat by this measure." Defending Cleveland's cautious approach, he even claimed the president had slowly and prudently prepared the public to understand the "supreme position" of the tariff.[6]

Other considerations, however, prompted Cleveland's action. The forces of a discordant decade had reached the White House, and they required more response than militant statements on civil service reform and honest government. Aggravating the situation even more was the fact that the economy slumped into a mild recession in May 1887, and seemed to be headed toward a depression. Hard times struck western and southern farmers with particular harshness; increasingly, they looked to monetary solutions. At the same time, the Treasury surplus continued to mount, thus reducing the amount of funds available to the private sector. Keenly aware that the monetary issue could rupture their party—as in fact it did in 1896—Democratic leaders turned hopefully to tariff reduction to unite the party and appease discontented voters in the west and south. These leaders also understood that destroying the Democratic protectionists was less risky than open warfare over the monetary standards.

The Democratic leaders used the Treasury surplus to buttress their tariff reduction campaign. Thus, Cleveland and his advisers stubbornly refused several expedients (redeeming government bonds before they were due, expanding federal expenditures, substantially reducing internal taxes, or depositing the excess funds in private banks) for lessening the surfeit in the Treasury. Such a position allowed them to add the pressure of the surplus to their drive to achieve general tariff reduction. Hence, as the meetings at Oak View began, an economic and fiscal cloud hung over the conferees.[7]

Cleveland's political future was not much brighter. The presidential election was drawing near. The first Democratic administration since 1860 had compiled a mixed record and no major accomplishment. That record reflected the severe limitations of Cleveland's imagination and political theory. He had shown some political courage, if not wisdom, but he had affronted several important groups in the United States. By vetoing a large number of special pension bills and the Dependent Pension Bill, Cleveland had angered Union veterans. To make matters worse, he had proposed the return of the Confederate regimental flags to the southern states. He had hedged on his public promise to follow civil service regulations rigidly. This action, along with his equivocation on the tariff, disappointed the Independents who were especially important in New York, where the administration had a special problem. Tammany Hall, an old Cleveland enemy, had allied itself with Governor David B. Hill, and the coalition threatened to destroy Cleveland's political base in his own state. The president angered some agriculturalists by his policies on silver, his failure to get European embargoes on American pork lifted, his withdrawal of grazing lands from the sheep and cattle industry, and his veto of the Texas Seed Bill. Cleveland did have an image of an incorruptible reformer, however, and in the 1880s this was a valuable asset.[8]

These considerations provided the background for the Oak View conferences in September 1887. Speaker Carlisle, Congressmen Mills of Texas and Scott of Pennsylvania, and Secretary of the Treasury Fairchild conferred with Cleveland; Randall was conspicuously absent. Although he was in Washington at the time and was informed about parts of the conference, Randall did not attend any of the tariff sessions. Most of the conferees were militant tariff reductionists, and their predominance indicated the direction Cleveland wanted to take. The group decided that the president would make a clearer commitment to tariff reduction, and that Mills, assisted by Carlisle, would begin to draft a tariff bill (later known as the Mills Bill). A circular detailing the need for tariff reduction was to be sent to trustworthy Democratic congressmen.[9]

After the conference, Cleveland asked Scott to meet with Randall to determine the protectionist's feelings toward tax reduction. Having refused to rout Randall completely at the August convention of the Pennsylvania Democrats, the president had left open a way for possible reconciliation. Scott later told Cleveland he had found a confident Randall. Although he had not fully developed his plans, Randall believed that he had enough Democratic votes from Virginia, North Carolina, Kentucky, and Tennessee—along with Republican votes—to get House approval of his plan to revise the tariff moderately and to reduce the Treasury surplus by repealing the tax on tobacco and cutting the levy on beer and whiskey. According to Scott, Randall hoped "thereby to catch not merely the tobacco men of the south, but the moonshiners of North Carolina and eastern Tennessee, and by such a policy to escape the hue and cry that would be raised against him should he favor free whiskey." Randall virtually admitted he opposed any reduction of the tariff. "The impression created on my mind, growing out of this interview," Scott concluded, "is that today Mr. Randall feels very confident of his position and believes in his ability to defeat any programme which our party may bring forward in connection with revenue reform. I have no doubt that he has had assurances from Virginia and North Carolina that make him more confident than he would otherwise be." Scott advised Cleveland to attempt to outflank Randall by using Senators Zebulon B. Vance of North Carolina and John S. Barbour of Virginia and others to undermine Randall's following in the border states and the South.[10] Cleveland, however, developed a more direct attack; he made tariff reduction a test of party loyalty.

Following the Oak View meetings and the Scott-Randall conference, Cleveland left Washington for a tour to measure his political popularity and to ponder his future course. The administration announced that the president intended to make a presidential tour to learn more about the United States and the wishes of the electorate. But the presidential train passed very quickly through Pennsylvania and Ohio, strongholds of protectionism and Republicanism. He devoted a full day to Indianapolis, the capital of an important and politically doubtful state. From there he went to Illinois, St. Louis, Wisconsin, Minnesota, Kansas City, and parts of the Deep South. Several days of the twenty-two day tour were spent in Madison, Wisconsin, in Vilas' company. Throughout, Cleveland restricted his public utterances to mere pleasantries,[11] but his tour, and especially his conversations with Vilas, probably reinforced his determination to commit himself firmly to tariff reduction.

Vilas and other Democratic leaders in the Midwest saw the low tariff as a vote-getting device and a way to circumvent the monetary issue. Aside from this, they had few positive proposals to appeal to the increasingly disaffected western farmers. Most of these leaders sympathized with laissez faire and free trade, and they derived little direct economic benefit from protection. By attacking protective tariffs, they could launch sorties at corporations and appear to be friends of the farmer and laborer. These leaders believed tariff reduction would attract normally Republican voters in the Midwest to the Democrats and would assure the continuation of conservative control of the Democratic party in the Midwest. Vilas and his political friends were aware that western farmers were growing increasingly hostile to the Republican party, that many believed that increased foreign sales of their products were urgent, and that many viewed protective tariffs as a serious grievance. Undoubtedly, Vilas conveyed these ideas to the president.[12] The midwestern Democrats read the public mood accurately, especially in Minnesota and Nebraska. Knute Nelson, the popular Republican congressman from Minnesota, had already come out openly for tariff reduction. He and several of his Republican colleagues from Minnesota had voted for the Morrison Bill of 1886. Major midwestern newspapers, including the *Chicago Tribune,* a major Republican newspaper, the *Minneapolis Journal,* the *Kansas City Times*, the *St. Paul Pioneer Press*, and the *Omaha Herald,* supported low tariffs. Republicans in Nebraska also demanded lower tariffs.[13]

But tariff reduction alone lacked adequate appeal for midwestern and Plains states farmers. Some of these farmers were protectionists, and many others were indifferent to tariff policy. Those who did oppose high tariffs, such as the Populists, saw the tariff as only one of several important issues. Democratic leaders like Vilas failed to understand the meagerness of their program compared with agrarian needs and desires. Cushioned against financial vicissitudes by his successful corporate law practice and restricted by his laissez faire philosophy, Vilas could not grasp the world view of the farmers. Not surprisingly, Vilas later found that neither he nor his political allies could control the western Democrats.[14]

When the president returned to Washington in November after his western tour and his extended conversations with Vilas, he worked on his 1887 annual message which he would send to Congress in December. Well aware that Cleveland was giving a great deal of attention to the tariff, protectionists and tariff reductionists alike poured letters into the White House. Two weeks before publication of the message, George Hoadly urged the president to " 'go slow' " on tariff revision. He suggested that a milder program of tariff revision—reduction of the duties on raw materials and imposition of duties on luxury items—"is a perfectly safe position to stand on before the country.'' Hoadly, obviously writing from his Ohio experiences, warned that the danger of alienating ''large bodies of workingmen, who are thoroughly organized, whose ignorance is crass, and whose employers are extremely jealous of any danger of loss of profits, is to my mind the danger of the situation. You have both the manufacturer and the Knight [*sic*] of Labor to be afraid of.'' If Cleveland listened to such extremists on the tariff as Frank Hurd and Henry Watterson, volatile editor of the *Louisville Courier-Journal*, he would lose the 1888 presidential election.[15]

A. K. McClure offered similar advice. At the invitation of the president, the editor of the *Philadelphia Times* visited the White House in late November. Speaker Carlisle was also present. Cleveland gave them some inkling of the contents of his message. When McClure pleaded for moderation, the president firmly refused to deviate from what he thought was his duty and was willing to do so ''regardless of the personal consequences to himself.'' The *New York Herald* also became anxious. An angry Watterson then attacked the *Herald*, which replied by appealing to the Democrats to avoid a tariff battle before the 1888 election: ''The *Herald* has urged tariff reform as earnestly as the *Courier-Journal*, but this reform has been so long bungled and so often lost by Mr. Watterson's friends in Congress that we would rather have delayed another year or two than, by an untimely attempt now, to risk next year's election.'' Did Mr. Watterson believe, the *Herald* asked, that Cleveland's reelection was in the national interest, could he assure the Democrats that a new general tariff reduction bill would help them in the next election, was he willing to risk the loss of New York and New Jersey—two supposedly protectionist states—to the Republicans, and was he confident that the Democratic leadership had adequately educated the public about tariff reduction? If the educational work had not been done, ''would it not be wise to do this before proceeding to action, and especially on the eve of a Presidential election, if the Democrats lose . . . tariff reform and all other reforms will undoubtedly receive a discouraging blow.''[16]

But Cleveland was determined, perhaps because of the results of the fall elections. After a campaign which had emphasized the tariff, the Democrats had carried New York State by comfortable margins. Many Democrats concluded that it was a victory for tariff reduction. The Democratic protectionists suffered losses elsewhere. Clearly, the tariff reductionists were gaining the upper hand in the Democratic party. One of the most persistent reductionists, Secretary of State Bayard, believed that "makeshift" efforts to reduce the Treasury surplus had been exhausted. Sound tariff reduction, he believed, would cut the surplus, the amount of imports, and the cost of food to the American consumer. And, lastly, he thought tariff reduction would give the United States great access to "*foreign* markets." More than political and economic calculations, however, swayed Cleveland, and he expressed it cogently when he told one of his advisers: "What is the use of being elected or reelected, unless you stand for something?"[17] Thus, both political expediency and the president's sense of duty were served.

The president carried his moral tone to his annual message. While he sounded familiar tariff reductionist themes, he gave particularly dramatic effect to his address by the unprecedented tactic of dwelling upon one topic, the tariff, and by emphasizing the dangers of the Treasury surplus. A relatively brief document, the message was used as a campaign broadside. Like an Old Testament prophet, Cleveland proclaimed: "It is a *condition* which confronts us, not a theory." He charged that the present tariff functioned as an unjust, unnecessary tax upon the overtaxed populace and as unwonted favoritism to certain industries at the expense of the average American. Cutting internal taxes, enlarging appropriations, or reducing the tariff only modestly (such as removing the duties on luxuries and merely reducing the tariff on raw materials) were inadequate solutions to the problem of excess government revenues.

He dismissed protectionism and free trade as irrelevant labels and denied that tariff reduction endangered the well-being of either laborers or manufacturers. In fact, laborers and other groups, such as farmers, would gain, as would consumers from price decreases and manufacturers from cheaper raw materials. Thus, he appealed to a broad coalition for support. Coincidentally, the president sharply attacked the alliance between the woolens makers and the wool growers, and the trusts which he was convinced protectionism fostered. He noted that the nation was celebrating the centennial anniversary of the Constitution, and was hailing the impressive growth of American industry. "Yet," he said sardonically, "when an attempt is made to justify a scheme which permits a tax to be laid upon every consumer in the land for the benefits of our manufacturers, quite beyond a reasonable demand for governmental regard, it suits the purposes of advocacy to a call our manufacturers infant industries [*sic*] still needing the highest and greatest degree of favor and fostering care that can be wrung from Federal legislation." He then attacked the duties on wool, a keystone of protectionism. Asserting that the small wool growers were not economically dependent upon their sheep, Cleveland charged that the tariff on raw wool was callous favoritism and resulted in a higher cost of living for all Americans. Such a tariff, he continued, is "a burden upon those with moderate means and the poor, the employed and unemployed, the sick and well, and the young and old."[18]

Cleveland devoted little attention to two goals of the Democratic tariff reductionists: opening the way for increased agricultural exports and providing for free raw materials so that American industry could expand its exports. He had planned to say more about tariff reduction as a device to increase American foreign trade. For some unexplained reason, his advisers urged him to delete most of the passages relating to exports.[19] They may have thought that such references might detract from the emotional impact of the message; the American public might be unmoved by a lecture on international economics. But it probably could easily grasp an attack on high taxes and the Treasury surplus, and would react favorably to proposals for a tax cut.

At least two recipients of the message, A. B. Farquhar and M. D. Harter, saw a direct relationship between Cleveland's call for tariff reduction and economic expansion. Farquhar, a Pennsylvania agricultural implements maker and political activist, had seen a resumé of the message before it was made public. After the publication of the message, Farquhar praised Cleveland and assured him, "Yes, a reduction in duties placing raw materials [,] certainly wool, coal, timber and ore [,] upon the free list would result in a largely increased export trade, and where one man was temporarily injured a thousand would be benefitted." Later, at Cleveland's request, Farquhar tried through personal interviews to discover the reaction of big businessmen to the president's message. Harter, treasurer of the Altman and Taylor Company, praised the president. Harter, whose farm implements company had at least one foreign sales agent, saw the message as the first step toward "a Tariff for Revenue only." He believed that when the United States had reached that position it would "practically control the world's markets for most lines of manufactured goods. What manna and quail were to the Children of Israel tariff reform will be to the working classes."[20]

Later, Cleveland gave more emphasis to the relationship between tariff reduction and exports. He developed this theme in June 1888 in a campaign letter written to Tammany Hall, and devoted much of his acceptance letter to the same subject. Costly raw materials, he explained, prohibit "the sale of our productions at foreign markets in competition with those countries which have the advantage of free raw materials. We know that, confined to a home market, our manufacturing operations are curtailed, their demand for labor irregular, and the rate of wages paid uncertain." To emphasize his point, he reiterated that the Democrats "propose . . . by extending the markets of our manufacturers to promote the steady employment of labor, while cheapening the costs of the necessaries of life we increase the purchasing power of the workingman's wages and add to the comforts of his home."[21]

The rhetoric of Cleveland's 1887 message had little immediate impact on international economics, but it set the stage for the "Great Tariff Debate" and the 1888 presidential election. Cleveland's stand gave the Democrats a clearcut issue and the appearance of being champions of the average American straining under a heavy burden of taxes. Given the political and social assumptions of the Democratic leadership, tariff reduction was the most positive program they had to present. Moreover, the Democrats finessed the especially divisive currency issue. The president transformed the apathetic political mood, and by committing the Democrats to tariff reduction, he created the means for a party loyalty test and for achieving considerable party unity. In doing so, Cleveland gave the Democrats, too often merely a collection of feudal lords, a national leader.

But his message alienated significant Democratic leaders—in particular, Randall and Senator Arthur P. Gorman of Maryland, key figures in Cleveland's 1884 election. Randall sat out the 1888 election, and Gorman's support was lukewarm. Both had been vital to Cleveland's election in 1884 and their inactivity in 1888 hurt the president's chances for reelection. Their important organizational skills and Randall's appeal to the labor vote were lost.[22] Furthermore, their departure created the illusion that Cleveland was a tool of the tariff reductionists.

The disaffection of another Democratic protectionist may have been more significant. Henry G. Davis, West Virginia's most powerful Democrat, put his large interests in the Baltimore and Ohio Railway and West Virginia mining above party loyalty. Davis persuaded Stephen B. Elkins, his son-in-law, a major Republican leader, and a devoted follower and friend of Blaine that the Indiana Republican Benjamin Harrison was the most suitable opponent for Cleveland. They expressed these feelings and their reaction to the message to Harrison during a private conference at the Davis-Elkins West Virginia retreat. Harrison expressed only cautious interest.[23] Very likely he was impressed by the political power and campaign money that Davis and Elkins represented. Harrison also must have sensed that the political wind was blowing away from Blaine.

Randall tried to heal the breach in the Democratic ranks, but his timing and the nature of his proposal gave the appearance of being an open challenge to Cleveland's leadership. The day Congress received the president's address, December 6, Randall offered a compromise plan that resembled the platform compromise of 1884: reduction of internal taxes, which, he admitted to a reporter, "the President does not seem to favor," and an allegedly "large reduction . . . in the rate of duty on imports." Although he conceded that the free list had to be expanded, he was vague about what kinds of imports would be affected. Randall closed the interview by warning that a "radical course" of action—the plan Cleveland presented in his address—would not be accepted by Congress.[24] Randall's assessment was realistic. His compromise might have kept more Democratic protectionists in the Democratic fold, and might even have kept Cleveland in the White House. But he had waited too long to act, and his proposal was too different from Cleveland's plan. The last opportunity for reconciliation had passed in September, if not earlier.

Cleveland had gone too far to alter his course now. His tariff message, in fact, left him in a dilemma. The address allowed the psychological satisfaction of assuming a bold posture, but his address made any compromise very difficult. Until Randall's attack upon his message (a major policy statement), Cleveland had vacillated in hopes of avoiding a complete break with the Pennsylvanian. In August 1887 he had prevented a thorough defeat of Randall at the Pennsylvania State Democratic Convention. Then, in late November, before Randall's attack, he had rebuffed suggestions that he no longer allow Randall any influence with the administration in the dispensing of patronage or favors. But now, having been so openly challenged, the president could no longer postpone a complete rupture. Randall's diminishing power virtually disappeared in the House and in the Pennsylvania Democratic party.[25]

The Solid South also began to show divisions in its ranks. Henry Watterson acknowledged that "the old Whig is there in all the [southern] states." Few southern politicians defended protectionism as openly as Senator Joseph Brown, the industrialist, a New South devotée, and member of Georgia's "Bourbon Triumvirate."

The editors of New South newspapers—the *Atlanta Constitution,* the *Augusta Chronicle,* the *Birmingham Age,* the *Macon Telegraph,* the *Richmond Whig,* and the *Nashville American*—were not so timid. Some southern industrialists and their allies also favored high tariffs. Among these were W. H. Skaggs, a bank president from Telladega, Alabama; Baker P. Lee, editor of *The Industrial South,* from Richmond; Samuel Noble of Clifton Iron Company, Anniston, Alabama; John H. Caldwell, an Alabama lawyer; R. H. West, a Dallas lawyer; and Major J. F. Hanson of the Bibb Manufacturing Company in Macon, Georgia (one of the largest textile firms in the South) and owner of the *Macon Telegraph.* Hanson was confident the South would divide on the tariff, but he warned, the "fear of Negro supremacy is ever present with a Southern man. . . . But for its existence the Solid South would dissolve like a rope of sand." Although the *Savannah News* claimed that there were few southern protectionists and that these were a mere "noise," the strength of protectionist sentiment in the South was reflected in the drafting of the Mills Bill.[26] But Hanson's warning, as the Republicans found out in the election of 1888, was well-founded.

Favorable reactions to the 1887 message came from a variety of sources. A member of the New York Stock Exchange wrote Cleveland and assured him of his support. Eastern importers backed the president. Like the agricultural implements makers, other manufacturers were attracted by the prospect of cheaper raw materials: Atlantic seaboard iron manufacturers, the large Bridgeport arms makers, some typewriter manufacturers, the Wheeler and Wilson Sewing-Machine Company, some wool manufacturers, and a white lead manufacturer. Congressman Clifton R. Breckinridge, Henry George, and Silas W. Burt, all active politicians, wrote enthusiastic praise of the president. Many other politicians must have done so verbally. Wheeler H. Peckham, prominent attorney, concurred, as did most of the Independents. The Independents, along with some Republicans and Democrats, held large meetings in Boston, New York, and Philadelphia in January to applaud Cleveland and to promise to back his program. One laborer interpreted the message as evidence of Democratic interest in the welfare of workingmen. Samuel Pellatier, a member of the United Labor party, promised to vote for Cleveland in 1888. The *Chicago Tribune* and the *St. Paul Pioneer Press,* the *New York Times* and most Democratic newspapers gave their editorial backing, but not some of the New South editors or Charles A. Dana of the *New York Sun,* a bitter enemy of Cleveland.[27]

Cleveland's stand on the tariff united most Republicans. Factions and personal feuds had splintered the GOP for several years, but, stimulated by the president's pronouncement and by James Blaine's militant response (the "Paris letter"), they began to rebuild their party. In his "Paris letter," Blaine adroitly combined an attack on England with an appeal to the American consumer and a recitation of orthodox protectionism. The London newspapers, he noted, were calling Cleveland's message a "Free Trade Manifesto" and were rejoicing in anticipation of increased sales of British goods to the United States. Blaine cleverly refuted this charge, saying with obvious sarcasm that Cleveland was not a free trader—he was just a tariff-for-revenue-only man. He buried the hook by emphasizing Cleveland's retention of domestic taxes. "For the first time in the history of the United States the President recommends the retaining of an Internal Tax in order that the Tariff may be forced below the fair revenue Standard." Blaine offered solicitude to the average American male who either chewed or smoked by advocating repeal of the federal tax upon tobacco. Avoiding the fury of the temperance movement, he supported the federal liquor tax. He recommended spending the surplus on modernizing the American coastal defenses. If the Treasury surplus remained, it could be distributed to the states. Blaine conceded that Cleveland's policy might lead to a small increase of American exports. While this was desirable, imports would increase tenfold. He thought that expanding American trade was important, "but it is vastly more important not to lose our great market to our own people in the vain effort to reach the impossible. It is not our foreign trade that has caused the wonderful growth and expansion of the Republic. It is the vast domestic trade."[28]

Blaine's "Paris letter" was widely publicized in the United States. Whether or not he was aiming for another try for the White House, his sense of political timing was superb, and his letter became a rallying cry for the Republicans. Their basic policy—protectionism—had been challenged, and they drew together in defense of a common cause. The Republican National Committee reflected this unity. It met on December 15 to set the dates for the 1888 Republican national convention. When it announced its decision, the committee broke a precedent. Instead of the usual, simple announcement of the dates set, the committee called Republicans to gather in Chicago in June 1888, to defend the "American principle of a protective tariff."[29]

Most of the Republican press praised the president's courage, but agreed with the *Philadelphia Press* that Cleveland's message was an "unequivocal avowal of his extreme free-trade purposes." Other Republican leaders soon followed Blaine's lead in denouncing the president. A number of manufacturers, including some Democratic industrialists, joined the outcry. One of them, Edward Risborough, a Philadelphia manufacturer, spoke for many: "This thing will kill Cleveland." The major New York bankers divided evenly over the issue.[30]

The virulent reaction of businessmen and Republican politicians and newspapers to his speech must have surprised and disconcerted Cleveland. Soon after he delivered his message, he began a strategic retreat; he carried his retreat through the national Democratic convention and the election. But he could not escape the free trade label. Secretary of the Treasury Fairchild planned a major address to the prestigious Massachusetts Tariff Reform League in Boston in January 1888, to which a large contingent of free traders had been invited. At the insistence of the president, Fairchild canceled his appearance. Cleveland also acted to restrain the more vigorous low tariff Democrats in Congress, and he attempted to counter accusations that he was a free trader. He even tried, unsuccessfully, to get a mild tariff statement into the 1888

National Democratic platform—milder than his 1887 message. Finally, he selected Ohio's Allen G. Thurman, a protectionist, as his running mate, and he entrusted his presidential campaign to two Democratic protectionists, Calvin S. Brice of Ohio and William H. Barnum of Connecticut.[31] But Cleveland's retreat failed. He could neither appease the alienated protectionists in his own party nor blunt Republican free trade charges.

Between the tariff message and the presidential campaign of the following year, Congress had ample opportunity to stew over the tariff. Congressional activity focused on two measures, the Mills Tariff Bill and the Allison Tariff Bill. The first provided for a lower tariff and was passed by the Democratic-controlled House. The second, drafted by the Republican Senate, reduced internal taxes and the sugar duty, and left protection intact.

Work on a draft for a new tariff began when the Oak View meetings ended in September 1887. Roger Mills, chairman of the House Ways and Means Committee, worked for six months on the legislation. Speaker Carlisle and former Secretary Manning assisted him and, along with Cleveland, restrained the zealous tariff reductionist.[32] On April 2, 1888, Mills published his report along with the Republican minority report, written by Representative William McKinley. Mills began by warning of the dangers of the Treasury surplus and the wrongs of burdensome taxation. Because of the surplus, he declared, money needed for the economy was unnecessarily tied up in the Treasury, and the excess funds tempted Congress to make unwarranted expenditures. Such "extravagant and reckless" spending would "breed corruption in public life and demoralization in private life." As a solution, he proposed that Congress reduce import duties and lower a few internal taxes. He dwelled on the former at length. He defended lower tariff duties as being in the national interest and in accordance with the most accurate analysis of the American economy. He elaborated on the technology-over-production-depression thesis that David Wells had developed and elaborated, and on the farmer's need to increase his export sales in order to guarantee his prosperity. Mills concluded by demanding tariff reduction in order to increase foreign trade.[33]

Congressman McKinley denounced the Mills Bill as a radical measure that threatened the American farmer and the prosperity and industrial independence of the United States. He decried the foreign market as "delusory," and claimed that no foreign market compared with the domestic market. "Let us first of all possess" the home market, he said.[34] In the 1880s, however, McKinley was not against overseas economic expansion per se. Protectionists and tariff reductionists often agreed on the importance of foreign trade; they disagreed on *when* the United States should make a concerted drive for overseas economic expansion and how it could best be done. McKinley did not suddenly change in the 1890s from a position of disinterest in the foreign market to one of strong emphasis on overseas expansion. He disagreed over timing and methods, not over desirability. Political pressures may have led him to talk about the overseas market earlier than he had wished, but he did not suddenly adopt a new position in the 1890s.

McKinley also challenged Mills on the surplus. He questioned whether lower import duties would reduce government revenues. He asked why, if the president was so alarmed about the Treasury surplus, he did not use the excess funds to retire all the bonded indebtedness of the United States. Congress could substantially reduce excise taxes, but, he charged, the Democrats wanted to use the surplus as an excuse to enact lower tariffs or, even, "the British policy of free foreign trade."[35].

Mills and McKinley gave rough summaries of the positions of the two major parties, but much more was to come in the "Great Tariff Debate." Congress debated the Mills Bill (and loosed a stream of orations for campaign use) from April to June 1888. Mills opened the floor debate on April 17. He repeated the usual Democratic charges that the tariff was an unfair tax and that it yielded excessive revenues. "But, Mr. Chairman," he said, in an open challenge to the "home market" thesis, "the excessive taxation imposed on the people is not the largest injury that it inflicts upon them.'' Using a crude quantitative approach to foreign trade, he turned his attention to the discontented farmers of the West and the South.

> The greatest evil that is inflicted by it is in the destruction of the value of our exports. Remember that the great body of our exports are agricultural products. It has been so through our whole history. From 75 to over 80 per cent of the exports of this country year by year are agricultural products. . . . These are the things that keep up our foreign trade, and when you put on or keep on such [high tariff] duties . . . they limit and prohibit importation and that limits or prohibits exportation. . . . All the commerce of all the countries of the world is carried on by the exchange of commodities—commodities going from the country where they are produced at the least cost to seek a market in those countries where they can either not be produced at all or where they can be produced only at the highest cost of production.[36]

Mills claimed that the prosperity of American agriculture and the whole economy depended on exporting its surplus farm production, especially to Europe. In order for Europe to continue making heavy purchases of American farm products, the Europeans had to be able to sell more of their manufactured goods to the United States. They could not do this unless the United States lowered its tariff wall. If the agricultural sector of the economy was prosperous, then the entire economy would thrive: manufacturers would have a stronger domestic market, labor would find continuous employment, and tariff reduction would open new markets for American manufactured goods. But Mills did not put great stress on export of industrial products in his speech. Other Democrats who helped introduce the Mills Bill concentrated on the relationship between the tariff and increased exports of manufactured goods. In addition to assuring a vigorous economy, Mills concluded that lower tariffs promised a lower cost of living.[37]

Mills' political and economic assumptions and his commitment to tariff reduction clouded his vision. He assumed that exports and imports existed in equal parts, and that the one could not increase without the other increasing. The economic facts of his own day refuted the assumption. On the one hand, the United States had a sustained favorable balance of trade beginning in 1876 under the tariff schedules Mills was attacking. On the other, Europe did not necessarily have to expand its sales to the United States in order to buy more American farm products. In fact, by the 1880s, England had established a strong triangular trade involving the United States, Great Britain, and Latin America. British merchants exported industrial goods to South America, sold South American sugar and coffee to the United States, and imported American agricultural products.[38]

Mills also assumed that exports of American farm commodities could be greatly expanded. But in view of the increasingly competitive world agricultural market, especially in wheat and cotton, the amount of expansion he envisioned was doubtful. Mills wanted to help American farmers within the limited alternatives that he thought were available to the federal government. His alternatives—like most others proposed then and since—could not cope with American wheat and cotton production, which greatly exceeded the demands of the market.

While Chairman Mills emphasized agricultural exports, other prominent Democratic congressmen concentrated on industrial exports. Benton McMillin of Tennessee, Speaker Carlisle's first lieutenant in the House, urged a policy of free raw materials to enable American manufacturers to increase their foreign sales. He claimed that the "United States must have other and broader markets" if labor were to be content and the nation prosperous. He warned coastal cities, such as Boston, that the railroads allowed cities in the interior to dominate the inland market. In the future, the coastal cities would have to turn to foreign trade or stagnate.

McMillin ignored the fact that the bill left coal and iron ore—both southern products—on the dutiable list. This, along with the provision for free cotton ties, gave the bill a distinct tone of favoritism to the South.

Others echoed McMillin's analysis. William D. Bynum, a high-ranking Indiana Democrat and a close adviser of the Cleveland Administration, argued that the large American labor force, assisted by rapid technological change, produced much more than the home market consumed. Continuous employment depended on overseas trade. He pleaded: "Give American labor a chance; give to it equal facilities and equal opportunities, and it will take care of itself at home and abroad." With free raw materials, he assured his colleagues, American business could "take advantage of the changes . . . in production, trade, and commerce." Then, the United States would "enter the markets of the great and growing countries south and to the southwest, and there dispose of that surplus of products, which is a constant disturbance and menace to all classes and industries at home."[39]

Republican congressmen clung to the home market like nervous biddies. William Kelley, the grand old man of the Pennsylvania protectionists, extolled the virtues of the home market. Julius Caesar Burrows of Michigan defended protectionism as a means to industrial development and economic independence. He denied that foreign markets promised sustained prosperity to American agriculture. The domestic market offered greater stability and required fewer expenditures for transportation. The interest of the American farmer lay in "ultimately" finding "a home market for the entire product of his farm." Agriculture should therefore support efforts to increase the industrialization of the United States; it should support protective tariffs.[40] Like the Democrats, the Republicans tried to appease and serve both industrial and agricultural interests. This was difficult under the best of circumstances. Considering the rate of expansion in American farm production and industry, it was problematic whether the farmer could hope, for years to come, to sell all his production domestically. Farmers, especially in the South and West, wanted immediate relief and Burrows' "ultimately" phrase provided small comfort.

Thomas Reed turned his invective on the low tariff-economic expansion thesis. He professed to see the hand of the New York international merchants behind the Democrats' rhetoric. The jeremiads on economic stagnation and unjust taxation came, he said, from the poverty-stricken brownstone houses of New York. He ridiculed Mills and other Democrats for drawing a misleading picture of the world market as a "vast vacuum, waiting till now for American goods to break through, rush in, and fill the yawning void."[41] Nelson Dingley, Jr., of Maine delivered the most comprehensive critique of the foreign trade strategy of the Democrats. He argued first that agricultural exports to Europe did not necessarily correlate with how much Europe sold to the United States. Europeans "will buy what they need where they can buy the cheapest, as we do, without regard to whether they can or cannot sell their manufactured products to us." To substantiate his point, he referred Mills to the commercial reports of the Bureau of Statistics. These, he said, showed that "our exports to each foreign country do not have the slightest reference to our imports from that country." Dingley thus neatly demolished the simplistic quantitative trade assumptions of Mills.[42]

Dingley next struck the Democrats at a particularly vulnerable point. If American manufacturers were really eager for foreign trade, then they could use the drawback provisions enacted by Congress. Under Section 3019 of the Revised Statutes, the duty on imported materials used in exports was subject to a 90-percent refund. Moreover, the Republicans promised to pass legislation to eliminate that tax altogether. Dingley had proposed a bill for this purpose in the Ways and Means Committee but, he added, "notwithstanding the apparent zeal of the majority of that committee for free raw materials in order to increase our exports, the bill sleeps the sleep of death in the committee-room."[43] Unlike some of his fellow Republicans, Dingley actively supported overseas economic expansion. He wished to do this without risking the home market, and for him, rejection of protective tariffs involved this danger. Dingley repeatedly urged measures to aid the revival of the American merchant fleet and the construction of a modern navy. He also sympathized with the expansionist plans of James Blaine.[44]

The drawback system struck hard at the logic of the Democrats. They had contended that American industry, with cheaper materials, could expand its foreign sales. Drawbacks promised to provide these cheaper materials. In fact, in its report on the Morrison Tariff Bill of 1886, the Democratic-controlled Ways and Means Committee recommended the continuation of this policy, but it criticized drawbacks as inadequate compared with free raw materials. On other occasions, the Democrats, coached by Wells, attacked the refunding operation as too complicated and for failing to apply the imported fuel used in manufacturing. Some businessmen concurred.[45]

Of course, the Democrats opposed (as it had spurned the 1884 reciprocity with Spain for Cuba) protectionism, modified by a drawback system, for practical political reasons. The most important factor was that the Democratic leadership had turned to the tariff issue to unite their party and expand its coalition and following. In addition, the drawback scheme did not encourage increased imports of European manufactured goods. Without these imports, the Democrats argued, increased farm exports would be impossible. They relied on free raw materials to appeal to the domestic and foreign sales interests of some American industrialists, particularly to eastern manufacturers. These industrialists, who used large amounts of imported materials for the American and world markets, found protectionism less attractive than did their competitors from the Midwest and the Middle Atlantic states. Finally, if the Democrats reversed their political commitment to tariff reduction, they risked even greater party division, especially if the silverites got the upper hand, and would have surrendered their major issue.

The "Great Tariff Debate" continued into June 1888, and then paused for the national nominating conventions. The Democrats renominated Grover Cleveland. After a resolutions committee fight, the convention emphatically pledged the national party to the lower tariff, and repeated the low tariff-exports liturgy. As indicated earlier, the president had wanted a more moderate tariff plank in order to mollify protectionists in the Democratic party, avoid the free trader label, and disassociate himself from the Mills Bill which, he believed, favored southern interests. In May 1888, Cleveland had called a White House meeting that included Manton Marble and Secretary of the Navy William C. Whitney, major figures in two factions of the New York Democratic party, Senator Gorman, an eastern protectionist, and Speaker Carlisle, a tariff reductionist. At that meeting, they had written a studiously bland tariff plank (the Marble-Gorman draft) that ignored the 1887 annual message and the Mills Bill. But the militant tariff reductionists had refused to compromise. Henry Watterson, an enthusiastic tariff reductionist and the principal author of the tariff plank, made the tariff resolution much more of a crusading pronouncement than Cleveland had wanted. The tariff resolution began with an endorsement of the tariff message and the Mills Bill. Then, like the Marble-Gorman draft, it vigorously attacked protectionism as "unjust and unequal taxation" and charged that "the cry of American labor for a better share in the rewards of industry is stifled with false pretenses, entreprise is fettered and bound down to home markets, capital is discouraged with doubt, and unequal, unjust laws can neither be properly amended nor repealed."[46]

Unlike the Marble-Gorman draft, the platform focused on allegations that high tariffs increased the cost of "necessities" and "permitted and fostered" "trusts and combinations" which "rob the body of our citizens by depriving them of the benefits of natural competition." Moreover, protectionism resulted in a Treasury surplus that went "far beyond the needs of economical administration" and that posed the threat of "extravagant appropriations." In contrast, the Marble-Gorman draft gave more attention to relating tariff reduction to export expansion while the platform attacked protectionism more generally and emotionally. The drafters of the platform, however, were cautious enough to promise a "fair and careful revision" of the tariff, "with due allowance for the difference between the wages of American and foreign labor." Such new tariff legislation "must promote and encourage every branch of . . . industries and enterprises by giving them assurance of an extended market and steady continuous operations." Both the platform and the Marble-Gorman draft declared the tariff was the great issue of the 1888 election.[47]

No such internal divisions over the tariff disrupted the Republicans. They boldly identified themselves with protectionism. Responding to the call of their national committee to meet in Chicago in June 1888, to defend protectionism, the wages of the workingman, and American economic independence, the Republican delegates declared they were "uncompromisingly in favor of the American system of protection." They also approved resolutions that asked Congress to grant subsidies to revive the merchant marine and appropriate funds for harbor improvements in order "to open new and direct markets for our produce." The Republicans criticized the Democrats for failing to pursue foreign markets in South America and the Pacific aggressively.[48]

The Republican convention nominated Benjamin Harrison, who was in perfect accord with the platform. A relatively unknown figure, Harrison was a devout protectionist, an earnest Presbyterian, a respected Civil War general, and a former senator. He was also seriously concerned about expanding American foreign trade. Later, during his campaign, Harrison talked about the flag and protectionism more than foreign trade, but, on at least two occasions, he declared that he and his party were anxious for overseas economic expansion. In a major campaign speech in Indianapolis, his home town, Harrison praised protectionism as a major factor in the creation of a strong domestic market. "But," he added, *"we do not mean to be content with our market. We should seek to promote closer and more friendly commercial relations with the Central and South American States."* He repeated these ideas in his acceptance letter of September 1888.[49]

Congress resumed the tariff debate once the national conventions adjourned. After each congressman had had an opportunity to make a tariff speech which could be reprinted and sent to the voters, the House voted. The Mills Bill was passed on a party-line vote (162-149). Only eight congressmen strayed from their party. Three Republicans—one from New York, one from North Carolina, and Knute Nelson of Minnesota—voted for the bill. One representative, who called himself an Independent Republican, joined them. There were four Democratic defectors—three from New York, the home of the president, and one from Pennsylvania. Congressman Randall, absent because of illness, was paired against the bill. The result, President Cleveland claimed, demonstrated "that we have a party."[50]

The Republican Senate gave the Mills Bill an entirely different reception. The Republican majority in the upper chamber had organized itself to alter the Democratic measure. As early as the previous January, they had anticipated the passage of a low tariff by the House. The Senate Finance Committee, led by William B. Allison of Iowa, Frank Hiscock of New York, and Nelson Aldrich of Rhode Island, had discussed various alternatives. If they killed the Mills Bill in committee, then they would be open to charges of failing to attempt to reduce the Treasury surplus and of lacking positive tariff proposals. They could simply amend the bill to restore protection and reduce internal taxation, but they might lose control of the measure in a conference committee. They had decided in July to write a new bill. The Allison Bill was the result. While they maintained high tariffs, the Republicans appealed to the voters with free tobacco and a 50-percent reduction of the raw sugar duty. (The latter would also significantly diminish the Treasury surplus). The Republicans hoped in this way to force the Democrats either to reject the Senate countermeasure or to abandon the low tariff. They did not expect the latter to happen.[51]

Two months later, in September, Senate Republican leaders became undecided again. Hiscock changed his mind and recommended that they avoid any detailed statement on the tariff. So did William E. Chandler of New Hampshire and Matthew S. Quay of Pennsylvania, two master politicians of the era. They thought that a specific tariff law offered by the Republican Senate would surely offend some voters and interest groups. Aldrich and Allison wanted to introduce the Allison Bill. They argued that the Republican party could not ignore Cleveland's tariff message and hope to attract enough votes in the presidential election.[52] The senators carried on this tactical debate in the midst of mounting anxiety in Congress to adjourn and give more attention to campaigning. Finally, in early October, the Republicans decided to report the Allison Bill.

The report of the Senate Finance Committee (written by Senator Aldrich) made a general attack on the Mills Bill, though it acknowledged the need for tariff revision to reduce the surplus. It also acknowledged the wisdom of removing the defects of the present tariff, modifying import duties to the changes in manufacturing and commerce, and providing more effective protection where needed. Basically, Aldrich indicated the Mills Bill as a free trade measure which threatened American industry and labor. He ridiculed free traders as naïve dreamers of "universal serenity and prosperity" in international trade. Putting raw materials on the free list was commendable, if they did not compete with American materials. Aldrich condemned the Mills Bill for showing favoritism to southern products.[53]

The Democratic minority of the Finance Committee replied with two reports. The first, signed by Isham G. Harris of Tennessee, Zebulon Vance of North Carolina, and Daniel W. Voorhees of Indiana, repeated the usual Democratic charges against protectionism, including the claim that the "enemies of industry" were those who limited the markets of the manufacturer by taxing his materials. James Beck, a zealous tariff reductionist from Kentucky, wrote a separate statement. He expounded the raw-materials argument at length. To conclude his remarks, the senator quoted a letter from J. M. Atherton. Atherton, president of the Distillers Association, defended tariff reduction, saying high tariffs restricted American industry to the domestic market. If this continued, production would exceed consumption, and the position of labor would deteriorate. Because the United States lacked an adequate amount of foreign trade, workingmen faced widespread unemployment. Neither self-employment nor farming offered them viable alternatives. The average worker had few opportunities to establish his own business because new industries required costly, modern machinery. Few laborers had the necessary capital. He denied labor could turn to farming, because "our public lands will soon be occupied and this outlet curtailed."[54] "The Republican policy," Atherton argued, "had so restricted foreign trade" that the country was like a "great steam boiler without a safety valve and in which the steam is made faster than used, and a destructive explosion must follow."[55]

Election pressures terminated the debate. Congressmen and senators rushed to their home districts without ending the tariff impasse. Fearing further internal divisions, the Republican leadership in the Senate never brought the Allison Bill to a vote. The Republicans used it, however, in the states west of the Mississippi to meet the growing restiveness of western farmers. In that region, at any rate, the GOP campaigned on the Allison Bill rather than the strong protectionist statement of the national platform.[56]

The tariff played an important part in the election of 1888. The issue united and stimulated the major parties. Either because of their sympathy for protection or their fear that the Democrats would reduce the tariff too drastically, businessmen rallied to the Republicans. This was crucial to Republican success, as business brought money and organizational talent into the GOP. The American Iron and Steel Association, for instance, distributed over one million protectionist pamphlets and made large monetary contributions to the Republicans. However, neither of the largest contributors to the GOP treasury was a steelman. John Wannamaker was a large Philadelphia merchant and Thomas Dolan's wealth came from utilities and wool manufacturing.

Sam M. Clark, president of the Iowa Press Association, shrewdly observed that Cleveland probably could have won the 1888 election if he had not taken such a forthright position on the tariff. Clark had thought Cleveland "would play a foxy game as to the tariff so that the manufacturers would not be scared to the extent of opening their purses. Now they will pay for making the fight.''[57] As Clark implied, a self-styled Democratic reformer had facilitated the growing alliance between the GOP and the increasingly powerful industrialists. Moreover, organized labor also supported high tariffs. The tariff issue may have affected voter behavior, but not as an issue: party tariff positions were apparently more useful in rallying the party faithful than in changing voter attitudes.[58]

The Republicans tried to revive southern Whiggism in order to crack the Solid South. The Republicans used protectionism in 1888 to appeal to the New South impulse. This strategy had been evolving since the mid-1880s in an attempt to capture some of the southern electoral votes and to construct a white Republican party. Blaine, for example, had linked southern industrial development to Republican protectionism in an appeal to the southern vote in 1884. In 1884 and afterwards, most Republican leaders agreed to wave the "bloody shirt" less and give more emphasis to Blaine's approach. James Swank, president of the American Iron and Steel Association, expressed their assumptions when he told Senator Justin Morrill in 1886 that "we need no longer . . . wave the 'bloody shirt,' but rather, as vastly more politic, press the tariff issue upon our Southern brethren." While some GOP leaders, like William Chandler and Joseph B. Foraker, wanted to keep sectional feeling alive, others toured the South in 1887 to tap the protectionist sentiment that clearly existed there.[59]

In the 1888 election, the Republicans worked vigorously to spread the high tariff gospel in the South, especially in Virginia and West Virginia. They enjoyed their greatest success in West Virginia, where they lost by only 505 votes. They lost by 1,605 in Virginia, 13,311 in North Carolina, and 19,721 in Tennessee. Protectionism, particularly in West Virginia, may have influenced these results. That West Virginia's most prominent political leaders, Henry Davis and Stephen Elkins, were protectionists must have helped the GOP. Despite their considerable efforts, the Republicans got no southern electoral votes. White unity, racism, and the myths of Reconstruction kept the South solid. The Republicans, Senator Wade Hampton of South Carolina noted, were "trying to win by introducing the Economic question in the South. But as long as the matter of local self-government demands our attention our people cannot divide on this issue. Whether a man is a Protectionist or a Tariff Reformer, the safety and welfare of his home is paramount to the tariff." Thus, even before the ballots were cast in 1888, Henry Grady, a major New South herald, awkwardly brought the *Atlanta Constitution* into the tariff reductionists' camp.[60]

Most voters probably voted without particular regard for the tariff as an issue, although the political leaders believed they did. Except in times of serious economic stress, most voters do not make economic issues paramount, and there is no evidence from the 1888 election suggesting that the electorate behaved otherwise then. Religious and ethnic group affiliations, as well as the Republicans' stronger organization and bigger treasury, probably affected the 1888 result more than party tariff stands. The tariff may have mobilized the party faithful, however, for voter turnout was considerably larger in 1888 than in 1884.

Other factors were present. Although Cleveland had the public image of incorruptibility, he had an unimpressive record, and Harrison's image was also clean. In addition, the president had disappointed the farmers, angered Union veterans, and had aroused northern sentiments about the Civil War. The Canadian fisheries, the pending Bayard-Chamberlain treaty (which included a reciprocity agreement), and alleged British interference in the election (the Sackville-West incident) seemed to substantiate Republican charges that Cleveland was pro-British in general as well as in regard to his tariff policies.[61] Among the Irish, this was the worst of political sins.

Cleveland lost New York and Indiana, two states he had to have to win. The tariff probably did not play a decisive role in either state. While the president lost New York by a narrow margin, David B. Hill, the Democratic nominee for governor, won handily. Cleveland's dispute with Tammany Hall very likely cost him the state. Indianans, on the other hand, found the prospect of one of their own in the White House attractive. When the returns were tabulated, Benjamin Harrison had defeated Grover Cleveland in the electoral college, even though he had lost by about 100,000 votes in the popular count.[62] Both sides claimed a victory for their party and their tariff stand, but the Republicans had the White House. They also retained control of the Senate and elected a majority to the House. The equipoise had ended temporarily. Thus, Republicans were in a good position to raise the tariff even higher.

For the first time since 1882, one party dominated the executive and legislative branches. President Cleveland used his last annual message to deliver a bitter tirade against protectionism, the machinations of business, and Republicans in general.[63] The Republican leadership ignored him. President-elect Harrison was prepared to support the protective tariff and to pursue economic expansion aggressively. He asked James Blaine, who shared his ideas on the tariff and on economic expansion, to join his administration. Harrison and Blaine then worked vigorously and intelligently to advance American economic interests abroad.

6

The Harrison Administration and the Pan-American Conference

The election of 1888 brought the temporary eclipse of the tariff reductionists and assured the continuation of a protectionist policy for four more years. But it did not change the fundamental assumptions that underlay American foreign policy. The administration of Benjamin Harrison accepted the emphasis on economic expansion that the Arthur and Cleveland administrations had made. President Harrison and his Secretary of State, James G. Blaine, of course, linked their expansionist program, as had President Arthur and Secretary Frelinghuysen, to protectionism. When Harrison and Blaine could not accomplish a commercial *zollverein* embracing Latin America and the United States, they revived the tactic of individual reciprocity treaties. More than either of its predecessors, however, the Harrison Administration had a tightly integrated plan and moved with vigor and skill to implement that plan.

Political and economic circumstances prompted and allowed the Republican administration and Congress to act quickly. Control of the White House and both congressional chambers for the first time since the forty-seventh Congress (1881-1883) gave the Republicans more freedom to move than the first Cleveland Administration had had, but their political position was far from secure. Not only was Harrison's victory very narrow, but, as late as September 1889, the Republicans doubted they had enough votes in the House to organize it under their leadership. More significantly, the electorate in the late 1880s and early 1890s began to reveal deep anxiety and discontent. Thus, the GOP, victorious in 1888, suffered setbacks in local elections in 1889.[1] In such an atmosphere of political instability, the Democrats and their low tariff dogma loomed as clear and present dangers.

A more immediate danger threatened from the South and, more importantly for the Republicans, from the West. The increasing discontent of western and southern farmers threatened both major parties after 1889. Thousands of farmers and their families found poverty instead of an idyllic life on the family farm. Some managed to cut costs, develop new products, and adjust to an increasingly complex commercial structure, but others failed. In the western wheat-growing and southern cotton-growing regions, failure exacted a tragic economic and human toll. Many farmers in those areas despaired of obtaining the bounty promised in the American dream.

Finding little solace in the rhetoric and actions of either the Democratic or the Republican parties, they turned to the Alliance movement and eventually to the Populist party. Their desertion created a crisis for both major parties. The Populists, President Harrison believed, were a greater danger to the Republicans than the Democrats because they, more than the Democrats, threatened to change basic voting patterns in the Plains and Mountain states. These states, including Idaho, North Dakota, South Dakota, Montana, Washington, and Wyoming, either had traditionally voted Republican or, during their history as territories, had been dominated by the Republicans. But in the emerging political flux of the day, many established patterns were being reshaped. The Populists could capture some or all of these states, or the People's party might attract enough Republican voters to give these states to the Democrats. Unless western farmers were appeased, Harrison thought, the Republicans would be defeated in 1892.[2] Harrison's careful attention during his presidency to agricultural interests reflected these thoughts.

Other groups, organized labor and the middle class, shared the feelings of the irate agrarians. In the 1880s and the 1890s, organized labor fought internal as well as external conflicts. Not only did unions confront a generally hostile management, but they debated among themselves about the means and ends of the labor movement as well. In the 1880s this found expression in the struggle between the Knights of Labor and the American Federation of Labor, and in the 1890s, in the conflict between the Socialists and Samuel Gompers and his allies. While engaged in this crucial ideological struggle, unions became involved in a dramatically increasing number of work stoppages.[3]

In the latter part of the 1880s, many middle class Americans read the immensely popular *Looking Backward, or 2000-1887* by Edward Bellamy and joined Nationalist clubs. Others added to the growing strength of the Social Gospel movement. The alarm Grover Cleveland had expressed in his 1888 annual message was more than merely that of a defeated incumbent; Cleveland had spoken for anxious Americans who were being buffeted by the rapid transformation of the American economy. Remarkably enough, he had even questioned his own laissez faire assumptions.

In the one hundred years since the ratification of the Constitution, President Cleveland said in December 1888, American cities had become "the abiding places of wealth and luxury," and "our manufactories" had yielded "fortunes never dreamed of by the fathers of the Republic." Americans were proud of this achievement but were deeply disturbed by the contrast between "the wealth and luxury" and the "poverty and wretchedness and unremunerative toil" found in their cities. Rapid urban growth reflected "the impoverishment of rural sections and discontent with agricultural pursuits. The farmer's son, not satisfied with his father's simple and laborious life, joins the eager chase for easily acquired wealth."

Cleveland, an urbanite whose business experience was limited to the legal profession, continued by warning that manufacturing fortunes were

> no longer solely the reward of sturdy industry and enlightened foresight, but . . . [the] result [of] . . . the discriminating favor of the Government and exactions from the masses of our people. The gulf between employers and the employed is constantly widening, and classes are rapidly forming, one comprising the very rich and powerful, while in another are found the toiling poor. . . . Corporations, which should be the carefully restrained creatures of the law and the servants of the people, are fast becoming the people's masters.[4]

Harrison responded to these mounting, diverse pressures by defining overseas economic expansion as the best and most appropriate solution. He developed a program in accordance with this definition, and he acted on his program. The available evidence suggests that the methodical Hoosier's program was not hastily conceived. Most of Harrison's 1888 campaign rhetoric was conventional for a Republican candidate: orthodox protectionism, which focused upon the domestic market, and rhapsodies about the miracle of American productivity—largely, of course, the result of Republican protectionism. But as indicated earlier, in one of his major campaign speeches, he emphasized foreign trade, especially with Latin America. And he repeated this theme in his acceptance letter of September 11, 1888.[5]

When he asked Blaine to join his cabinet as secretary of state, Harrison wrote: "We have already a pretty full understanding of each other's views as to the general policy which should characterize our foreign relations. I am especially interested in the improvement of our relations with the Central and South American States. We must win their confidence by deserving it. . . . In all this I am sure you will be a most willing coadjutor, for your early suggestion and earnest advocacy have directed public attention to the subject." "As to our relations with European governments," Harrison continued, "they will, I hope, be easy of management, and in the main formal." He left no doubt that he saw such an approach as the way to meet the problems of American society, and thereby "preserve harmony in our party. . . . [and the] continuance of Republican control for a series of presidential terms."[6] Blaine accepted the invitation to the cabinet, replying that he was in "heartiest accord" with Harrison's plans and "especially pleased" with Harrison's comments on foreign affairs.[7]

Harrison's response and program were imaginative and comprehensive but well within the limits of nineteenth-century American ideology. Private enterprise capitalism was sacred; the government ought to encourage it by subsidization. Thus operating from a positive, though circumscribed, view of government, as opposed to the more negative perspective of Cleveland, Harrison readily used the overflowing Treasury. His use of those funds was alternately crude and sophisticated. The Dependent's Pension Act savored of largesse, and the same can be said of many of the projects funded by the generous rivers and harbors bills of the "Billion Dollar Congress."

President Harrison was far more than a "machine" oriented politician using the pork barrel to satiate the faithful. He wanted to use the Treasury to subsidize the reconstruction of the American merchant fleet and the completion of the program to modernize the American navy. In 1891, the president told Congress that the United States needed a modern navy "for the protection of its citizens and of its extending commerce." He blandly assured the European powers that they needed "no assurance of the peaceful purposes of the United States." The United States had to reconstruct its naval forces because "we shall probably be in the future more largely a competitor in the commerce of the world, and it is essential to the dignity of this nation and to that peaceful influence which it should exercise on this hemisphere that its navy should be adequate both upon the shores of the Atlantic and of the Pacific."[8] Harrison also supported some rivers and harbors appropriations, such as the one for Galveston, that were not mere sops to local opinion. In order to secure an American-dominated isthmian canal in Central America, he urged Congress to allow the government to guarantee the financial security of a private American company, the Maritime Canal Company, that planned to build such a canal in Nicaragua. In a related program, the Harrison Administration actively sought naval coaling stations in the Western Hemisphere.[9]

The Agriculture Department reflected the vigorous mood and sense of urgency of the president. Headed by Jeremiah M. (''Uncle Jerry'') Rusk, who was especially popular among western farmers, the Agriculture Department was keenly aware of agrarian discontent. While it did not embrace the Alliance program, the department did attempt to help the farmers in accordance with its understanding of its duties and of the American economy. Expanding agricultural exports became the major program of the department under Rusk. The secretary created a section in his department which gave its entire attention to increasing the foreign sales of American agriculture. Working closely with President Harrison, Congress, and large meatpackers, Rusk helped obtain passage of the first federal meat inspection act. The primary purpose of this legislation was the elimination of the European embargo against meat imported from the United States. Several European governments had alleged that American meats were unsafe. Hopefully, United States inspection would eliminate unsafe meats from the export trade and any grounds, real or imagined, for the European charges.[10]

Coincidentally, the Agriculture Department hired Colonel C. J. Murphey to tour Europe as a special ''Indian Corn Agent.'' Murphey's primary responsibility was to convince Europeans that American corn could be ''a palatable, satisfying, and economic'' addition to their diet. Market expansion was also mixed with philanthropy. When famine struck Russia in 1891, the department and Murphey saw the calamity as a unique opportunity for American humanitarian relief that could eventually lead to a major increase of American agricultural sales to Russia.

With an eye to disenchanted agrarians, Rusk and Harrison loudly publicized and acclaimed the work of the department.

"From the time of my induction into office," the president justifiably asserted to Congress in his 1890 annual message, "the duty of using every power and influence given by law to the executive department for the development of larger markets for our products, especially our farm products, has been constantly in mind, and no effort has or will be spared to promote that end."[11]

Not surprisingly, the Harrison Administration pursued more aggressive diplomatic tactics than its predecessors in acting upon the traditional assumptions underlying American foreign policy —American hegemony in Latin America and the vital national interest of the United States in playing a primary role in the Pacific. Some of Harrison's diplomatic moves—the tripartite agreement over Samoa, the attempt to annex Hawaii, the military crisis with Chile—followed logically. These moves and their underlying assumptions dovetailed neatly. Deviating slightly from the geographical limitations set by the strategy of its foreign policy, the Harrison Administration employed firm diplomacy to assist Liberia in its territorial dispute with France. But more consistently, the administration, implying that Africa was a European province, refused a Portuguese offer to establish coaling stations and trading posts in Mozambique, Angola, and Lisbon. Despite his firm rejection of the Portuguese offer, President Harrison showed some interest in a reciprocity treaty with Portugal. He took pleasure in reports of growing American investments and trade in the Congo, and he supported Horace Allen, an American missionary who coupled commerce with the Gospel in Korea.[12] These moves and their fundamental premises coincided with the attempts to rebuild the navy and the merchant marine, to find coaling stations in the Western Hemisphere, and to construct an isthmian canal. They were also consistent with the most important diplomatic efforts of the Harrison Administration: the Pan-American conference (1889-1890) and reciprocal trade treaties.

Both of these efforts were largely the handiwork of James Blaine. While the president was usually dominant in formulating and executing the foreign policy of his administration, he followed and supported Blaine with respect to the Pan-American conference and the reciprocity treaties. In the latter case, after initially following Blaine's lead, the president assumed an active and crucial part. He helped secure congressional approval for the reciprocity amendment to the McKinley Tariff, and then he established the strategy for negotiating a series of reciprocity treaties involving the Western Hemisphere and parts of Western Europe.[13]

The First International Conference of the American States, as the conference was formally entitled, reflected James Blaine's personality: it was optimistic, visionary, vague, and gregarious in intent. Yet, it involved a concrete, reasoned purpose: the United States wanted to use the conference to expand its political influence and its economic stake in Latin America, and to displace Great Britain as the major foreign economic power in Latin America. Blaine also sincerely wished to end the frequent wars in the area. Accordingly, he envisioned the creation of an arbitration mechanism to prevent these conflicts. He of course realized the connection between peace and economics. Most of the Latin American countries welcomed the conference; they too wanted peace and economic development.[14]

The gregarious Blaine seemed to equate the conference with a family gathering. Goodwill, he apparently believed, would overcome differences and obscure several important organizational lapses. The conference began on October 2, 1889, and lasted until 1890. A dispute immediately developed over who should be president. During the dispute, Argentina showed a marked coolness toward the United States, and maintained this attitude throughout the conference. After some haggling and bitter exchanges, the delegates elected Blaine. It was later discovered that the United States had not provided for a bilingual secretary for English and Spanish translations of the minutes.[15]

These differences were temporarily obscured as the delegates (except the Argentines who did not go) left for a 42-day, six thousand mile tour of the United States that featured American industrial centers. The clear intent of such a tour was to impress the delegates with modern economic development. One delegate, however, regarded the "excursion" as "barren."[16] That the tour was carefully planned and advertised was revealed in the advance publicity for the conference and the preparatory papers of the State Department.

Blaine's manipulative hand was obvious. Before and during the meeting, as during the tour, he skillfully created a favorable public response to the conference and tour. Throughout he used the *New York Tribune* as a vehicle for publicity. Blaine also managed to get positive reactions from the business community. The State Department polled various economic groups in the United States, especially local chambers of commerce, to discover their views of the conference. An agent of the department visited several cities to drum up a favorable response to the Pan-American meeting.[17] Chambers of commerce, boards of trade, business associations, and businessmen from all sections of the country caught Pan-American fever. Several individual businessmen already involved in export trade in Latin America gave enthusiastic support.

The agricultural sector was represented by the American Short-Horn Breeders Association, the Indiana Millers' Association, and the National Millers' Association. E. E. Perry, secretary of the Indiana Millers' Association, told the State Department after the Pan-American meeting that "we would like to know what we can do to extend our trade in South American countries *now.*" The National Farmers' Congress, acting on its own initiative, praised the conference as a first step toward getting increased exports from the United States to Latin America.[18]

The W. R. Grace Company and Flint and Company (both active traders in Latin America), Standard Oil, the Pusey and Jones Company of Wilmington, Delaware, the United States and Brazil Mail Steamship Company, the New England Shoe and Leather Association, and the Stationers' Board of Trade expressed their interest in the conference. William I. Martin, chairman of the last-named group, assured Blaine that the "large majority" of stationers were "interested in the Export Trade," and were "ready and willing to sell goods to Central and South America." Adequate transport for goods and "a satisfactory way of collections" on the sale of goods, however, had to be established before the trade would flourish. Andrew Carnegie, a close friend of Blaine and later a delegate to the conference, joined the chorus and gave particular support to a customs union, which offered advantages "so great as to justify considerable disturbance of our present system."[19] If the agricultural implements makers, usually vigorous supporters of economic expansion, were consulted, there is no record of their reaction.

Groups in Brunswick (Georgia), Chicago, Tampa, Chattanooga, and Richmond gave the State Department circulars more than perfunctory attention. Tampa businessmen saw their city as a port for an enlarged United States-Latin American trade. A committee from the Chicago Board of Trade visited Tampa in 1889 to discuss building a railroad between the two cities in a direct trade route from the Midwest to Latin America that would compete with established routes. The committee concluded the scheme was sound, and it forwarded its conclusions to the State Department. The Chattanooga Chamber of Commerce claimed that its city was developing commercial links with Latin America, and it welcomed the Pan-American meeting. The city council of Brunswick, Georgia, eagerly pushed a claim as a port in Western Hemisphere trade. The Richmond Chamber of Commerce said that the conference was "very important," and declared that wheat growers and millers in that area needed Brazil as a flour market. They had to obtain "any market which affords a steady demand for any portion of our large surplus of breadstuffs."[20]

The Spanish-American Commercial Union of New York, whose members were active in commerce in South and Central America, the West Indies, and the Philippines, gave valuable assistance to the preparations for the conference. When the union was founded, the members invited Blaine to address them. At the last minute, Secretary of the Interior John W. Noble replaced Blaine, who was detained in Washington. John Foster, who had diplomatic experience as the American minister to Mexico and Spain, and in 1890 helped line up the votes for the reciprocity section of the McKinley Tariff, also spoke. Two years later, he became Harrison's second secretary of state.[21]

Secretary Noble began his speech with the fanciful image of "Freedom and Equality" uniting all Americans. He then restated the concern of the Harrison Administration for economic expansion and the president's wish to establish rapid communications within the Western Hemisphere. The secretary explicitly linked the economic future of the Mississippi Valley and Latin America. The United States had, he said, enjoyed remarkable growth and development in its first one hundred years under the Constitution; now the country needed a new frontier. With notable facility, the secretary interpreted the land frontier of the past as having been the arena for American economic expansion; then consciously or unconsciously, Noble deftly redefined and relocated the frontier. In place of the simple frontiersman, he substituted the modern American Christian capitalist. The achievements of the past century, he claimed,

are now projecting into the future the mighty strength of the Republic; and the question of the hour is: 'What are you to do with it? ['] In Oklahoma, so great is the pressure for homes, that although we have had this vast continent before us, a town of five thousand inhabitants springs up between the time the sun crosses the meridian and sinks behind the prairies in the west. (Cheers). Is that a lesson? These vast multitudes of laborers; this army of men of intellect in the social ranks; what shall become of them? That is the question, gentlemen, that you must answer as commercial men. A greater commerce must be built; that commerce must be created, not by armies in this age, nor by statutory enactments; but by enterprise, by intellect, by industry, intelligence, honesty and truth, and justice to the regions yet to be developed.[22]

Despite his anxieties over the loss of excess land on the frontier, Noble explicitly rejected any American colonial designs for Latin America. Instead, he transformed it into a commercial safety valve.

Foster specifically addressed his remarks to a brief discussion of the relationship of the tariff to economic expansion in Latin America. Politely, but candidly, the former minister spoke about the central issues of the mounting Republican feud over the domestic market-oriented protectionism as opposed to a growing interest in overseas economic expansion. First, he claimed that the system of protective tariffs in the United States was a "fixed fact." Neither party, he thought, would significantly alter the system. Second, the tariff "has stimulated the production of skillfully manufactured goods to such an extent that it has become a necessity to seek a foreign market for the surplus, and there is no better field for that surplus than the Central and South American countries; and there is no better or surer method of securing that field than by means of reciprocity treaties." Without specifically naming those Republicans who opposed reciprocal trade agreements, he decried efforts to put raw sugar on the free list (as some congressional Republicans wanted to do) because this would destroy "our best source of securing reciprocity of trade." Finally, he concluded with praises for steamship subsidies and the Spanish-American Commercial Union, which could "crystallize . . . public sentiment" behind a program for economic expansion into Latin America.[23] In the minds of some Republican leaders, export expansion had clearly become more important than avoiding a bitter intraparty fight.

Several American members of the Spanish-American Commercial Union later served as delegates to the Pan-American conference. Charles R. Flint, the self-proclaimed "Father of the Trusts," who had extensive experience in Latin American trade and revolutions, received a place at the conference. He enjoyed a close association with Baring Brothers of London, had been a partner in the W. R. Grace and Company, and, in 1889, headed Flint and Company. Although he was a Tilden Democrat, he used his knowledge to lobby successfully for a major role in the planning and the execution of the First International Conference of the American States. Other union members who attended the conference were Cornelius N. Bliss and J. F. Hanson. Bliss, president of the Protective Tariff League and a prominent Republican, ran a large textile firm in the northeast. Hanson was an adamant southern protectionist, who turned his newspaper, the *Macon Telegraph*, into an outspoken protectionist organ in the South. Like other leaders of the southern cotton textile industry, he supported export expansion vigorously, linking this expansion to a demand that the United States improve its merchant marine.[24]

On November 18, 1889, following its tour of industrial America, the First International Conference of the American States began serious discussions on an agenda prepared by the United States. Its overly ambitious program encompassed inter-American arbitration, a customs union, ways to provide better steamship communications, and methods to establish uniform systems for customs regulations, port dues and charges, invoices, valuation of merchandise, weights and measures, and ship sanitation and quarantine. The United States also wanted to mint a common silver coin for commercial transactions, to make mutual agreements to honor copyrights, patent rights, and trade marks, and to arrange for the extradition of criminals.[25] This elaborate program amounted to an attempt to organize the Western Hemisphere into a closed system dominated by the United States. As extensive as it was, the proposed system involved no formal violation of the political sovereignty of any nation. This was economic, non-territorial expansionism garnished with expressions of Pan-American goodwill. It suited the assumptions of the Harrison Administration perfectly.

The American strategy promptly encountered opposition, led by Argentina. The friendly atmosphere that Blaine had carefully cultivated was quickly dispelled. The Argentines had remained in Washington during the industrial tour, and they were prepared to resist the blandishments of the United States. Argentina was the natural leader of the opposition; of all the Latin American nations, its economic interests and its drive for economic development most nearly paralleled those of the United States. Argentina wanted to imitate American industrialization. After years of internal turmoil, Argentina had begun in the 1880s to concentrate its energies and develop its resources. It exported meat, hides, wool, and wheat, and in return imported capital and manufactured goods from Europe. Argentina began exporting wheat in 1876, and its foreign sales of grain rose rapidly during the following decade. Thus, her exports placed Argentina in competition with the United States in the world market. While Argentine trade with Europe grew rapidly during the decade, its trade with the United States had declined since 1867. The Argentines blamed this on the American wool tariff of 1867, and they bitterly resented the legislation.

The leaders of Argentina welcomed Europe to the Western Hemisphere, and they often crossed the Atlantic to refreshen their ties. Intellectually, they drew heavily from Europe. They also needed European capital to finance their development, and immigrants from Europe to populate the Argentine expanses. Some of the Argentine leaders were themselves recent immigrants from Europe. In the 1880s, a new, aggressive generation of Argentine aristocrats arose who, unlike their elders, did not lionize the United States but rather had ambivalent attitudes. They admired American economic power, but they did not want that power to dominate them. They began to see Europe as a counterweight to American force in South America, and they criticized the Monroe Doctrine as a rationalization for interference. Argentina had also entered a period of intense nationalism; it desired a place among world powers. The Argentines resented the American bid to lead the hemisphere; they themselves wished to head a Hispano-American movement—a movement which would exclude the United States.[26]

Led by the Argentines, the conference vitiated Blaine's arbitration proposal. The conferees approved arbitration when it did not interfere in the national interests of the individual nations. Chile, perhaps with an eye toward Peruvian mines, strongly supported Argentina in this instance. The customs union plan had an equally short life. It threatened to greatly reduce import duties, the major source of revenue of the Latin American nations. In addition, they feared that an invasion of American manufactured goods would destroy their domestic industries. They wanted to imitate American protectionist policy to facilitate their own economic development. Finally, Argentina reasoned that the customs union was an American attempt to exclude Europe from the Latin American market, and Argentina emphatically rejected this. Eventually, the conference simply recommended the negotiation of separate reciprocity treaties among the American states.[27]

Republican tariff policy also disrupted the proceedings of the International American Conference. While the conference was in session, the House Ways and Means Committee announced that it put raw sugar on the free list and would impose substantial duties on raw wool and hides. Both of the latter were important Argentine products. The Argentine delegation immediately accused the United States of hypocrisy: even as the United States conducted an international congress on extending commerce, it was moving to pass legislation which would hamper international trade. Blaine intervened with the Ways and Means Committee. Though he persuaded it to put hides on the free list, he could not budge the committee on the politically sensitive wool issue.[28]

The secretary favored lower import taxes on hides and wool, but he opposed putting raw sugar on the free list. Duty-free sugar was presumably very acceptable to Latin American sugar-exporting countries. Thus, in its attempts to placate western Republican demands for free sugar, the Republican-controlled Ways and Means Committee had unintentionally struck a blow for Pan-Americanism. But Blaine believed, as Secretary of State Frelinghuysen, the Central and South American Commission (1884-1885), and John Foster had concluded earlier, that the large American demand for imported sugar gave the United States leverage for demanding trade concessions from the Latin American (and some European) countries. The free sugar proposal threatened to squander this advantage. Eventually, the Republicans compromised the sugar dispute when they amended the McKinley Bill to include a provision for reciprocity treaties which were linked to duty-free sugar.

The episode was only the first of a series of clashes between administration and congressional Republicans over the tariff and economic expansion. Republican leaders were not united concerning the urgency and the tactics of economic expansion. The episode also demonstrated the close connection between the administration version of Pan-Americanism and its view of American economic interests.

When the Conference of American States adjourned on April 19, 1890, its accomplishments fell far short of the program outlined in its agenda. The Argentines successfully led resistance to the most far-reaching schemes of the United States. The economic necessities and aspirations of the Latin Americans killed the customs union plan. Committees of the conference met on the various items of the agenda; they discussed and wrote reports which were lodged on shelves. In an editorial prior to the conference, *Bradstreet's* had sensed the outcome. "Immediate practical results from the conference are not very hopefully anticipated in commercial circles." The recommendations of the delegates would have little influence on the United States Congress or the governments of Latin America. Some value could come from the conference if it resulted in the "further spread of information about the facts and principles involved in the commerce of this continent."[29]

Some Republican leaders interpreted the conference more favorably. During the meeting, for example, the United States minister to France, Whitelaw Reid, told Blaine that the Europeans believed that it was doing "good work for us." "They have had a great dislike and suspicion of it from the start." The *New York Tribune* (Reid's newspaper) hailed the conference in April 1890 as "one of the most notable events of contemporary history." But the *New York Times* asked: "Does anyone know what the Pan-American Congress has accomplished."[30] The *Times* was nearer the truth, at least in judging the short-run result.

The first Pan-American meeting did produce some concrete

results. It opened the modern era of Pan-Americanism, and it influenced tariff and merchant marine policies in the United States. The conference recommended individual reciprocity treaties in place of the customs union scheme, and Congress later added the reciprocity amendment to the McKinley Tariff. The conference also urged steamship subsidies for improved communications, and the creation of an inter-American bank, inter-American railroad, and an international bureau to disburse economic information about the Americas. The United States Congress, by a voice vote and without a formal debate, passed a ship subsidies bill in the last days of the fifty-first Congress.[31] Efforts to create an inter-American bank and an inter-American railroad were abortive.[32] The Bureau of American Republics (which later became the Pan-American Union) was the one viable institution to emerge from the first congress of the American States. The Bureau collected and distributed data on economic conditions in the Western Hemisphere. In its early years, at least, the Bureau functioned as a virtual adjunct of the State Department. It displaced the Spanish-American Commercial Union, and, as one observer happily noted, the United States and the other nations represented at the Pan-American Congress paid the expenses of the Bureau.[33]

William E. Curtis became the first director of the Bureau of American Republics. A newspaperman by profession, he served on the Central and South American Commission in 1884. He started as secretary to the commission and finished as a member, and he then used his considerable energies to publicize United States-Latin American trade. He assisted in the preparation and execution of the Pan-American conference. Even after he became director of the Bureau, he operated more as an official of the State Department than of an international organization. For example, he worked on the details and on the politics of passing the reciprocity section of the McKinley Tariff. He received information about Latin American trade, and relayed advice about the reciprocity section of the McKinley Tariff to Senator Aldrich, the Senate Republicans' leader on the tariff.[34]

President Harrison and Secretary Blaine, having failed to implement their expansionist program through the Pan-American conference, turned their efforts toward Congress where they could exert greater influence. Reacting to and aided by mounting domestic pressures, especially from western agrarians, they significantly altered the McKinley Tariff and the Republican commitment to protectionism.

7

The McKinley Tariff and Reciprocity

The decorous toasts and inflated rhetoric of the Pan-American conference failed to produce a concrete approach for American economic expansion in Latin America. So President Harrison and Secretary of State Blaine turned to reciprocity treaties and developed a reciprocal trade program for Latin America. In their struggle with Congress and in their negotiations for reciprocity with various countries, the president and his secretary revealed the underlying assumptions and strategy of their program and a deep sense of urgency about the national position of the Republican party and the welfare of the American economy. So intense were their feelings of urgency that they were willing to risk a serious, open intraparty fight. Throughout, Harrison and Blaine demonstrated sophisticated thinking and vigorous, persistent leadership. Their achievement was impressive.

Congress, at administration urging and against its own inclinations, amended the McKinley Tariff Bill to allow the president unprecedented flexibility in negotiating reciprocal trade agreements. Then, after the passage of the bill, the Harrison Administration made reciprocity treaties with countries in Latin America. By cleverly manipulating the reciprocity amendment of the McKinley Tariff, the administration also succeeded in the partial removal of the European boycott against American meat products. In some cases, as in Cuba and Brazil, after reciprocity had been negotiated, sales of American imports increased significantly. But the brevity of the program which was terminated during the second Cleveland Administration, produced inconclusive results.

The reciprocity program of the Harrison Administration rested upon a defined set of assumptions. Neither the primacy of the home market nor the Republican commitment to protectionism was questioned. "You know I have, from the beginning," Harrison reminded Blaine in 1892, "felt that it was absolutely essential that we should confine our reciprocity negotiations with such limits as not to attack the protective system—in other words, to the admission to our markets of non-competing products, as much as possible."[1] But by 1890, and even before, Harrison and Blaine doubted that a home market-oriented protectionism was adequate. They assumed the United States had arrived at the point where overseas economic expansion was imperative. Thus, protectionism modified by reciprocity promised a secure domestic market and urgently needed foreign trade expansion.

The administration also shaped its reciprocity strategy and its rhetoric to fit party needs. It used reciprocity and protectionism to appeal to manufacturers, labor, and farmers. Most American industrialists and many laborers and farmers wanted to continue protectionism. Generally, manufacturers wanted a protected home market more than increased foreign trade. Such trade was welcome but not at the risk of the American market. Among the agricultural interests, wheat farmers in the Republican Great Plains clamored for increased foreign trade.[2] Accordingly, the administration arranged reciprocity treaties—especially one covering the Spanish West Indies—to increase exports of wheat and wheat flour. Harrison and Blaine defended their reciprocity strategy as necessary to maintaining the growth of American industry and providing steady employment for labor. Their program offered a lighter tax burden, reduction of the Treasury surplus, and some cheaper products, in particular, sugar, to the consumer. The program promised to maintain party unity, which rested on a protectionist foundation, and to avoid the divisive silver issue.

Latin America was to be the prime recipient of the overflow from the American cornucopia. Proximity and American pretensions to predominance in the Western Hemisphere aided in target selection. Latin America was believed to be peculiarly vulnerable to pressures to grant commercial favors to the United States. Like Arthur and Frelinghuysen, Harrison and Blaine assumed that as the major importer of Latin American sugar and coffee the United States had unique leverage to extract trade advantages from Latin America. Being non-industrial, Latin America also fitted into Harrison's and Blaine's scheme. They assumed that trade between the United States and Latin America would usually involve the exchange of manufactured goods for raw materials. The advantage rested clearly with those marketing finished goods. But the administration implemented its ideas only after it had won a pitched battle with Congress—a battle that further embittered an already factionalized GOP.

When the fifty-first Congress gathered for its first session in December 1889, neither the administration nor the Republican majority in Congress expected intraparty conflict. The House leadership turned immediately to the tariff. Hearings and intense labor on the draft of a new tariff followed. Believing that the 1888 election was a popular referendum on protectionism, Representative William McKinley and the Republican majority of the House Ways and Means Committee wrote a new tariff with generally increased import duties. To satisfy midwestern wool growers' demands, the duty on raw wool was increased. To strengthen the position of western Republicans, the committee placed a number of agricultural products on the duty list and put sugar on the free list, after appeasing domestic sugar producers with a bounty on raw sugar. Placement of more farm products on the protected list was designed primarily to restrict the importation of Canadian farm products into markets along the border. McKinley and his allies on the committee were responding to farm pressure from states along the Canadian border (Republican country). The sugar maneuver had other purposes. Since sugar was a table item, the American people could see solid evidence that the Republicans had secured lower taxes. Free sugar also meant reduced federal revenues, consequently reducing the troublesome Treasury surplus and eliminating one of the principal rationales of the tariff reductionists. Finally, the Republicans increased the drawbacks on raw materials used in American exports from 90 to 99 percent. They claimed that this measure should satisfy the tariff reductionists' argument that urgently needed foreign markets could be best secured by duty-free raw materials.[3]

As early as February 1890, the news about free sugar, the placement of hides on the dutiable list, and the increased duty on raw wool leaked out of the committee room. James Blaine was caught in an awkward predicament. Even as he was laboring in the Pan-American conference for increased United States-Latin American trade, the Ways and Means Committee seemed determined to destroy his efforts. At the same time the troublesome Argentine delegation raised doubts about the basic purpose of the conference. Noting the direction that the McKinley Tariff Bill appeared to be taking, Argentina, whose major exports included hides and raw wool, openly questioned American sincerity toward increased trade in the Western Hemisphere.[4]

Blaine quickly turned his persuasive skills toward the House. At his invitation, the Ways and Means Committee visited him at the State Department on February 10, and the secretary expounded his views on the tariff and trade. As Congressman Robert LaFollette remembered the discussion, Blaine spoke in an agitated manner. "At this time," LaFollette claimed, "Blaine had begun to see clearly the path along which the high protective tariff was driving us, and to realize the necessity of developing our foreign markets."[5] But Blaine had a weak hand to play.

Blaine concentrated his efforts on sugar. He explained to the committee that he wanted to use preferential sugar duties to force tariff concessions from the sugar-producing nations represented at the Pan-American conference. If Congress put sugar on the free list, it would take away his lever. But these nations (Cuba, a major source of American sugar, was not represented at the conference) could not supply enough sugar to meet American demands. Thus, Blaine could not guarantee that all sugar entering the United States would be duty-free, and western Republicans demanded free sugar in return for their support of the McKinley Tariff Bill.

For this and other reasons, the Ways and Means Committee resisted Blaine's appeals. It did leave hides on the free list, but it refused to give ground on wool or free sugar. Later, to enlarge the sources of sugar for the United States, Blaine broadened his reciprocity strategy to include the West Indies.[6] The West Indies and Latin America produced enough sugar to meet American needs. Thus, if the United States signed an adequate number of trade agreements involving free sugar, it would give the American consumer sugar without an import duty.

Some members of the House did give Blaine concrete support almost immediately. Congressman Robert R. Hitt, an old political ally, presented a resolution which called for reciprocity treaties that modified "duties upon the peculiar products of different countries by tariff concessions on both sides."[7] Such resolutions may have irritated McKinley and the Ways and Means Committee, but they had little initial impact.

Having aroused little support in the Ways and Means Committee, Blaine turned to the upper chamber. Liberally employing his dramatic skills, he reportedly told the Senate Finance Committee that the McKinley Tariff Bill did not contain "an item or line that will further or increase our foreign trade anywhere." Then, Blaine lost his temper and mutilated his new silk hat on a table in the Senate committee room.[8] In an unprecedented move, an administration leader had publicly attacked a congressional leader from his own party, McKinley. Blaine, who was ever sensitive to political shifts and attuned to broad historical and economic trends, believed that market expansion was urgently needed for political and economic reasons. He obviously thought these needs were more important than party harmony, and he sensed that overseas economic expansion and reciprocal trade agreements had considerable support outside Congress. Eventually, that support forced a reluctant Congress to amend the McKinley Bill to provide for reciprocity treaties.

John Foster reviewed the situation and found McKinley very cool toward reciprocity and furious at the secretary of state. The Blaine-McKinley feud grew worse before it died. When McKinley introduced his tariff bill in May, he remarked bitterly that "I am not going to discuss reciprocity or the propriety of treaties and commercial arrangements. I leave that to the illustrious man who presides over the State Department under this Administration and to my distinguished friend, the Chairman of the Committee on Foreign Affairs of this House [Hitt]. This is a domestic bill; it is not a foreign bill (Applause on the Republican side)." Such a public attack upon a fellow Republican was uncharacteristic of McKinley. The supposedly unemotional McKinley was so angry that as late as September 1890, he ridiculed the advocates of reciprocity on the House floor. House Republicans followed McKinley's lead. After conciliating Republican silverites with the passage of the Sherman Silver Purchase Act, the House passed the McKinley Tariff Bill with free sugar, dutiable raw wool, and a no reciprocity amendment on a party line vote on May 21. Only one Republican voted against the bill, and no Democrats voted for it. While they could not stop passage of the bill, the Democrats delighted in the Republican feud.[9]

McKinley's initial opposition to Blaine's reciprocity proposal probably stemmed from several sources. For one thing, Blaine could not assure him that the United States would have free sugar, and free sugar was part of an existing compromise with the westerners. McKinley was not concentrating, moreover, on expanding foreign trade. Blaine, in February 1890, was a possible presidential nominee and a political threat to McKinley, so he did not want to add to Blaine's public stature. McKinley later became the major Republican exponent of reciprocity treaties. He had said in the 1880s that he would support overseas economic expansion when the economy was ready for it. He apparently began to move in that direction during the fight over reciprocity in 1890. Between then and 1896, and after Blaine was no longer a presidential threat, he discovered how popular reciprocity had become with large segments of the American public. [10]

Blaine had no more success at first in the Senate than he had had in the House. The Senate Finance Committee reported the bill to the Senate on June 17 without changing either the wool or the sugar provisions. Convinced, as Blaine was, of the economic and political urgency of overseas expansion, President Harrison entered the public lists the same day. In a message to Congress, he sided with the State Department, criticized the free sugar provision, and claimed that the United States was giving something (a sugar market) and receiving nothing in return from sugar-exporting nations. This was hardly, the president argued, a wise bargain. [11] Thus, the fight was focused on sugar. Obviously, President Harrison agreed with Blaine about the urgency of market expansion. He also may have wanted to preempt a major program of a principal political rival.

Harrison included a long letter from Blaine with his message to Congress. The secretary reviewed American motives for calling the Pan-American meeting, emphasizing the concern to expand commercial ties. Circumstances had required the rejection of the customs union plan, he explained, and the conference had recommended bilateral reciprocity treaties instead. In refusing to cooperate, he scornfully noted, Congress threatened the positive results of the Pan-American meeting, angered the Latin Americans, and deprived the United States of valuable, needed foreign markets. [12] Harrison and Blaine thus initiated vigorous efforts to secure congressional approval for a reciprocity amendment to the McKinley Tariff.

The same day, Eugene Hale, senator from Maine, offered a resolution "hastily" drafted by Blaine for a reciprocity amendment to the McKinley Bill. The Hale Amendment authorized the president,

without further legislation, to declare the ports of the United States free and open to all the products of any nation of the

American hemisphere upon which no export duties are imposed whenever and as long as such nation shall admit to its ports, free of all national, provincial (state), municipal, and other taxes, . . . all articles of food, lumber, furniture and all other articles of wood, agricultural implements and machinery, mining and mechanical machinery, structural steel and iron, steel rails, locomotives, railway cars and supplies, street-cars, refined petroleum, or such products of the United States as may be agreed upon.[13]

If this resolution were taken literally, a Republican administration had proposed a significant alteration of protectionism—even a sweeping reciprocity treaty with Canada. Actually, the Hale Amendment, as Blaine acknowledged to the chairman of the Senate Finance Committee, Justin Morrill, was merely an opening gambit. Later, in September, when the Republican leadership lined up behind a less ambitious reciprocity amendment, Democratic Senator George Gray reintroduced the Hale Amendment. It was defeated, largely by Republican votes, including Hale's.[14] Hale also consistently denied that his resolution applied to Canada. The administration never favored a reciprocal trade agreement with Canada, but it was successful in using the Hale Amendment to build public support for reciprocity and to force concessions from Congress.

The immediate reaction indicated that reciprocity had some real support in the Senate. Other senators quickly presented similar resolutions. Republican Gilbert A. Pierce of North Dakota, perhaps prompted by the administration, presented a formal reciprocity amendment. Clearly aiming to quiet western anxieties about reciprocity with Canada, Pierce presented a more limited, starkly simple proposal that was focused on major sugar-exporting countries: Congress would empower the president to reimpose sugar duties on those countries which failed to grant adequate concessions on American exports. The *New York Tribune* reported quick and favorable reaction to the Pierce Amendment. Senators and congressmen, especially those from the Northwest and Pacific slope, found strong support among their constituents. Alliance officials in particular made strong pleas for reciprocity. They, according to a *Tribune* news release on July 26, liked free sugar, but they also "desire[d] to secure a market for their products." The day after the *Tribune* report, Senator John H. Mitchell, Oregon Republican, followed suit. Blaine's reciprocity scheme was drawing increasing support from Congress, but by supporting reciprocity, the protectionists exposed a weak flank to the reductionists. If the American market needed expansion, the Democrats asked, why did it need protection? At the same time, they graciously congratulated the Republicans on accepting expansionism, one of the principal arguments for lower tariffs. Connecticut's Orville H. Platt, of the Republican Old Guard, was "afraid" reciprocity would "be the beginning of the end of the protective system."[15]

Such qualms did not disturb Blaine. He was busily engaged in orchestrating a public relations campaign. He sent out circulars to chambers of commerce, boards of trade, and trade associations, many of which responded favorably. Newspapers from all sections of the country echoed them. Farm groups and political conventions passed resolutions demanding reciprocity and increased trade with Latin America. Even Cubans, concerned about their principal sugar market, supported the secretary of state. William Curtis, probably with State Department approval, released an account of Blaine's dealings with the Ways and Means Committee. It pictured Blaine fighting a noble battle for American economic interests against stubborn, narrow-minded congressmen. As Thomas Reed later said, Blaine put McKinley on "the point of his knife."[16]

Blaine also wrote letters, including several to Senator William P. Frye of Maine, that were carefully released to the press. Frye played the student, and the secretary was the instructor elaborating his ideas. On July 11 Blaine told the senator that the State Department had just learned that Spain had increased duties on American wheat flour shipped to Cuba and Puerto Rico. The change would effectively block this profitable trade. The secretary saw no reason why the United States should put sugar on the free list and thus lose a lever to force the Spanish to rescind the changes in their tariff. While the McKinley Bill was "in many respects" a "just measure," there was, he charged in a widely publicized line, "not a section or a line in the entire bill that will open a market for another bushel of wheat or another barrel of pork." He concluded by pointing out that the European market for American breadstuffs was shrinking. The rapid development of Indian and Russian wheat was primarily responsible for this shrinkage.[17]

Frye then asked how the administration proposed to guarantee free sugar to the domestic consumer under its reciprocity program. Blaine answered that "only six years ago the Prime Minister of Spain, in his anxiety to secure free admission to our markets for the sugar of Cuba and Puerto Rico, agreed to an extensive treaty of reciprocity with John W. Foster."[18] Blaine wrote similar letters to the mayor of Augusta, Maine, and W. W. Clapp, editor of the *Boston Journal*. Clapp had wanted the secretary to speak to the Boot and Shoe Club of Boston about reciprocity and trade expansion in Latin America. Blaine declined, but he used the opportunity to defend reciprocity as a policy which favored both the farmer and the manufacturer. If Congress failed to enact reciprocity, then western farmers would demand free trade. "The enactment of reciprocity," he argued, "is the safeguard of protection. The defeat of reciprocity is the opportunity of free trade."[19]

The State Department simultaneously released for publication letters supporting the secretary. Most of these were published by the *New York Tribune*, the faithful outlet for the secretary's ideas. The *Tribune* pointed to some of the tactical problems of the administration. The administration could not reveal too much about concrete proposals and chances for reciprocity treaties with the West Indies, which would assure the United States of duty-free raw sugar. It contended, in an effort to ease intraparty disharmony, that Blaine was not completely opposed to the McKinley Bill.[20]

Thus, Blaine astutely shifted his position to meet the arguments of his critics. To meet congressional demands for free sugar, he had expanded his program to include Cuba, Puerto Rico, and Santo Domingo. These, added to other Latin American sugar-producing countries, could provide tax-exempt sugar for the United States. Blaine also met pressure exerted by American flour millers. In June 1890 Spain had changed the flour tariff covering West Indian colonies. By altering import duties, it gave preference to Spanish flour exporters. Alarmed American millers claimed that this move endangered their valuable trade with Cuba. "This," J. F. Imbes, president of the National Millers' Association, told Blaine in June, "would prohibit any possible flour trade between the United States and Cuba. The millers are consequently agitated." The western demand for free sugar, the secretary deftly countered, threatened to undermine administration efforts through "a system of reciprocity, to secure, in exchange for the repeal of this [sugar] duty, the free admission of their breadstuffs and provisions into the markets of 40,000,000 of people, including Cuba. In my opinion this is the most profitable policy for the Western farmer."[21] Blaine's strategy (one Harrison approved) was to counter "the opposition of his party, through his direct personal appeal in the public prints to the people, especially the farmer, who was quick to perceive its direct benefit to him."[22] Within a few weeks, Blaine's plan began to enjoy some success.

While Blaine caught the public's eye, President Harrison was behind the scenes, devising and negotiating the political compromise that made the reciprocity amendment to the McKinley Tariff possible. While he and Blaine were counseling each other about sugar and reciprocity, the president turned to the Republican House leadership (McKinley, Reed, and Nelson Dingley) and to the most powerful figure in the Senate, Nelson Aldrich.[23] Aldrich, the president's former Senate colleague and good friend proved especially helpful. Aldrich, who himself in 1886 had proposed that the United States manipulate the sugar tariff to gain trade concessions, worked with Harrison to draft a reciprocity amendment. They were convinced after meeting with key congressmen and senators that free sugar was too popular to set aside. Accordingly, they conceived a plan to get both free sugar and reciprocity. In the amendment he brought to the Senate Finance Committee, Aldrich proposed "that the exemptions from duty of sugar, molasses, coffee, tea, and hides, provided for in . . . [the McKinley] act, are made with a view to secure reciprocal trade with countries producing these articles.'' The president was to have the power to reimpose the duty on these articles if reciprocal concessions were not forthcoming.[24] On August 28, the Senate Finance Committee accepted the amendment offered by Aldrich to the original McKinley Bill.[25] The amendment had several advantages. Free sugar remained, yet it could be used to obtain preferential treatment for American products. Moreover, the president did not have to win congressional approval for each reciprocal trade agreement. Thus, the executive could avoid the congressional obstacles which had hindered Arthur and Cleveland.

Two days after Senator Aldrich introduced his amendment, Blaine fired his biggest shot. As a part of the congressional election campaign of 1890 and before an audience of 5,000 gathered on his home ground at Waterville, Maine, the secretary delivered a brief, blunt address. As he began he said:

> I wish to declare the opinion that the United States has reached a point where one of its highest duties is to enlarge the area of its foreign trade. Under the beneficent policy of protection we have developed a volume of manufactures which, in many departments, overruns the demands of the home market. In the field of agriculture, with the immense propulsion given to it by agricultural implements, we can far more than produce breadstuffs and provisions for our people; nor would it be an ambitious destiny for so great a country as ours to manufacture only what we can consume, or to produce only what we can eat.[26]

Blaine denied that the United States desired new territory and claimed that his reciprocity program was ''supplementary'' to protectionism. After he pointed to the unfavorable trade balance of the United States with Cuba, Brazil, Mexico, and South and Central America in general, he declared that it was a serious mistake to repeal American duties on tropical products without seeking favors in return. Blaine's call for an "open door" economic expansion reached a national audience through the newspapers.[27]

Praise came from many quarters. The *New York Tribune* provided a loyal echo, and free traders and tariff reductionists welcomed Blaine to the economic expansionist faith.[28] Henry Watterson, a militant tariff reductionist, extended the genial hand of a Kentucky colonel and welcomed Blaine as the "new apostle of Free Trade." "I agree with him," Watterson declared, "that the home market is no longer sufficient; that we must find sales for our surplus production; that the system of foreign exchanges, which I have always advocated and he now advocates is becoming indispensable."[29]

The *Tribune* scorned the tariff reductionists and free traders, but the paper accepted one of the basic themes of their argument. "The common sense of the whole matter is this: protection aims to build up American industries and to increase the demand for American labor, not necessarily by enlarging the home market only, but also by opening foreign markets where that is practicable."[30] Blaine and the *Tribune* had torn a leaf from David Wells' book. Many of the participants in the debate over the McKinley Tariff Act, like most observers since, failed to see this consensus.

Despite the accolades for Blaine's Waterville speech, the administration still confronted a hostile Congress. The Republican leadership worked feverishly in the late summer to graft a reciprocity section to the McKinley Bill. Foster, Curtis (of the Bureau of American Republics), and Charles Flint advised Senator Aldrich during August and early September on various aspects of the reciprocity amendment. Flint mailed over two thousand letters to businessmen to drum up support for the Aldrich Amendment, and he personally called on important New York merchants. Public pressure, partly created by the State Department, helped. One congressman who opposed the plan complained that the idea swept his district like "a prairie fire." Speaker Thomas Reed, who detested Blaine, scoffed at the scheme—perhaps because he feared Blaine had presidential ambitions. But not even Reed could stem the tide.[31]

A large number of Republican and Democratic newspapers from Washington to St. Louis supported the reciprocity program, as did a number of commercial associations, boards of trade, chambers of commerce, and farm groups. Political conventions including some Democratic state conventions, meeting in the politically critical West and Northwest, concurred. Even where the Democrats rejected reciprocity, they used Republican rhetoric to attack Republicans. In a bid to take advantage of Republican division and win farm votes, the Ohio State Democratic Convention assailed the McKinley Tariff, in Blaine's words, for failing to "open a market for another bushel of wheat or another barrel of pork."[32]

The struggle over the McKinley Bill and the reciprocity section continued through August and most of September. The Senate passed the reciprocity section of the McKinley Bill on September 10, 1890, on a party line vote of 37-28. But the House balked. Several conference committee meetings and seven days of Republican caucuses were required to get final congressional approval. The silverites enjoyed the same leverage they had earlier when they were able to demand passage of the Sherman Silver Purchase Act before the Senate could act on the McKinley Bill. The silverites, who were indifferent to the tariff, joined Senate Democrats to block the McKinley Tariff until the Senate postponed action on the Lodge election bill, stigmatized as the "Force Bill." (The election bill was killed during the next session of Congress.) Finally, the House accepted the McKinley Bill with a reciprocity section. Confronted by an adamant administration and a determined group of Republican senators, and pressed by mounting public opinion, especially from western farm areas, House Republicans capitulated on September 27. Many Republican politicians felt no urgent concern about overseas economic expansion, but some prominent GOP leaders did. "It is believed by distinguished leaders of our party," McKinley sardonically told the House in September, "to whose judgment we have always given the greatest weight, that large advantages will come from this provision and all of us indulge the hope that the fullest expectation in this direction will be realized."[33]

The reciprocity section of the McKinley Tariff represented a major achievement of the Harrison Administration. Congress allowed the president to sign trade conventions without its approval, granting the executive a part in the process of levying taxes. Seldom has Congress been so generous: Harrison and Blaine had persuaded Congress to modify one of its most jealously guarded prerogatives. They also had overcome the objections of some protectionists that reciprocity—especially through the more traditional interpretations of most-favored-nation clauses—would be a dangerous break in the protective tariff wall. In addition, they had surmounted the fear that reciprocal trade agreements suggested entangling alliances. After 1890, the Republican party welded reciprocity to protectionism, and both President Harrison and William McKinley became vigorous exponents of reciprocal trade agreements.[34]

The Harrison Administration succeeded where the Arthur Administration had failed for several reasons. First, although the Republicans divided over reciprocity treaties, they did control both the Senate and the House in 1890. They did not in 1884. Second, although both administrations were committed to overseas economic expansion, Harrison and Blaine gave especially vigorous and able leadership to the drive to obtain reciprocity treaties, and they moved faster and earlier in their administration than Arthur and Frelinghuysen had. Harrison and Blaine were willing to risk an intense intraparty conflict, and they persisted in the face of sharp resistance. Third, a number of congressional Republicans shared their commitment. Fourth, unlike the Arthur Administration in 1884, the Harrison Administration had not lost a presidential election. Congressional Republicans, in August and September 1890, did face elections, and they knew that their prospects were poor. Fifth, as Blaine had realized, overseas expansion attracted increasing numbers of agrarians and industrialists by 1890, and Republican reciprocity promised both a secure domestic market and expansion. Finally, the most important reason was that, while there was no general depression in 1890, there was acute depression in much of the agricultural sector of the economy. The growing antagonism of western farmers to the Republican party, fed by their economic difficulties, provided a major impetus for securing favorable congressional action on the reciprocity amendment to the McKinley Bill. Western agriculturalists, traditionally Republicans, were on the verge of deserting the party of Abraham Lincoln. Republican politicians hoped to prevent this desertion.

"The tariff is passed," sighed one weary senator. The legislators plodded home to wage the 1890 congressional elections. The Republicans faced great odds. Local issues in Pennsylvania, Wisconsin, Iowa, and Illinois worked against them. In Ohio, McKinley had to campaign in a district which had been gerrymandered unfavorably to him. Southern and western agriculture and some of New England industry had slumped badly. The Populists threatened Republican strongholds. The Force Bill, the high duties of the McKinley Tariff Act, the largesse of the "Billion Dollar Congress," and the heavy-handed tactics of Speaker Reed hardly helped. Finally, Harrison was not popular with his party and the public, and he had not united the badly factionalized Republicans.[35]

The GOP suffered a crushing defeat in 1890. Some Republicans blamed the McKinley Tariff, but other factors were probably more important. The agricultural depression in the Great Plains and parts of the Midwest hurt, and so did local issues in Wisconsin, Illinois, Iowa, and Ohio. Reciprocity, however, won some public approval. One Minnesota Republican declared in October 1890 that the McKinley Tariff was very unpopular in his state but that there was very strong support for the reciprocity section of the act. "We think," he said, "that it [reciprocity] will be the only means that can relieve the agricultural interests (which is [sic] the mainstay of these Western states) from its present depressed condition." But he thought that the remainder of the McKinley Tariff was so unpopular that the Republicans would lose in Minnesota in 1890. Voting analyses of the 1890 elections, though limited in the states covered, indicate the tariff did not significantly alter voter attitudes or behavior. In the Midwest, religious and cultural issues had greater importance.[36] At the time, Democratic and Republican politicians saw the McKinley Tariff as a major determinant in the election results. Cleveland Democrats read the vote as a mandate for tariff reduction.

The 1890 congressional elections gave the political initiative to the Democrats and left a bitter, divided Republican party. With their control of the House and Senate, the Democrats kept the GOP on the defensive. They maintained a steady attack on the Harrison Administration, and they focused on the McKinley Tariff.[37] The Republicans had splintered into warring factions before their 1890 debacle; their crushing defeat only worsened matters.

Goaded perhaps by the erosion of his political power, obviously concerned with agrarian discontent in the West, and armed with an expansionist analysis of the needs of the American economy, the president energetically pushed overseas economic expansion through reciprocity treaties. In the Western Hemisphere alone, he and Blaine negotiated and signed reciprocal agreements with Brazil, Spain (for Cuba and Puerto Rico), Santo Domingo, Nicaragua, Guatemala, Honduras, Costa Rica, El Salvador, and the Caribbean possessions of Great Britain. The Brazilian agreement was the first, and it set the pattern for the later arrangements. According to one member of the administration, Brazil was "to be the test case of success or failure." The United States agreed to keep Brazilian coffee, hides, tea, molasses, and sugar on the free list. In return, Brazil allowed American manufactured goods, commodities, and processed agricultural products to enter Brazil duty-free or at a 25-percent reduction.[38]

The State Department apparently considered attempting to get congressional approval of the 1883 Mexican reciprocity treaty, but the Harrison Administration let the matter remain dormant. Negotiations for another treaty with Mexico were unsuccessful. The McKinley Tariff left little room for maneuver with Mexico. Unless Harrison allowed the State Department to go beyond the limits of the McKinley Tariff, the United States could offer only one significant concession to Mexico—admission of hides (without wool) duty-free. The new tariff also kept import duties on silver-lead ores, a major Mexican export.[39]

Except for Cuba and possibly Brazil, these reciprocity treaties failed to stimulate marked trade increases between the United States and Latin America. They were in force only two years at the most, and during part of that time, the United States and Latin America experienced major depressions. American exports to Cuba increased from $12 million in 1891 to $18 million in 1892 and to $24 million in 1893. Cuban exports to the United States grew from $62 million to $78 million and to $79 million in the same years. This trade decreased somewhat in 1894, the second year of the depression of the 1890s. After the abrogation of the reciprocal agreement, trade declined sharply. United States exports fell from $20 million in 1894 to $13 million in 1895, and Cuban exports to the United States declined from $76 million to $53 million.[40] While the depression undoubtedly accounted for part of this decline, the *de facto* repeal of the reciprocity agreements by the Wilson-Gorman Tariff of 1894 was an important factor, as the marked decrease in 1895 compared with 1894 indicates. Moreover, the disruption of Cuban-American trade undermined the Cuban economy and set the scene for the Cuban revolution of 1895-1898.

In a report in 1892, the State Department claimed that reciprocity treaties accounted for the significant increase of trade with Cuba and for modest increases of American exports to Brazil, Puerto Rico, Santo Domingo, and British Guinea. (There had been a slight, "unexplainable" decrease in exports to the British West Indies.) This trade expansion occurred, the department added, despite economic dislocations in Brazil and Puerto Rico, and in the case of Santo Domingo and Brazil, British exports declined as a consequence of the growth of American trade. As the increase of shipping services between Latin America and the United States indicated, according to the department his was merely the beginning of an enlarged American economic penetration of Latin America. If this trend were to continue, American businessmen must have a greater interest in and resourcefulness for the foreign market. To encourage American business, the government should help by eliminating American dependence on European shipping, banks, and currency in the Latin American market.[41]

But the reciprocity strategy of the Harrison Administration encompassed more than Latin America. After the passage of the McKinley Tariff in 1890, Blaine acted to strengthen American dominance in Hawaii. He opened discussions with the Hawaiian minister to the United States, H. A. P. Carter. The timing of the talks was prompted by the free sugar provision of the new tariff, a provision that hurt Hawaiian sugar which had previously received favored treatment. Blaine had moved quickly to exploit the opportunity. In return for placing the Hawaiian sugar producers on an equal footing with domestic sugar growers, the secretary asked for a permanent treaty that would include a perpetual, exclusive concession of a naval station at Pearl Harbor, a pledge that Hawaii would not make any treaties with another power without first informing the United States, and the right to land troops in Hawaii to restore order in the islands.[42]

The last provision was obviously conceived of as a response to the problem of political instability in Hawaii as well as another means to insure American preeminence in the islands. In 1891 Hawaii became more unstable. That year Queen Liliuokalani came to the throne. She soon moved to restore some of the political prerogatives of the monarchy, support Hawaiian nativism, and restrain the growing power of the Americans who lived in Hawaii and who, by 1891, were economically dominant. The American settlers also derived considerable political power from their position in the island economy.

Initially, the Hawaiian government appeared willing to accept all of the treaty except the provision concerning American military intervention. Then, the queen rejected the new treaty altogether, and the negotiations collapsed. She was undoubtedly influenced by a determination to maintain Hawaiian independence and to buttress the position of the natives, while constraining the American settlers. Another factor may have been the intrigue of the Canadian government, which allegedly wanted to undermine United States dominance in Hawaii. The settlers, with the encouragement or at least the tacit approval of Washington, then made determined efforts to gain complete control of Hawaii. They revolted, and then appealed to the United States to annex the islands. The American minister, one of Blaine's old associates, abetted their revolution, and Harrison made a vigorous but unsuccessful effort to drive the annexation treaty through the Senate before he left office.[43] Events had rapidly transformed the issue from reciprocal trade relations to annexation, from informal empire through reciprocity to formal empire. This change was significant, but it was in accordance with the traditional American policy of preeminence over the Hawaiian Islands.

The administration also conducted reciprocal trade talks with Canada. On the American side, they were a sham. Generally, the Republican party had opposed any attempt to revive reciprocity with Canada since the Canadian-American reciprocity convention of 1857 had lapsed in 1866. President Harrison did not deviate from that course. He expressed his views to Blaine on the eve of new trade talks: "I have never seen how we could arrange a basis of reciprocity with Canada short of a complete customs union, by which they should adopt our tariff and everything should be free between the two countries. This would be an absolute commercial union, and is probably not practicable unless it is accompanied by political union." The president added that he did not especially want to annex Canada, but did suggest that he and Blaine believed the United States would eventually incorporate that country.[44] The Republican leadership opposed a reciprocal agreement with Canada on other grounds. Northern business and agricultural interests, especially those in upper New England and in the wheat-producing states of the Great Plains, feared Canadian competition in farm markets or large increases of British manufactured products entering the American market through Canada. The party paid particular attention to these Republican strongholds on these matters.

The Harrison Administration reluctantly opened reciprocity

negotiations with Canadian representatives in February 1892. As domestic pressures against high tariffs increased, the administration decided to go through the motions. If the talks failed, the Republicans could claim they tried. Blaine assured the desired result by making his minimum demands more than the Canadians would accept. The secretary asked for substantial tariff reductions on a long list of items, including manufactured articles. Many American goods were to be placed on the free list, a privilege that not even Great Britain enjoyed. Canada rejected these stipulations because of her close economic ties with Great Britain and her reliance upon import duties as a major source of income.[45] So, reciprocity with Canada, along with such issues as the boundary between Canada and Alaska, the northeastern fisheries, and seal hunting in the Bering Sea, remained unresolved.

The Harrison Administration also used the reciprocity section of the McKinley Act to secure European concessions on imports of American pork into Europe. Most of the European governments had banned these imports in the early 1880s. The governments charged that American pork and pork products were unsafe. Thus, they protected their farmers against competition from cheaper American pork, but American farmers and meat packers lost a valuable market. Before 1890 all attempts by the United States to get European prohibitions removed had failed.[46]

The Harrison Administration acted to meet the European sanitation charges, and then threatened retaliation against European beet sugar. The Meat Inspection Act of 1891 provided for microscopic inspection of meat that was to be exported. After they were pressed by the American government, Germany and Austria-Hungary agreed in 1891 to remove their bans on American pork. A prime consideration in this action was their fear that the president would reimpose a duty on their sugar exports to the United States. Harrison then used their concessions to coerce the French, who removed their ban in 1891. Finally, the administration considered, but did not negotiate, a reciprocal trade agreement with Portugal. The French found other means—a prohibitive import tax —to block American meat imports. But the Harrison Administration could claim success with other European countries, especially Germany. Exports òf American pork products to Europe had increased from 46.5 million pounds in June 1891 to 85.7 million in June 1892.[47]

In his last annual message, and after his defeat in the 1892 election, the president acclaimed the reciprocity treaties program and asserted that his administration, through efforts to secure greater foreign sales for American agriculture, had shown real sensitivity to the needs of the American farmer. The foreign trade figures he cited appeared to substantiate his claims. Total export trade had risen from $730 million in 1889 to a new plateau (over $1 billion for the first time) in 1892. A favorable balance of trade had been regained—from minus $3 million in 1889 to plus $203 million in 1892.[48]

The significance of Harrison's achievement can be lost by giving too much attention to his defeat in 1892 and the brevity of his White House tenure. Harrison and Blaine had met the challenge of David Wells and the Democratic expansionists: they had developed a program to keep protectionism and, at the same time, to expand the American market. In an election eve article, Blaine claimed that the United States had brought Cuba and the British West Indies into its commercial nexus through reciprocity treaties. Cuba provided the best example of the blessings of Republican foreign trade policy. Blaine recited the figures of the expanded Cuba-United States trade. Then, addressing himself to western farmers who were deserting the GOP for the Populist party, he gave particular emphasis to the growth of American flour exports to Cuba. Whereas in the first six months of 1891 Cubans imported only 14,000 barrels ($175,000 worth), they bought 337,000 barrels ($4 million) in a comparable period in 1892. The Harrison reciprocal trade program made this dramatic increase possible by obtaining removal of $5.75 per barrel of American flour shipped to Cuba. Blaine boasted that the Republicans had obviated the Democratic "bad" neighbor policy of annexing Cuba by force. The Republicans through reciprocity had found a "more excellent way to capture'' Cuba. Some day ''commercially the two countries will be one.''[49]

Andrew Carnegie, a close friend of Blaine and a delegate at the Pan-American conference, applauded the Brazilian treaty for providing an opportunity for greater sales for the American wheat farmer and the American manufacturer. But Cuba was ''the most notable illustration of the force of this reciprocity clause.'' (Originally, he had written ''Reciprocity weapon.'') Assuming that the Cuban economy was dependent on the American domestic market, the State Department had used this dependence to force Spain to remove its restrictions on American exports to Cuba. Carnegie claimed that Spain had to make these concessions or be faced by Cuban demands for annexation to the United States. These concessions, Carnegie asserted, meant that ''Cuba will hereafter be of as little good to Spain as Canada is to Britain . . . and probably will become the source of serious trouble and danger to Spain.''[50]

Such ideas were not limited to the upper ranks of the Republican party. In April 1890 *Bradstreet's* had remarked laconically that, as in the case of the Hawaiian agreement, reciprocity treaties led to virtual annexation. If the 1883 treaty with Mexico had been approved, a similar result would have occurred. *Bradstreet's* added that ''the same thing is to be anticipated from any future arrangements that may be entered into with the countries of South America.''[51]

But more than two years was needed to convince important interest groups and to get Republican unity behind reciprocity. Consequently, reciprocity did not become a major issue in the election of 1892. Moreover, other factors made Harrison's reelection very doubtful: the unpopularity of the McKinley Tariff, the Homestead Strike, discontented farmers who turned to the Populists, and local issues that had a very important bearing in several Republican states. To complicate matters further, the Republicans were factionalized. Blaine, plagued by illness and at political odds with the president after 1890, resigned from the State Department in June 1892. Subsequently, he lent little of his campaign skills to the election. Harrison, preoccupied with the death of his wife in September 1892, failed to provide urgently needed leadership and oratory. Still, while Cleveland won by an impressive margin (5,557,000 votes to 5,176,000 for Harrison), it was not a landslide. James B. Weaver, the Populist candidate, received 1,041,000 votes[52], many of which were normally Republican votes. The 1892 election results meant that the tariff reductionist forces temporarily displaced the forces for protectionism and reciprocity.

Despite the Republican defeat of 1892, the Harrison-Blaine reciprocity scheme achieved a broad appeal within four years. In 1896, the House Ways and Means Committee, once again in Republican hands, measured reactions to the repeal of the reciprocity section. A wide variety of groups and individuals—boards of trade, chambers of commerce, manufacturers of various finished goods, merchants, processers of agriculture products, and the New York state legislature—supported the reestablishment of the reciprocity program. The dissenting voices were very few.[53] The Chamber of Commerce of Pittsburgh spoke for the majority when it declared:

At no time in the history of our country has a commercial question of equal importance presented itself. We have reached a point in both manufactures and agriculture so great that (call it overproduction or whatever you please) we can not consume our output, and the necessity of finding new markets is an imperative one. At this juncture of affairs the acts of 1890, providing an enlarged traffic with our Spanish-American Republics, came into existence most opportunely for all parties in interest.

The treaties, the Pittsburgh Chamber claimed, allowed the United States to gain in a European-dominated market which "promised to become an integral part of our commerce." The abrogation of the treaties caused "an almost total suspension of commercial relations.'' The abrogation ''was simply partisan politics run mad.'' As a result, the Chamber asserted, Pittsburgh lost orders with Central and South America worth over $200,000 a month.[54]

The Republicans sensed the popularity of reciprocity in 1896. Their national convention of that year emphatically declared itself for reciprocity.[55] William McKinley, a White House aspirant, became an outspoken exponent of the program. He acknowledged and praised Harrison's leadership of the reciprocity scheme, and publicly defended the policy before and after he became president. ''In the revision of the tariff,'' he told the inaugural audience of 1897, ''especial attention should be given to the reenactment and extension of the reciprocity principle of the law of 1890, under which so great a stimulus was given to foreign trade in new and advantageous markets for our surplus products.'' His last public address was a vigorous endorsement of greater trade between Latin America and the United States based on reciprocity treaties.[56]

Whatever their attitudes toward the reciprocity program, Harrison's successors, Cleveland and McKinley, accepted his emphasis on overseas economic expansion. Harrison supported a vigorous, commerce-oriented foreign policy that included, in addition to reciprocity, a Pan-American conference, an American-controlled isthmian canal, the acquisition of a modern navy and coaling stations, harbor improvements, and similar measures. After 1892, Harrison faded into political obscurity, but not before he had made a significant contribution to the growing interest in expansion in the 1890s. Thus, rather than being a mere four-year interlude, the Harrison Administration formed an important prelude to the outward thrust of the United States in the last decade of the nineteenth century.

8

The Tariff and
Foreign Trade Expansion:
The Struggle over Tactics

In less than a decade Congress passed three general tariff acts; yet the results were anticlimatic. After the modest reductions of the Wilson-Gorman Act (1894), Congress returned to the higher levels of the McKinley Act when it passed the Dingley Tariff in 1897. The hopes of the tariff reductionists rose with Democratic election victories in 1890 and 1892 and fell with the Democrats during the depression of the 1890s. The hyperactivity about the tariff was also anticlimatic in that both Republican and Democratic leaders agreed by 1890 that expansion of American exports was necessary and could be achieved by manipulating the tariff. "Protectionists and free traders [tariff reductionists] seem to have at last arrived at a common point," *Iron Age* noted in October 1890, "as both classes now profess to be desirous of enlarging our foreign trade. They are, of course, not in harmony with each other as to the means to be adopted in securing this purpose."[1] The "means" occupied much of the thinking and efforts of the second Cleveland Administration and the two McKinley Administrations.

The expansionist consensus became explicit during the enacting of the Wilson-Gorman Tariff and in the foreign policy of the newly elected Cleveland Administration. The legislative history of the Wilson-Gorman Tariff has often been detailed,[2] obviating the need of yet another elaborate narrative. No new issues or arguments appeared during the tariff debates of 1893-1894. Reductionists did give greater stress to the charge that high tariffs fostered monopolies, which were becoming a major issue in the 1890s.[3] The generally dull rhetoric seemed out of place in 1894. As Congress droned on with its set speeches, the severe depression continued. Feelings excited by the Pullman Strike and Coxey's Army deepened anxieties about the economy and the nation's future.

The Democratic majority of the House Ways and Means Committee, led by William Wilson, drafted a bill with substantially lower duties designed to reduce the cost of consumer goods and to implement the Democratic doctrine of free raw materials. Wilson proposed to add hides, wool, lumber, coal, and copper and iron ore to raw sugar on the free list. This, it was claimed, would benefit the American economy and most Americans by reducing the cost of consumer goods and by facilitating the development of a more stable industrial production. Thus, the Democrats astutely linked their tariff policies with greater economic stability, a chronic need in the fluctuating, expanding American economy in the late nineteenth century. During the depression of the 1890s that chronic need became an urgent one. And, happily, the Democrats had a strategy that promised to satisfy it by imposing even fewer government restrictions.

The Democrats sought to modulate the fluctuations of the American economy through a free market approach—in the domestic market and through overseas economic expansion based upon their free raw materials strategy. Thus, they followed the scheme largely devised and articulated by David Wells and Abram Hewitt, along with Edward Atkinson in the 1880s. The Democrats admitted that tariff reduction might temporarily hurt some groups, but they claimed that a more stable economy was worth the short-term losses. Even if wages, for example, fell somewhat as tariffs were reduced, the Democrats argued, the loss would be more than offset by continuous employment and the availability of cheaper consumer goods. Lower production costs secured through reduced raw materials costs, the Democrats asserted, would allow American manufacturers to compete more effectively with one another and especially with foreign manufacturers in both the national and the international markets. This greater competition would also check the growth of monopolistic practices in the United States.

Agriculture was not neglected. A healthier domestic market would strengthen domestic farm prices, and as the United States engaged more freely in international commerce, commodity farmers would be able to increase their foreign sales. The Democrats felt ideologically comfortable with their free raw materials strategy. They had consistently attacked protectionism as unconstitutional government paternalism which threatened American individualism and self-reliance. Tariff reduction also suited the free market assumptions that most Americans accepted, even if they failed to live by them.[4]

The Democratic tariff strategy had a grandiose aura; nevertheless, it rested upon some hard-headed analyses. Commodity farmers relied heavily on foreign sales, and by the early 1890s, certainly during the 1890s' depression, American manufacturers developed an intense interest in foreign trade. In the past this interest had been sporadic, except in some cases like the agricultural implements makers and some processors of farm products. By 1894 the expansionist rationale developed in the 1880s by David Wells, Edward Atkinson, Abram Hewitt, and James Blaine had won acceptance from leaders in agriculture, industry, commerce, and both major parties. A "conservative consensus" had concluded that overproduction was a permanent condition. Once manufacturers worked at foreign trade by "fits and starts" merely to weather short-term economic dislocations; that day, according to the consensus, had passed. The *when* of economic expansion was no longer an issue, for America's dislocated economy must expand *now*. There was no other acceptable alternative.

As *Bradstreet's* commented in May 1896: "The need of developing adequate foreign outlets for surplus products of American industry has been written and talked about so much as to have it almost a truism." Where once manufacturers saw foreign markets as providing occasional relief, they now envisioned exports as a means of obtaining more regular sales and, thus, greater industrial stability. In view of the fluctuations of the American economy in the late nineteenth century, the appeal of this conception of expansion is understandable. President Cleveland grasped this when he assured William Vilas that the free raw materials policy would surely attract broad support. This policy would, he claimed, release American enterprise and ingenuity, open the doors of foreign markets, and give "continuous and remunerative employment to American labor."[5]

The Democratic tariff strategy was also based on shrewd political thinking. The Cleveland Democrats used the duty-free list cleverly. To gain a wider following, the Democrats employed duty-free raw materials as a divide-and-conquer tactic; this, as Wells among others suggested, allowed the reductionists to attack protected interests individually rather than in concert. As various interests lost their protected positions, they supposedly would join the low tariff forces.[6] Thus, one of the major elements of the Wilson Bill was a carefully expanded free list.

The proposed free list of the Wilson Bill, nicknamed by some "the New England Manufacturing Bill," reflected an awareness that the Democratic party was showing signs of rebirth in New England, especially in Massachusetts. The Democratic leadership understood that as the New England economy slumped in the late nineteenth century, Yankee distaste for extreme or "Pennsylvania" protectionism grew to considerable bitterness. Free iron ore, coal, and wool, as well as lower duties on tin, appealed to New England industrial and commercial groups. The iron and steel makers of that region looked to foreign sources for iron ore and coal (in particular, to nearby Nova Scotia for coal) in order to compete with industry giants in Pennsylvania, Ohio, and Illinois.

The competitive position of the New Englanders would also be enhanced by the Democrats' proposal to put lower duties on scrap iron.[7] Other iron and steel makers on the middle Atlantic seaboard stood to share in these benefits. Moreover, unlike the Mills Bill of 1888 which had favored southern interests, the Wilson Bill was less subject to charges of southern sectionalism. But the Democrats had to please the South and the West. The Ways and Means Committee had to offer more than duty-free raw materials for industry.

Substantial reduction on a number of manufactured products was therefore the other major element of the Wilson Bill. These reductions, along with cheaper production costs which would supposedly be secured through free raw materials, promised cheaper goods to domestic consumers. As American foreign trade in manufactured goods grew because of tariff reductions on raw materials, the Democrats argued, agricultural exports would also increase as a result of the growth of international trade. The promise of lower domestic prices and the prospect of expanded farm exports, the Democratic leadership hoped, would appeal to the South and West in particular. Thus, the Democrats aimed much of their tariff reduction strategy, along with a provision for a federal income tax, at southern and western agrarians at a time when these segments of the electorate were being drawn toward Populism and free silver.[8] The Cleveland Democrats relied on their strategy to recoup their declining fortunes among the increasingly disenchanted farmers. A new tariff would ease the bitter reactions in the South and West to the Democratic leadership's role in repealing the Sherman Silver Purchase Act. (That repeal was, of course, popular in New York and New England, where bimetallism, but not free silver, had some significant support.)

Having supposedly eliminated free silver as an issue, the Cleveland Democrats sought through tariff reduction to erect an alliance between New England and the South, along with New York and parts of the Midwest. The growing ties among southern and New England Democrats involved Wells and Atkinson, Representatives Wilson (West Virginia), Clifton R. Breckinridge (Arkansas), W.

C. P. Breckinridge (Kentucky), John E. Russell (Massachusetts), Benton McMillin (Tennessee), Roger Mills (now a Texas senator), and Governor William E. Russell of Massachusetts. Appropriately, William Russell went to Atlanta in 1890 to deliver a memorial address in honor of Henry Grady who had died shortly after speaking to a Boston audience. The next year, Mills, Wilson, and McMillin came to Massachusetts to help in a state election. If the Democrats consolidated their 1890 gains in New England and the Midwest,[9] the new coalition might mature. Then, the Cleveland Democrats would make a strong bid to continue leading the Democratic party and the nation.

The Democratic battle plan, however, had serious weaknesses. Two major problems presented themselves in the South. Silver, not tariff reform, held first place in the minds of most of the southern agrarians whose dismal fortunes got even worse in the 1890s. Among a smaller, but more vocal and wealthier group of southerners, free raw materials, particularly free coal and iron ore, seemed to be an attack upon the New South (into which large amounts of New England capital had flowed). Alabama and West Virginia reacted most strongly against the free coal and iron provisions of the Wilson Bill. The southern textile industry had at least one strong voice for protection: J. F. Hanson of the large Bibb Manufacturing Company of Macon, Georgia and the *Macon Telegraph*. The *Manufacturers' Record* of Richard H. Edmonds became the main vehicle for expressing southern protest. The *Record* went so far as to open a special Washington office to lobby against the Wilson Bill. The strategy of the Cleveland Democrats had taken the agrarian South into account, but not the industrializing South.[10] To return to an overworked but valid truism: there was a serious breach in the "Solid South."

The weak footing of the New England Democrats also hindered the emerging alliance. The Democratic party had done very well in the 1890 election, yet most New England voters still believed the party represented a conglomeration, primarily supported by immigrants, particularly the Irish. In fact, Massachusetts Democrats had already lost ground by the 1892 elections. Whether the Democratic tariff strategy could reverse the tide was doubtful. Free raw materials attracted some Massachusetts industrialists but repelled others. Self-interest, narrowly or broadly conceived, was a determinant. Free wool, for instance, threatened what some protectionists believed was the keystone of protectionism and a vital working relationship among protectionists, the wool growers, and wool manufacturers alliance. This combination—developed in the 1860s and institutionalized in the Wool Tariff of 1867 and by the close cooperation between the National Wool-Growers Association and the National Association of Wool Manufacturers—had been sustained largely by the efforts of John Hayes, executive secretary of the manufacturers' association.[11] The element of direct interest was also involved. The attitudes of Massachusetts wool manufacturers toward duties on raw wool reflected the type of wool they used and the availability of an adequate supply from foreign sources. Finally, New Englanders took offense at tariff reductions on their manufactures and, especially, at the income tax provided for by the Wilson Bill.[12] Like most people, they defined good tax policy as that policy which favored them.

In pursuing their free wool strategy, the Cleveland Democrats also risked losing support in important midwestern states, particularly Ohio and Indiana. Other problems included their general insensitivity toward agrarian and silverite agitation in the Midwest. They had made impressive election gains in 1890 in Iowa, Wisconsin, Illinois, and Michigan largely as a result of local, not national, issues. Thus, their position in the Midwest, as subsequent elections demonstrated, was vulnerable.[13]

The Cleveland Democrats believed their tariff reduction strategy was not only worth the risks involved, but in view of the available alternatives that was perhaps their only hope. As early as March 1892, Cleveland confided to a close associate that the Democrats must avoid free silver and do something constructive with the tariff if they were to succeed. The tariff was "the only issue upon which there is the least hope of carrying the country."[14] Democrats thus integrated domestic politics with the foreign policy of non-territorial expansionism which they had followed in the 1880s and continued to follow in the 1890s. Their free raw materials strategy was designed to meet both urgent domestic political and foreign policy needs, including alleviating a severe economic slump in accordance with the technology-overproduction-depression analysis first articulated by Wells.

President Cleveland also defined tariff reduction as a moral crusade. At least one leading Democrat, West Virginia's Wilson, knowingly risked his political future when he supported adding coal, a major West Virginia product, to the free list.[15] Cleveland and some of the other Democratic leaders demonstrated less courage. The president often obscured his political motives with an unctuous self-righteousness; he may have been confused about his own motives. His contemporaries were divided. Some saw him as a selfless man doing his duty, others as a sanctimonious politician. Historians have since shared this confusion.

If the battle lines of the Cleveland Democrats on the Wilson Bill were weak, their timing was atrocious, and the president's tactical execution was even worse. He saw himself in the heroic image of Andrew Jackson and preferred frontal assaults. Cleveland chose to engage the silverites first, then the protectionists. This reflected the thinking of those Cleveland Democrats who were primarily from the East. They believed free silver was a greater danger than protectionism. Convinced that resolution on the monetary issue cast doubt on American morality and threatened an economy that was sagging badly in 1893, Cleveland called a special session of Congress, to meet in August 1893, to repeal the Sherman Silver Purchase Act—but only after squandering valuable time while he vacillated for nearly four months (from March 4 until June 30).[16]

The Republicans stood aside and watched the Democrats fight a prolonged, internecine war over the standards. Cleveland waded in with a liberal use of patronage.[17] After a three-month struggle, he obtained repeal in November, which was of dubious benefit to the economy.[18] He also got an even more divided party, ill-prepared to do battle with the protectionists. Midwesterners, one Democrat commented angrily, believed "that the silver question . . . [had been] relegated to the rear and the Tariff question given the right of way . . . for the special purpose of enabling Mr. Cleveland to be nominated [and] elected President. The [successful] attempt, now that the election is over [,] to place the silver issue in front and Tariff reform in the rear is arousing a bitterness that is liable to cause a landslide in the Congressional elections of 1894."[19]

Cleveland's influence with many congressional Democrats was as spent as his patronage leverage. In 1893, in the midst of an extremely serious economic slump, Wilson reported the new tariff bill on December 19 during the regular session of Congress. Displaying a degree of unity unusual for them, House Democrats passed the Wilson Bill on February 1, 1894, on a party line vote amid a widely joyous scene on the House floor.[20]

Joy and unity disappeared when the bill reached the Senate. The Democrats lacked the large voting margin in the Senate (44 Democrats, 38 Republicans, 3 Populists and 3 vacancies) that they had in the House. They also lacked the vigorous leadership of John Carlisle, an outspoken tariff reductionist. Cleveland had drawn Carlisle from the Senate to be his secretary of the Treasury. The president's tactlessness made a bad situation worse. He failed to flatter senatorial egos in intimate social gatherings or to devote appropriate attention to important nominations requiring Senate approval. In the case of his old New York political foe, Senator David Hill, the president twice—once in 1893 and again in 1894—nominated New Yorkers for the Supreme Court without first consulting Hill. The Senate rejected both nominees. The administration was not prepared to conduct the negotiations and to make important concessions if the Wilson Bill were to pass the Senate.

Thus, when the Wilson Bill reached the Senate, Maryland's Arthur Gorman took command. The results reflected his moderate protectionism. After 634 amendments, a drastically changed Wil-

son Bill went to the conference committee. The provision for an
ad valorem tariff schedule had been replaced by a specific duty
schedule, and sugar, coal, and iron ore were no longer duty-free.
Any semblance of Democratic harmony was shattered. Gorman's
opponents promptly stigmatized him as a traitor who obtained personal profit from higher tariffs. These charges had the appearance
of fact. Gorman was associated in business and politics with his
cousin, Henry Davis, former West Virginia senator and heavy
investor in railroads and the coal mines of his state. Whether, as
was charged, Gorman speculated in refined sugar and therefore
had a personal stake in higher duties on processed sugar is doubtful. That he disliked Cleveland, that he was a career politician
who necessarily gave priority to his own survival, and that he
believed that the small, but important, high tariff faction of the
Democrats had to be appeased in the interests of party harmony
were true. Gorman knew that the public was wary of tariff reduction and tariff reductionists, and that several Senate Democrats
were not members of the low tariff faction of their party.[21]
Perhaps, then, it would be fairer and more accurate to see Gorman
as a compromiser working to preserve his own political position
and to harmonize differences on the tariff. Whatever the assessment of Gorman's role in the evolution of the Wilson-Gorman
Tariff, the result of his efforts did not please the low tariff Democrats.

Initially, the conference committee was deadlocked on the tariff
bill. At this point the president dropped any pretense of non-
involvement in the legislative process of the bill and boldly intervened. In a letter to Wilson, which he allowed Wilson to read
from the House floor, Cleveland lent his support to the House-
passed version of the bill. There was one notable exception: he
approved the duty on sugar, raw and refined, provided by the
Senate's action. He defended this as necessary for the urgent
revenue needs of the government. (No doubt, he was also impressed by the political power of Louisiana sugar planters.) He
concluded the blunt letter with the sharp warning "that our aban-
donment of the cause of the principles upon which it [the Demo-

cratic party] rests means party perfidy and party dishonor.''[22] The president had intervened dramatically—but deviously and unwisely.

Cleveland's letter falsely presupposed a consistent presidential course on the tariff. Not only had he wavered during his first administration, but he followed a similar course during the 1892 election and during the negotiations on the Wilson-Gorman Tariff. In 1892 he had opposed a militant low tariff resolution in the national Democratic platform. He severed relations with Henry Watterson after the assertive editor of the *Louisville Courier-Journal* led a successful floor fight in the convention to commit the Democrats to a militant tariff reductionist position. In his own acceptance letter for the 1892 campaign, Cleveland carefully avoided the extremes of his party's platform. Later, the administration participated in the negotiations to settle House and Senate differences over the tariff bill. Cleveland approved of these conversations and even attended some of them.[23]

Cleveland's course was distinctly erratic and hardly courageous. More than that, it was foolish. By publicly stigmatizing the Senate, and by implication, its Democratic leader, Gorman, the president held the Senate up for public scorn and made any Senate compromise appear to be a humiliation. Finally, he inaccurately equated the Wilson Bill (House version) with the Democratic tariff stance. Gorman replied promptly and vigorously. In a lengthy Senate address, the Maryland senator recalled Cleveland's personal history on the tariff. He denied that the unamended Wilson Bill reflected the tariff position of the Democratic party, and he claimed that the bill could not be passed without the Senate amendments. The Senate remained firm. In order to pass any bill the House and the president had to acquiesce. Eventually they did.[24]

Cleveland reluctantly allowed the tariff bill to become law without his signature. Pointing to its modest reductions and to the raw materials (lumber and wool) added to the free list, the president declared that the measure was at least an improvement upon the McKinley Tariff. A partisan critic had described the Democrats' predicament while the bill was still in Congress: "The Democrats are not engaged in explaining the bill, or making one which rests on intelligible principles. They are merely trying to pass something which they can call a tariff."[25] Whatever merits Cleveland found in the first general tariff the Democrats had enacted since 1857, the performance of the Democrats did not match its rhetoric. If newspapers reflected public opinion, public bitterness toward the Democrats became even deeper. The *Richmond Times* (Democratic) claimed the Democrats had at least improved upon the McKinley Tariff. "Nevertheless," the paper admitted, "the bill has not met the popular demand." The Populist *Denver News* commented more prophetically, if somewhat prematurely:

> The new Tariff bill . . . will remove free trade and protection discussions from politics long enough at least to allow the coming campaign to be fought out on the money question. . . . This is now the real issue before the people. The Wilson bill cannot become a law too quickly. One year after the repeal of the Sherman [Silver Purchase] law, the country is no better off. It won't take six months to prove the terrible tariff question cuts mighty little figure in the present depression. Silver's the thing."[26]

The president remained deeply committed to the free raw materials strategy for market expansion designed to end the tragic depression of the 1890s and give long-range stability to the economy. He persisted in his hope that the list of free raw materials would be expanded in the future. In particular, as he had during the negotiations for the Wilson-Gorman Tariff, he repeatedly requested that coal and iron ore be added to the free list. When the Wilson-Gorman Tariff became law, Cleveland told Thomas C. Catchings, chairman of the House Rules Committee, that to regard duty-free raw materials "as only related to concessions to be made to our manufacturers" was erroneous. Rather, the impact of free raw materials was "so far-reaching" that without them there could be no tariff reform. Not only would consumers benefit from lower prices, but, as he had told Vilas earlier, when "we give to our manufacturers free raw materials we unshackle American enterprise and ingenuity, and these will open the door of foreign markets to the reception of our wares and give opportunity for the continuous and remunerative employment of American labor.'' He reiterated these themes in his annual messages. (He also noted that the free wool provision of the Wilson-Gorman Tariff had provided a basis for a new commercial treaty between Argentina and the United States.) In December 1894 the president linked Democratic tariff policy with both domestic and foreign policy when he applauded "the advent of a new tariff policy not only calculated to relieve the consumers of our land in the cost of their daily life, but to invite a better development of American thrift and create for us closer and more profitable commercial relations with the rest of the world.''[27] Other Cleveland Democrats made similar arguments.[28] They offered little else to the beleaguered nation.

The Wilson-Gorman Tariff undermined both the reciprocity agreements negotiated by the Harrison Administration and the Cuban economy. By removing sugar from the free list, the Wilson-Gorman Act abrogated the agreements. Originally, neither the White House nor the House Democratic leaders had wanted to do so. Representative Wilson explicitly denied that the free sugar provision of the Wilson Bill destroyed the agreements then in force. Literally, Wilson was right. The treaties could have remained in force even if the final tariff bill passed had, as Wilson and Cleveland originally intended, contained free raw sugar. But such a tariff would have destroyed the power of the executive to maintain a treaty by threatening to reimpose the duty on sugar against a particular country. Moreover, whatever their initial stand on raw sugar, the administration and several leading House Democrats compromised on the sugar duty. They returned sugar to the dutiable list without providing for removing the duty by reciprocal agreements. In doing so, they ignored warnings of adverse reactions in the Midwest and elsewhere if reciprocity was repealed.[29] Along with the 1890s' depression, the new tariff legislation hurt American farm exports, especially in Germany and France, and struck hard at the vulnerable Cuban economy. The slump in the Cuban economy helped set the stage for the Cuban Revolution that was ultimately transformed into the Spanish-American War.

The expansionism explicit in the free raw materials strategy was consistent with the other major facets of Cleveland's foreign policy. Generally, like the first Cleveland Administration, the second administration, while rejecting the Republican reciprocity strategy, assumed that the United States should have predominance in the Western Hemisphere and enjoy greater power in the Pacific. Thus, the diplomatic strategy of the second administration was similar to that of the Harrison Administration, although tactics and mood differed. The Cleveland Democrats were more reluctant to annex territory. The Harrison Administration, however, showed more imagination in its foreign policy.

Despite a serious depression and a determination to reduce government spending, President Cleveland supported his secretary of the navy, Hilary A. Hebert, when he asked for increased appropriations to continue the construction of a modern navy. The second Cleveland Administration vigorously backed its interpretation of the Monroe Doctrine and American interests during the abortive Brazilian coup d'etat of 1893 and the Venezuelan boundary dispute of 1895. It showed due concern for America's claims with respect to a Central American isthmian canal, and carefully watched the Cuban Revolution that began in 1895. Although the administration refused to annex Hawaii in 1893, it also rebuffed suggestions that, since the United States had helped dethrone Queen Liliukalani, it should restore her to power. It persistently pleaded for a more efficient consular service. Finally, the Cleveland Administration made some efforts to enhance American interests in China.[30]

Secretary of Agriculture J. Sterling Morton, as Rusk before him, believed farm prosperity was dependent on foreign sales, but neither he nor Cleveland was as imaginative as Rusk or Harrison. The administration did send an agent to Europe in 1893 to investigate foreign market demands for American agricultural products, the tobacco laws in Europe, and "the subject of the sale of meat products in Germany and France." But the abrogation of reciprocity by the Wilson-Gorman Tariff undermined such efforts, and the gains secured by the Harrison Administration were lost. Adversely affected farmers sharply criticized the Democrats. Morton offered little else to distressed agrarians except untimely lectures on self-reliance and the recommendation that they read Adam Smith's *The Wealth of Nations,* which was "to political economy what the New Testament . . . [was] to the Christian religion." Many farmers interpreted this as a cruel joke;[31] they probably felt the same about the entire Cleveland Administration.

Following the Democratic waves of 1890 and 1892, the Cleveland Democrats had envisioned low tariffs and other future victories. Instead, they absorbed crushing defeats, first in the 1894 congressional elections and then in the 1896 presidential election. The first gave the Republicans control of Congress as such Democratic stalwarts as Wilson were defeated. Henry Davis had his revenge on Wilson, his former protege, for his free coal heresy. Then, in 1896, the silver forces captured the Democratic party. The Cleveland Democratic strategy of avoiding free silver by stressing tariff reduction had failed to prevent the Democratic silverite triumph or to meet the nation's needs in the throes of an economic collapse.

In the election of 1894 and after, the Republicans discerned that it would be unwise to sever the connection between protection and reciprocity that Blaine and Harrison had finally consummated after the earlier, unsuccessful attempts of the Hayes and Arthur administrations. Protection plus reciprocity had become too popular and too valuable a political weapon to ignore or deemphasize. But as long as the Democrats held the White House, the Republicans could not enact new high tariff legislation. They could, however, attack the Wilson-Gorman Act. The GOP did not, as the Democrats had done during the 1891-1892 congressional session, propose a series of individual ("pop gun") tariff bills. Instead, the Republicans made an issue of reciprocity. They knew what they were doing. In 1895, the Republican-controlled House Ways and Means Committee polled manufacturers, commercial associations, and farm groups on reciprocity, and found a great deal of support for the policy.[32] The assurance that the Republicans intended to continue protecting the domestic market only partly accounted for this favorable response. Republican reciprocity also found favor because it fitted into the emerging conservative consensus about the urgency for foreign trade expansion. This consensus found institutional expression in 1895 in the founding of the National Association of Manufacturers and in the opening of the Philadelphia Commercial Museum in the heart of protectionist country. At its first convention, the NAM announced that American manufacturers must enlarge their exports and that that was the main function of the organization. William McKinley, then governor of Ohio and the leading Republican presidential candidate for the 1896 election, was the keynote speaker at the convention. Now firmly committed to protection and reciprocity, McKinley told an enthusiastic audience that protectionism was one of the "plain and natural rights" of Americans. The United States wanted to dominate its own market and export its agricultural and industrial surpluses without "degrad[ing] our labor" with low wages. "We want a reciprocity which will give us foreign markets for our surplus products and in turn that will open our markets to foreigners for those products which they produce and we do not."[33]

As his party's presidential nominee, McKinley tried to focus the 1896 campaign on the themes of his address to the NAM—protectionism and expansion through reciprocity. In his letter accepting the nomination, he firmly defended "sound money" and declared that the tariff and reciprocity were preeminent issues. As late as October in a major campaign appearance in Ohio, McKinley revealed his serious concern about trade expansion. He told the Commercial Club of Cincinnati that, "It should be our settled purpose to open trade wherever we can, making our ships and our commerce messengers of peace and amity." But this was to no avail. William Jennings Bryan, the Democratic candidate, succeeded in making the standards the central, dominant issue of the election.[34]

The results of the 1896 election restored the Republicans to the

White House and left them in control of the House and Senate, a position of power they had seldom enjoyed since 1874. The elections of 1894 and 1896 indicated that the political equipoise of the Gilded Age had been broken. With few exceptions, the Democratic party fell back to the Old Confederacy and some of the Border States. Most of the exceptions were northern urban Democrats whose ethnic following allowed them to win local elections.

Republicanism and protectionism were triumphant. The Republicans moved quickly and decisively in late 1896 and in a special session of Congress in 1897 to produce a new tariff by July 1897, rationalizing their haste by claiming that urgent revenue needs required swift restoration of tariff rates higher than those of the Wilson-Gorman Tariff.[35] Their preoccupation with implementing a high tariff initially obscured their interest in reciprocity. As was often the case, the legislative branch showed more concern with the interests of their constituents than with foreign policy. The Republican Congress returned most duties to the levels of the McKinley Tariff and made some provisions for reciprocal trade agreements. But the Dingley Tariff did not put sugar or hides (or, as the Wilson-Gorman had, wool, a keystone of protectionism) on the free list. The basis for reciprocity treaties with Latin America was therefore limited as compared with the McKinley Tariff. The sugar duty reflected the desire to increase government revenue and domestic sugar production. (From 1890 to 1897 production rose to 321,538 long tons, an increase of more than 100 percent. The greatest increase came from beet sugar). Even without serious concern about revenue needs, the political power of the sugar producers might have precluded using the domestic sugar demand of the United States as a lever in international trade.

The new tariff provided for three types of reciprocal trade agreements. In the first two, under Section Three of the Dingley Tariff, Congress allowed minimal concessions. Neither required congressional approval. For equivalent concessions, the United States would reduce duties on such important household necessities as brandies, wines, vermouth, paintings, statuary, and crude tartar (used in wine making). The executive also could retaliate against countries that were believed to be discriminating against American exports: the president could reimpose duties on coffee, tea, vanilla, and tonka beans. With the possible exceptions of coffee and tea, this was not much of a threat. The four treaties of the first two types (with Italy, Portugal, Germany, and France, including in effect Switzerland) were negotiated and implemented by the McKinley Administration and had little economic significance. The French agreement, however, may have helped conclude a second, much more comprehensive agreement between France and the United States.

Congress enacted a third, much more substantial type of reciprocity treaty. For equivalent concessions, the United States would reduce some or all of its duties as much as 20 percent. This apparent generosity was tempered by the stipulations that these treaties be approved by the Senate and the House, negotiated and in force within two years of the date the Dingley Tariff became law, and remain in force only five years. Moreover, it was alleged that the rates of the Dingley Tariff had been put even higher in anticipation of some reductions due to trade agreements. Section Four of the Dingley Tariff actually gave the president no treaty-making power that he did not already have under the Constitution. The major intent of Congress was to move the French government toward an international agreement on bimetallism. Congress hoped Section Four would demonstrate American flexibility on tariffs and bring France into a new monetary agreement. But the tactic failed.[36] Section Four of the Dingley Act also allowed congressional Republicans to affirm their party's commitment to reciprocity and at the same time indicate the acceptable limits for reciprocal trade agreements. The action demonstrated that congressional Republicans were only mildly inclined to deviate from rigid protectionism.

The McKinley Administration was less inhibited than Congress. President McKinley pressed the Senate Republicans about reciprocity during his first term, but he avoided a serious reciprocity battle with the Senate until his second term. Circumstances allowed the McKinley Administration to pursue a more cautious course than that of the Harrison Administration. Populism had collapsed; prosperity had slowly but steadily returned; and other matters required more immediate attention than did expansionism through reciprocity. The administration had to establish itself, and it faced the residual strength of the silverites in the Senate where they were able to logroll the Dingley Tariff[37] and to prevent the passage of the Gold Standard Act until 1900. At the same time, the Cuban revolution, the Spanish-American War, and European threats to fragment and preempt the China market preoccupied the diplomatic efforts of the president and his advisers.

The State Department was too busy in 1897 to devote adequate attention to the negotiation of reciprocal trade agreements. Responding to "great" domestic pressure, however, McKinley appointed a Reciprocity Commission in October 1897. He chose an able group. John Kasson, leader of the commission, had an impressive record of congressional and diplomatic experience. He represented Iowa for six terms in the House where he rose to a leadership position. His diplomatic experience included serving as United States Minister to Austria-Hungary and to Germany and as an American representative to the Berlin West African Conference and to the 1889 international conference on Samoa. Coleman Chapman, an experienced minor diplomat with linguistic skills and a serious interest in economics, assisted Kasson. (The second secretary, John Ball Osborne, was a strictly political appointee.)[38]

Shortly after his appointment Kasson served as a member of the Canadian-American Joint High Commission. In early 1898, he opened reciprocity talks with Spanish and Cuban representatives, but circumstances were not favorable. By March, Kasson despaired of success. In a remarkably frank private memorandum ("WHY THE U.S. ARE SPECIALLY INTERESTED IN THE RESTORATION OF ORDER IN CUBA") to the president, Kasson indicated that his, and probably the administration's, patience was being exhausted. Kasson pointed to the loss in American trade to Cuba, the destruction of American property there, the costs of patrolling against Cuban fillibusters using the United States as a base, and "political. . . . and moral disturbances" resulting from the brutal nature of the Cuban revolution and Spanish efforts to repress it.[39] Whatever the impact of Kasson's memorandum, the Spanish-American War and its result precluded further negotiations with Spain.

The Reciprocity Commission had more success with other negotiations. In all, the commission negotiated seventeen treaties, most of which they reported to Congress in December 1899, after the two-year limit had been extended. Four of these, which did not require congressional action, have already been discussed. The commission negotiated the remaining thirteen in accordance with the fourth section of the Dingley Act. Of these thirteen, only those with France, Ecuador, Argentina, and Great Britain (for Jamaica) had any economic significance or constituted a clear challenge to protectionism.

Domestic interest groups, already concerned that a great influx of products from Cuba, Puerto Rico, and the Philippines would be one ramification of the victory over Spain, sounded the alarm. California fruit growers claimed that increased imports of Jamaican fruit meant disaster. Wool growers predictably charged Kasson had given "away an important American industry" in the treaty with Argentina which provided for the full 20-percent reduction of the duties on sugar, hides, and wool. That McKinley allowed the Argentina treaty to be reported indicated that he was no longer as sensitive to pressures from the wool growers. The agreement with Ecuador, much like that with Argentina, attracted little public attention.

The same cannot be said of the agreement with France. The French had passed a new tariff in 1895 which reflected the growing protectionist sentiment in Europe. The new French tariff had a maximum and a minimum schedule which allowed them to retaliate against countries charging high duties on French exports. Only Portugal and the United States sent their exports to France under the maximum schedule. Kasson hoped to change this. In return for reductions averaging less than 10 percent on French imports, he got the French to agree to shift most American products to the minimum schedule, a reduction of about 26 percent.

The French did exclude several important American products from the treaty: boots, shoes, and machine tools. Whether or not the United States had struck a good bargain, this was not "tropical" reciprocity of the Harrison Administration that was directed toward Latin America and made concessions on items not produced in the United States.

The McKinley Administration was venturing upon new terrain, and it elected to make the French treaty the test case for any reciprocity program that had real significance. The treaty also provided a clear opportunity to determine if there was adequate domestic support to reverse the growing tendency to erect trade barriers between industrial Europe and the United States. Would the United States move to ease this facet of an intensifying international economic rivalry? The answer was no.

Support for the French treaty came from the NAM, agricultural implements makers, locomotive manufacturers, wagon makers, petroleum and cotton seed oil companies, some iron and steel manufacturers, and some companies engaged in refining and smelting. But a combination of interest groups and intransigence in the Senate prevailed. Along with the Boston Home Market Club, the American Protective League, and the American Iron and Steel Association, strong opposition came from such northeastern industries as braids paper, brushes, spectacles and optical instruments, and knit-goods which were especially well represented at Senate hearings on the treaty. Groups opposing other treaties and the general fear that reciprocity threatened the security of the domestic market helped the opponents of French agreement. A more important factor was that the opponents could count on several of the Senate's most powerful figures: Nelson Aldrich, Orville Platt, Mark Hanna, and William Allison. (Midwestern support for reciprocity later forced Allison to modify his position.)[40]

Kasson warned the Senate Foreign Relations Committee that the high rates of the Dingley Tariff had been adversely received by European governments, that European leaders were openly discussing ways to close their markets to American exports, and that without a more consistent pattern for economic expansion the

United States would experience "the usual closing of factories and disaster." "I have had that in mind," he went on, "that we must under this reciprocity clause, do what we can, and do it promptly, to open the markets of the world securely to our exports." The only alternative was serious economic dislocation which the United States had had "several times" during Kasson's "public life." Kasson admitted that the French treaty was not strictly in accordance with the Blaine-Harrison, or perhaps even the early McKinley, conception of reciprocity strategy, which was to secure advantages for American exports by granting concessions on products not produced in the United States. Also, Kasson shifted the emphasis from farm to industrial products: "We are not regulating an old trade and market, but making a new one for American manufacturers. We are getting advantages on old trade, but that is nothing as compared with the new trade that is coming to relieve the plethora which will soon be on our home market." He concluded by cautioning the committee that without firm diplomatic agreements the United States could do little to prevent European governments from suddenly and arbitrarily increasing tariffs against American exports. Reciprocity treaties could help assure more stable international trade and defuse the threats of retaliation. But such warnings had little impact amid the boom of the American economy in 1900. The *Protectionist* had the last word—at least in 1900. "If . . . no reciprocity can be obtained except at the injury or sacrifice of some American industry then let us resolve to dispense with it altogether."[41]

The president did not force the issue in 1900. It was an election year, and serious dissension had begun to develop in Republican ranks over reciprocity. McKinley preferred to wait until his 1900 election victory. "I can no longer be called the President of a party", he boasted, "I am now the President of the whole people." In his annual message in December 1900, he urged the Senate to act favorably on the pending reciprocal trade agreements, and repeated this recommendation in his second inaugural address of March 1901. Later that month, when he tried unsuccessfully to dissuade Kasson from resigning from the Reciprocity Commission, the president promised to continue the fight for reciprocity.[42]

In April McKinley took the fight to the public, an explicit challenge to the Senate. The president and Mrs. McKinley began a six-week tour of the country on April 29. Their train carried them through the South and as far west as San Francisco to launch the U.S.S. *Ohio*, a major addition to the rapidly expanding American fleet. They planned their last stop for the Pan-American exposition at Buffalo. McKinley had hoped that his entourage would include all the cabinet officers, but only Secretary of State John Hay and Postmaster-General Charles Emory Smith could go. Secretary of the Navy John D. Long, Secretary of Agriculture James Wilson, and Secretary of the Interior Ethan Allen Hitchcock were to join the party in San Francisco. At every opportunity, McKinley dwelled on two themes: national unity (which had supposedly displaced the disunity of the Civil War and Reconstruction years), and the need for and the readiness of the United States to expand its foreign trade. But, in early May, Mrs. McKinley became critically ill, and the president had to cancel the remainder of the tour. Only after Mrs. McKinley's recovery and a vacation in Ohio did McKinley go to Buffalo (in September) for a speech that he believed would be "an epoch-making oration."[43]

The main theme at Buffalo was expansion through reciprocity. The president emphatically rejected the commercial isolationism that some protectionists had espoused when he declared to a receptive Pan-American audience that "the period of exclusiveness had past." Domestic production so exceeded domestic consumption that "the problem of more markets requires our urgent and immediate attention." He defended reciprocity as "the natural outgrowth" of the industrial development the United States had experienced under protectionism. He closed with a call for a modern merchant marine, a Pacific cable, and a Central American isthmian canal.[44]

McKinley's tragic assassination the following day obscured certain aspects of his remarks. He blunted the effect of his remarks at Buffalo when he called protection "the domestic policy now firmly established." Reciprocity treaties, he promised, would be "sensible"; they would "not interrupt our home production" or "harm . . . our industries and labor." McKinley may have felt that he had to mollify the critics of reciprocity with some protectionist clichés. His private secretary, George B. Cortelyou, recalled that, "I never saw him more determined on anything." During some of his more lucid moments on his deathbed, the president asked about newspaper reaction to his speech.[45] McKinley intended to lead his party away from extreme protectionism, but how far is not clear.

Whatever McKinley's intentions about reciprocity were, he had not deserted the economic nationalism that so permeated the thinking of protectionists and tariff reductionists. He may have believed that "commercial wars are unprofitable," that international trade bred "good will," but he once told Robert LaFollette that his "greatest ambition" was the commercial supremacy of the United States.[46] He, like so many of his contemporaries, missed the irony of a trip that embraced both an occasion to laud international brotherhood (Buffalo) and the launching of the U.S.S. *Ohio*. McKinley also assumed that overseas economic expansion was the only viable alternative for an economy whose production, he believed, exceeded domestic purchasing power. McKinley's position was neither novel nor courageous; clearly, he was part of the conservative expansionist consensus of his time.

The shot that took McKinley's life killed the drive for reciprocity within the Republican party. Without strong presidential leadership, the reciprocal trade agreements program had little chance in Congress. With the exception of the reciprocal agreements with Cuba (1903) and with Canada (1911)—neither of which were representative cases—intense interest in reciprocity subsided. Congress finally ratified the Cuban treaty in spite of vigorous opposition. This, no doubt, came largely as a result of the settlement of the war with Spain. The Canadians refused to ratify the 1911 agreement.[47]

McKinley's successor, Theodore Roosevelt, lacked both the inclination and the personal political power in his first term to obtain Senate approval of the French or any other agreement negotiated under Section Four of the Dingley Tariff. Roosevelt also lacked the electoral mandate that McKinley had enjoyed, and he was suspect among some Republican leaders. In general, Roosevelt had far less interest in the tariff than McKinley had had. Thus, both the tariff and the Republican reciprocal trade agreements program quickly lost preeminence. Intense interest in reciprocity was not revived until the great economic crisis of the 1930s, under Franklin D. Roosevelt.[48]

But the Republican Roosevelt and Congress were under some pressure to accept reciprocal trade agreements. Although various groups supporting reciprocity remained rather active until 1904 or 1905, the most significant instance of support came in 1901. The day after President McKinley was shot at Buffalo, the NAM —perhaps with unseemly haste—called for a national reciprocity convention to meet in Washington in November. The meeting attracted a wide range of industries, trade associations, boards of trade, and chambers of commerce from virtually every part of the country. Led by the farm implements industry, the delegates formed a chorus of support for reciprocal trade treaties and for McKinley's phrase, "The period of exclusiveness is past." The impact of the assassination could not, however, smother all discord. Led by representatives of the knit-goods industry, which was opposed to the French treaty, a few delegates shunned foreign trade and rhapsodized upon the home market. Even fewer of those present who did support reciprocity were willing to make concessions that might endanger their own interests. Anxieties about the domestic market appeared again as they had throughout thirty years of tariff debate and legislation.

A convention that attracted both the Home Market Club and the American Free Trade League offered little promise of agreement on a reciprocity program of real consequence. As could be predicted, the convention came out in favor of reciprocal trade agreements that would do no "injury to any of our home interests of manufacturing, commerce or farming." The delegates also recommended that Congress create a new cabinet level "Department of Commerce and Industries" which would include a new Reciprocity Commission that would have only investigative powers. A delegation from the convention carried these resolutions to President Roosevelt.[49]

With the return of prosperity, reciprocity lost its most important economic rationale. As new gold discoveries lowered the price of gold and as farm prices rose impressively and consistently, agrarian discontent eased. American exports, especially manufactured goods, made impressive gains from 1895 to 1901 (from $921 million to $1,605 million). Balance-of-trade figures indicated a dramatic gain of more than 500 percent (from +$133 million in 1895 to +$680 million in 1901). As early as February 1898, the *New York Times* proclaimed "A New National Era." Others concurred. The expansionist NAM had lost some of its sense of urgency even before the November reciprocity convention. Theodore C. Search, president of the NAM, told the national convention of the association in June 1901, that the crucial issue was not "further extension of trade," but holding present gains in exports. In September of that same year, the Bureau of Statistics of the Treasury Department complained happily that American export trade had grown so rapidly that it could not keep up with the pace of export growth. Coincidentally, Americans increased their foreign investments, particularly in Canada. They had discovered that by locating branch plants abroad they could take advantage of the protective tariffs of other countries, something Europeans who built subsidiaries in the United States had long known. Large American manufacturers, strengthened by new technology and large-scale, centralized operations, found steady production more profitable than a pattern of high production interrupted by shutdowns while overstocked inventories were slowly sold off. Excess production was then "dumped" on the international market.[50] Finally, the Democrats had very obviously become the minority party, its decline now signaling the end of significant tariff reduction as a political issue. The Republicans did not need to risk a divisive struggle over a comprehensive reciprocity program. Other issues, such as the danger of concentrating large aggregates of financial and industrial power in relatively few hands, eclipsed the tariff—at least until the William H. Taft Administration.

*   *   *

For more than twenty years the tariff had persisted as a major political issue. National political leaders had focused on an issue that accorded with their needs and ideology, that fitted the Gilded Age and its political and economic circumstances. From 1874 to 1896, neither the Republican nor the Democratic party could assert its dominance; in fact only the peculiar circumstances of the Civil War and Reconstruction gave the GOP the upper hand from 1860 to 1874.

Breaking the political balance of power became an urgent, primary task for the political leadership. To do so they needed a suitable issue. Severe ideological restraint on the national government restricted their choice. Most of the recurrent political issues of the nineteenth century—the Civil War and Reconstruction, monetary policy, prohibition or temperance, railroad regulation, civil service reform, immigration restriction—lacked national voter appeal or were seriously divisive issues. "Monopoly," the place of large concentrations of private capital and industry in American society, became a major issue only late in the Gilded Age, and the complexities of the monopoly question undermined its political value.

With all the other issues discounted, only the tariff was left. So the parties turned to their pasts. Prior to the Civil War, in 1846 and again in 1857, the Democrats generally had followed a low tariff policy. The Republicans reversed this course in 1861. Afterwards, the GOP remained consistently protectionist despite strong complaints within the party. During the 1880 presidential election, when James Garfield equated protectionism with Republicanism, the GOP firmly identified itself with high tariffs. After the 1882 congressional elections, the tariff reductionists seized the initiative in the Democratic party. Though they were a majority in the Democratic party, the reductionists nevertheless had to struggle with a strong faction of protectionists within their own party led by Congressman Samuel Randall and Senator Arthur

Gorman. They also confronted the persistent political power of the Republicans, the intransigence of vested interests that had a stake in maintaining high duties on particular items, and the powerful silverite element in their own party. Abortive efforts at tariff reduction resulted: the Morrison bills of 1884 and 1886 and, after Cleveland's noted 1887 tariff message, the Mills Bill of 1888. Then came the "Great Tariff Debate" and the election of 1888. Finally, in 1893, the Democrats got control of the White House, the Senate, and the House for the first time since the 1850s. A debacle followed—the depression of the 1890s, repeal of the Sherman Silver Purchase Act, passage of the Wilson-Gorman Act, and the election of 1896. Republicanism and protectionism had triumphed.

Both parties demonstrated considerable partisan unity on the tariff after the 1870s. The final congressional roll call votes on the tariff and the congressional debates fell into sharply partisan patterns. Unlike the tariff debates of the 1820s, when the general economic development of the United States was still an issue and the two national parties had not yet emerged, the congressional tariff debates after 1880 were partisan exercises.[51] In the latter case, senators and representatives directed their concern to swaying voters, not one another. Tariff orations served as party identification badges, in an era when both the leaders and the voters were intensely partisan. Congressmen and senators in the Gilded Age endlessly reiterated well-known tariff positions. With their franking privilege, they then scattered ample copies of their remarks to the electorate. It was, appropriately, a liturgical exercise. The faithful reaffirmed their doctrinal purity for others of the faith. Some constituents failed to have the proper worshipful attitude.

Mr. Dooley, fictional political savant, told his bartender friend that his congressman, who "looks after me inthrests well," had sent him a copy of a proposed tariff. "He knows what a gr-reat reader I am, I don't care what I read. . . . I've been studyin' it f'r a week. 'Tis a good piece of summer lithachoor. 'Tis full iv action an' romance. I haven't read annythink to akel it since I used to get th' Deadwood Dick series."[52]

But the tariff debates merit a more serious reading. They reveal the basic political and economic assumptions of the political leaders of the Gilded Age and how those leaders used the tariff for broad political purposes. In addition to the urgent business of breaking the political equipoise, they confronted a unique situation: they had to communicate with a mass electorate experiencing the agonies and confusion of rapid industrialization.

Cities, factories, railroads, and farms increased with amazing speed, but the economy frequently faltered or virtually failed. The mood of the country swung erratically from abounding confidence to deep fear and pessimism as a different America emerged in the late nineteenth century. An urban America divided by disparities in wealth and income and fragmented along ethnic and religious lines raised disturbing questions. The seeming tidal wave of "new immigration" from southern and eastern Europe reinforced such anxieties. Labor strife became more common. The massive rail strike of 1877 preceded the great increase of strikes and union membership in the 1880s. National confidence wavered badly with the Haymarket Riot of 1886, the Homestead Strike of 1892, and the Pullman Strike of 1894. The feeling of discontent and alienation swept through many farming areas. Where had the supposedly homogeneous days of Jacksonian America gone?

Some found solace by clinging to the myth of the self-made man or to traditional religion. Others turned to Henry George, the Nationalist clubs inspired by Edward Bellamy, the Social Gospel, Social Darwinism, or the socialists. But more Americans—and most political leaders—conformed to the fundamental American political and economic ideology. Private enterprise capitalism, aided by government ("the American system"), held out the promise of plenty which would bring the good life, contentment, social harmony, and a continuing social and economic rise. Most assumed that the national government had little responsibility beyond subsidizing private enterprise and supporting the relatively free forces of the market. Confronted by mounting discontent in 1892, Republican Senator Orville H. Platt, a protectionist, declared that all the "conservative" elements could do was to unite and wait out the storm.[53]

In response to these discordant decades, the politicians resorted to the tariff. The remarkably malleable qualities of tariff rhetoric allowed them to claim that their tariff positions offered something for everybody. Tariff reductionists promised that by selectively lowering tariff duties, consumers (most Americans) were assured of cheaper prices, but neither wage rates nor the domestic market for industry or agriculture would be threatened. Reduced tariffs would also facilitate overseas economic expansion which would benefit all Americans. Tariff reductionists thus appealed to a wide coalition. Tariff reduction also fit the more passive political philosophy of the Democratic party. This policy reflected the more rural nature of the constituencies most Democrats served. Finally, by stressing the tariff, Democratic leaders hoped to finesse the silverites.

The protectionists had a more activist philosophy that was more in keeping with the American past and American thinking—"the American system." Protectionists claimed that their policy assured high wages and secure domestic markets. As Henry C. Carey asserted, there would then be "a harmony of interests." "There is," one protectionist congressman said, "no difference between classes on this question. [The tariff] is either better or worse for all classes."[54] Many protectionists genuinely sought to serve a wide range of interest groups; they were not the pawns of any particular interest such as big business. The high tariff advocates, however, failed to grasp the consequences of the development of big industry and large financial institutions.

The protectionists enjoyed considerable advantages. Only once, in 1893-1894, did the Republicans fail to control either the White House or the Senate. The protectionists held the high ground of nationalism. They stressed the anti-European, especially the anti-British, thrust of their policy to an American audience that felt these emotions deeply. Once a tariff schedule became law, the protectionists acquired valuable allies—those who had direct interests in the duties.

But there were serious flaws. The "mixed economy" strategy allowed the more advantaged Americans to derive disproportionate benefits. Thus, Ohio Congressman Frank Hurd, a self-styled free trader, asked the protectionists: "On what ground shall the Government interpose to help the business of one at the expense of another? . . . I deny the right of the Government to build up one man at the expense of another."[55] But Hurd's criticism was a bit tardy: protectionism was just one aspect of Hamiltonianism, a public policy Americans had followed for a century.

Both protectionists and tariff reductionists came to assume, before the 1890s, that to sustain prosperity overseas economic expansion was necessary. The Democrats initially charged that high tariffs hindered the flow of American products abroad. First, they emphasized increasing agricultural exports, and, later, a small group of Democratic leaders, guided by David Wells and Abram Hewitt, turned to a free raw materials strategy designed primarily to expand the foreign sales of American manufacturers. Republican leaders—first James Blaine, then Chester A. Arthur and Frederick T. Frelinghuysen, and later Benjamin Harrison—answered with their reciprocity strategy. They hoped to keep protectionism largely intact while expanding overseas. Regardless of their approach, all hoped to expand their following in the electorate.

Such an expansionist course, as both factions knew, would greatly increase American dependence on the world market. For the protectionists, this contained a special irony. Over the years they had wrapped themselves in the flag, and had asserted that protectionism would give the United States economic independence. In 1892 McKinley told an enthusiastic Newark audience that American political independence had begun in 1776, and that its economic independence had begun when Congress passed the first protective tariff in 1789. Nine years later, he told a crowd gathered at the Pan-American exposition in Buffalo that overproduction in the United States must be relieved by "sensible trade arrangements which will not interrupt our home production. . . . The period of exclusiveness is past. The expansion of our trade and commerce is the pressing problem. Commercial wars are unprofitable. A policy of good will and friendly trade relations will prevent reprisals."[56]

Like most contemporary leaders, McKinley saw no contradiction between vigorous expansion of American exports and the desire to maintain international peace. In some mystical way international trade would have a harmonizing effect on international relations. That the outward thrust of the American economy might cause serious economic disruptions abroad (such as those resulting from the impact of American farm exports on European farmers) troubled neither protectionists nor reductionists. Moreover, those who favored protectionism plus reciprocity ignored the dangers inherent in their desire to keep the American market a virtual sanctuary while massively penetrating the markets of other countries. Brooks Adams, confidant of the powerful, recognized these perils. In August 1901, a month before McKinley's assassination, Adams realized that American economic power posed a vital threat to Europe. He saw only two alternatives for the future: "compromise or war."[57] Adams' vision may have been cataclysmic, but it was also wise.

Both protectionists and tariff reductions hoped they could pursue "Plenty" and "Progress" without creating an overseas territorial empire. Yet, both made or accepted preemptive moves with respect to Hawaii, Samoa, Latin America, and a Central American isthmian canal.

Generally, the expansionist model was Great Britain. As it had expanded, so would the United States.[58] The Gilded Age leaders believed non-territorial, economic growth to be both natural and necessary. Their religious beliefs, their cultural chauvinism, and their racism all supported expansionist views. In the early 1880s, the important political leaders, including both protectionists and reductionists, concluded that making an outward thrust was urgent. Agrarians had reached similar conclusions earlier. But elsewhere the expansionist strategies met considerable opposition. Some protectionists believed that reciprocity threatened the entire high tariff structure; they had especially strong congressional representation.

Groups which thought that reciprocal trade agreements or tariff reduction would affect their interests adversely vigorously opposed this form of expansion. Similarly, some fought any kind of tariff reduction, and others fought reductions on specific items.

Neither protectionists nor tariff reductionists could prevent monetary policy from becoming the major issue in 1896. America the Bountiful had become America the Depressed in 1893. The silverites forced both major parties to take a clear stand on the issue of the monetary standards in the 1896 election, and they seized control of the Democratic party. William Jennings Bryan and his followers forced the Battle of the Standards; when the smoke cleared, the political equipoise of the Gilded Age was shattered. Republicanism and protectionism—as well as the gold standard—held sway. Except for the Wilson interlude, the Republicans dominated national politics from the mid-1890s to 1930, and except for the Underwood Tariff of 1914, protectionism remained the fixed policy of the United States until after World War II.

McKinley's death climaxed efforts to add reciprocity to protectionism. His successor, Theodore Roosevelt, expediently shunned the tariff issue. Roosevelt turned from the wait-and-hope strategy of Orville Platt to the collective action approach of the Progressive era. In so doing, he weaned the Republican party from its heavy reliance on the tariff issue.

In 1919 an aged Henry Watterson lamented: "McKinley and Protectionism, Cleveland . . . and Free Trade—how far away they seem."[59] He was wrong. Vital issues connected with the tariff debates and legislation of the Gilded Age were not and are not dead. The wealthier, better organized groups, often with the aid of the government, still have significant advantages over other Americans. The tariff debates and legislation of the late nineteenth century provide crucial insights into how the political elite and the American people have dealt with severe domestic crises, especially the depression of the 1890s. The tariff issue also enhances our understanding of the motives and nature of American economic penetration in the world. Few citizens questioned the logic of American overseas economic expansion; they debated only its timing and its tactics—territorial or non-territorial imperialism. The outward thrust of the United States in the 1890s followed the policy outlined in the 1870s and the 1880s.

Notes

Introduction

[1] Walter Dean Burnham, "Party Systems and the Political Process," in *The American Party Systems, Stages of Political Development*, eds. William Nisbet Chambers and Walter Dean Burnham (New York: Oxford University Press, 1967), 295-298; Roy F. Nichols, *The Disruption of American Democracy* (New York: Macmillan Co., 1948); Joel Silbey, *The Transformation of American Politics, 1840-1860* (Englewood Cliffs, N.J.: Prentice-Hall, 1967); U.S., Department of Commerce, *Historical Statistics of the United States, Colonial Times to 1957* (Washington: Government Printing Office, 1960), 691; Michael Fitzgibbons Holt, *Forging a Majority: The Formation of the Republican Party in Pittsburgh, 1848-1860* (New Haven: Yale University Press, 1969), 304-313.

[2] Data used in the table are taken from Burnham, "Party Systems and the Political Process," in *American Party Systems*, 297. Also see Edgar Eugene Robinson, *The Presidential Vote, 1896-1932* (Stanford: Stanford

University Press, 1947), 47-53; Burnham, *Presidential Ballots, 1836-1892* (Baltimore: Johns Hopkins University Press, 1955), 246-257.

[3] My impressions of Irish-American voting behavior are corroborated by Thomas N. Brown, *Irish-American Nationalism, 1870-1890* (New York: J. B. Lippincott Co., 1966), 134-146; Robert D. Marcus, *Grand Old Party, Political Structure in the Gilded Age, 1880-1896* (New York: Oxford University Press, 1970), 91, 271.

[4] Supra, footnote 2; Walter Dean Burnham, "The Changing Shape of the American Political Universe," *American Political Science* Review, LIX, No. 1 (March 1965), 7-28; Paul Kleppner, *The Cross of Culture, A Social Analysis of Midwestern Elections, 1850-1900* (New York: The Free Press, 1970); Richard Joseph Jensen, "The Winning of the Midwest: A Social History of Midwestern Elections, 1888-1896" (Unpublished Ph.D. diss., Yale University, 1967); Samuel Thompson McSeveny, "The Politics of Depression: Voting Behavior in Connecticut, New York, and New Jersey, 1893-1896" (Unpublished Ph.D. diss., University of Iowa, 1965). Also see Seymour Martin Lipset, "Religion and Politics in the American Past and Present," in *Religion and Social Conflict*, eds. Robert Lee and Martin E. Marty (New York: Oxford University Press, 1964) 69-126; V. O. Key, Jr., *Southern Politics* (New York: Alfred A. Knopf, Inc., 1949), 75, 219-220, 280-282; John H. Fenton, *Midwest Politics* (New York: Holt, Rinehart and Winston, 1966), 5, 44, 118-122, 131, 140-141, 155-163, 184, 195; Duane Lockard, *New England State Politics* (Princeton: Princeton University Press, 1959), 122; Duncan Macrae, Jr., and James A. Meldrum, "Critical Elections in Illinois: 1888-1958," *American Political Science Review*, LIV, No. 3 (September 1960), 669-683; Thomas A. Flinn, "Continuity and Change in Ohio Politics," *Journal of Politics*, XXIV (1962), 521-544; Gerald W. McFarland, "The Breakdown of Deadlock: The Cleveland Democracy in Connecticut, 1884-1894," *Historian*, XXXI, No. 3 (May 1969), 381.

[5] Burnham, "The Changing Shape of the American Political Universe," *American Political Science Review*, 7-28; Samuel P. Hays, "The Social Analysis of American Political History, 1880-1920," *Political Science Quarterly*, LXXX, No. 3 (1965), 373-394; Angus Campbell et al., *The American Voter* (New York: John Wiley and Sons, Inc., 1960).

[6] See Richard Weiss, "Horatio Alger, Jr., and the Response to Indus-

trialism," in *The Age of Industrialism in America*, ed. Frederic Cople Jaher (New York: The Free Press, 1968), 304-316.

[7] Quoted in H. Shelton Smith, Robert T. Handy, and Lefferts A. Loetscher, *American Christianity, An Historical Interpretation with Documents* (New York: Charles Scribner's Sons, 1963), II, 322-324.

[8] Robert H. Wiebe, *The Search for Order, 1877-1920* (New York: Hill and Wang, 1967), 1-132.

[9] U.S., Department of Commerce, *Historical Statistics*, 99. John Higham has written very perceptively about the mood of the 1800s and 1890s. Higham, *Strangers in the Land, Patterns of American Nativism, 1860-1925*, Rev. ed. (New York: Atheneum, 1963), 35-105.

[10] Irwin Unger, *The Greenback Era; A Social and Political History of American Finance, 1865-1879* (Princeton: Princeton University Press, 1964); Walter T. K. Nugent, *Money and American Society, 1865-1880* (New York: Free Press, 1968); Allen Weinstein, *Prelude to Populism: Origins of the Silver Issue, 1867-1878* (New Haven: Yale University Press, 1970). Also see Robert P. Sharkey, *Money, Class, and Party; An Economic Study of Civil War and Reconstruction* (Baltimore: Johns Hopkins University Press, 1959).

[11] Jensen, "The Winning of the Midwest," 102-105; Kleppner, *Cross of Culture*, 158-171.

[12] Wiebe, *Search for Order*, 1-132; Samuel P. Hays, "Political Parties and the Community-Society Continuum," in *American Party Systems*, 152-181; Robert K. Merton, *Social Theory and Social Structure* (Glencoe, Ill: Free Press, 1949), 387-420. Both essays were very suggestive and helpful. For a succinct discussion of party programs as a nationalizing force, see William Nisbet Chambers, *Political Parties in a New Nation, The American Experience, 1776-1809* (New York: Oxford University Press, 1963), 47.

[13] William Appleman Williams, *The Roots of the Modern American Empire* (New York: Random House, 1969).

[14] Marcus, *Grand Old Party*, 91, 271.

[15] Paul Kleppner, "The Tariff as a Political Issue: The Democratic Case," Organization of American Historians, Los Angeles, April 1970.

[16] One scholar has established a clear relationship between voter behavior and partisan tariff appeals in the 1890 election in Wisconsin. Roger E. Wyman, "Wisconsin Ethnic Groups and the Election of 1890," *Wisconsin Magazine of History*, LI, No. 4 (Summer 1968), 269-293.

[17] Robert A. Lively, "The American System: A Review Article," *Business History Review*, XIX, No. 1, (March 1955), 81-96.

Chapter 1

[1] The composition of the new Congress graphically demonstrated the extent of the Republican defeat in 1874. In the 44th Congress, the Republicans had 109 seats compared with 194 in the previous Congress. On the other hand, the Democrats controlled 169 seats in the 44th Congress as compared with 92 in the 43rd. U.S., Department of Commerce, *Historical Statistics of the United States, Colonial Times to 1957* (Washington: Government Printing Office, 1960), 691.

[2] For typical views, see *New York Times*, January 1, 1877, 4; January 1, 1878, 4; *Commercial and Financial Chronicle*, XIX, No. 472 (July 11, 1874), 28-29; XXII, No. 550 (January 8, 1876), 29; XXIV, No. 602 (January 6, 1877), 3; XXVI, No. 654 (January 5, 1878), 13; XXVIII, No. 715 (March 8, 1879), 235

[3] U.S., Department of Commerce, *Historical Statistics*, 7, 114, 278, 294, 296-303, 409, 416-417, 425.

[4] *Congressional Record*, 7:5:4380 [hereafter cited as *CR*, 7:5:4380]; U.S., House, Select Committee, *The Causes of the General Depression in Business and Labor, 45th Cong., 3rd Sess., 1879), House Mis. Doc. No. 29* (Washington: Government Printing Office, 1879).

[5] *Bradstreet's*, January 19, 1884, 34. Also see *Commercial and Financial Chronicle*, XXX, No. 759 (January 10, 1880), 28. Algernon S. Paddock, Remarks of February 10, 1879: *CR*, 8:2:1158-1160; James D. Richardson (ed.), *Messages and Papers of the Presidents* (Washington: Government Printing Office, 1902), VIII, 578-579; Royal Cortissoz, *The Life of Whitelaw Reid* (New York: Charles Scribner's Sons, 1921), II, 3: William Appleman Williams, *The Roots of the Modern American Empire* (New York: Random House, 1969), 205, 207, 211, 215-216.

[6] Wells, *The Creed of Free Trade* (New York: n.p., n.d.), 4-6. (This is a reprint of an article that appeared in the August 1875, issue of *Atlantic Monthly*.) Wells, "How Shall the Nation Regain Prosperity? Part III," *North American Review*, CXXXV, No. 259 (November-December 1877), 544. His most elaborate statement of this position appeared in his *Recent*

Economic Changes (New York: D. Appleton and Co., 1890). Other Americans shared Wells' anxiety if not his analysis. See Samuel Rezneck, "Distress, Relief and Discontent in the United States During the Depression of 1873-1878," *Journal of Political Economy*, LVIII, No. 6 (December 1950), 494-512; Wells to William B. Allison, June 17, 1880 [?]: David A. Wells Papers, Library of Congress [hereafter cited as Wells Mss.]; Wells to Worthington C. Ford, June 3, [1884]; Ford Papers, New York Public Library.

⁷ Harris, Remarks of May 9, 1878: *CR*, 7:4:3341-3343, 3345.

⁸ Burchard, Remarks of June 4, 1878: *CR*, 7:Appendix:434; *New York Times*, February 1, 1876, 4; May 27, 1880, 4; Ivo Nikolai Lambi, *Free Trade and Protectionism in Germany, 1868-1879* (Wiesbaden: Franz Steiner Verlag GMBH, 1963); R. R. Palmer, *A History of the Modern World* (New York: A. A. Knopf, 1954), 608.

⁹ U.S., Senate Select Committee, *Transportation Routes to the Seaboard, 43rd Cong., 1st Sess., 1874, Senate Report No. 307, Parts 1 and 2* (Washington: Government Printing Office, 1874); Windom, Remarks of June 10, 1878: *CR*, 7:5:4364. The emphasis is Windom's.

¹⁰ Ibid.; *CR*, 7:5:4358-4367.

¹¹ Maxey, Remarks of June 4, 1878: *CR*, 7:4:4069-4071.

¹² *CR*, 8:2:1662; 8:3:2132; *New York Tribune*, October 12, 1877, 1; Leonard A. Swann, Jr., *John Roach, Maritime Entrepreneur: The Years as Naval Contractor, 1862-1886* (Annapolis: United States Naval Institute, 1965), 114-115.

¹³ *New York Tribune*, April 15, 1877, 5; July 7, 5; July 13, 2; *New York Times*, February 17, 1878, 8; U.S., Senate, *Postal and Commercial Intercourse between the United States and South American Countries, 1878, Senate Ex. Doc. No. 7* (Washington: Government Printing Office, 1879), 2-3; John S. Shriver, (comp.) *Through the South and West with the President* (New York: *The Mail and Express*, 1891), 29-32.

¹⁴ *CR*, 4:4:3037, 5572.

¹⁵ U.S., House Committee on Ways and Means, *Hawaiian Treaty, 44th Cong., 1st Sess., 1877, House Report No. 116, Part 1* (Washington: Government Printing Office, 1876), 4-11.

¹⁶ Ibid., 6-7, 9, 11; Ibid., *Part 2*, 5.

¹⁷ Ibid., *Part 1*, 6, 11; Ibid., *Part 2*, 5; Morrison to Wells, February 20, 1876; March 9, 16: Wells Mss.; Merze Tate, *Hawaii: Reciprocity or Annexation* (Lansing: Michigan State University Press, 1968), 108-

117; Sylvester K. Stevens, *American Expansion in Hawaii, 1842-1898* (Harrisburg: Archives Publishing Co. of Pennsylvania, Inc., 1945), 108-140; Wells, "Hawaiian Reciprocity Treaty Not a 'Fraud' or 'Swindle.' " (Boston) *Evening Transcript*, February 25, March 1, 1875: cited in Tate, *Hawaii*, 113. Ironically, William D. Kelley, arch-protectionist and bitter opponent of Morrison and Wells, signed the minority report. He viewed any reciprocal trade agreement as a dangerous breach of the tariff wall.

[18] Richardson, *Messages*, VII, 469; F. W. Seward to Edward F. Noyes, August 29, 1879: U.S., State Department, *Foreign Relations of the United States, 1879* (Washington: Government Printing Office, 1879), 343-344. *New York Times*, February 17, 1878, 8; *Bradstreet's* February 25, 1880, 5; Chester L. Barrows, *William M. Evarts* (Chapel Hill: University of North Carolina Press, 1941), 376-377.

[19] Charles I. Bevans (comp.), *Treaties and Other International Agreements of the United States of America, 1776-1949* (Washington: Government Printing Office, 1968), 63-67; Richardson, *Messages and Papers*, VII, 497. Thus, the Senate in effect reversed itself. During the Grant Administration, the Senate had refused to appropriate funds for a naval coaling station in the Samoan Islands. *CR*, 3:3:1096; Richardson, *Messages*, VIII, 168-169. See George Herbert Ryden, *The Foreign Policy of the United States in Relation to Samoa* (New Haven: Yale University Press, 1933).

[20] Richardson, *Messages*, VII, 585-586; U.S., House Select Committee on the Inter-Oceanic Canal, *The Monroe Doctrine, 46th Cong., 3rd Sess., 1881, House Report No. 390* (Washington: Government Printing Office, 1881), 8-9.

[21] *New York Tribune*, September 14, 1877, 8; U.S., House Committee on Foreign Affairs, *Treaty with Mexico, 45th Cong., 3rd Sess., 1879, House Report No. 108* (Washington: Government Printing Office, 1879); Remarks of Congressman Randall L. Gibson on joint resolutions H. R. Nos. 5, 6, 7, 8, October 29, 1877: *CR*, 6:178-179; Joint resolution H. R. No. 28 presented by W. C. Whitthorne, November 5, 1877: *CR*, 6:239; Samuel B. Maxey presented joint resolution S. R. No. 2, Nov. 13, 1877; *CR*, 6:362; Remarks of Abram Hewitt, December 10, 1877: *CR*, 7:1:102-103; Resolution of Roscoe Conkling, December 11, 1877: *CR*, 7:1:120; Remarks of W. C. Whitthorne, March 12, 1878: *CR*, 7:2:1701; John T. Morgan to John W. Foster, September 7, 1878: John

W. Foster Papers, Library of Congress; Abram Hewitt to John Hancock, October 14, 1879: Abram Hewitt Papers, Library of Congress; *The American*, II, No. 32, (May 21, 1881), 87; *Bradstreet's*, October 11, 1879, 4; February 11, 1880, 3; *Frank Leslie's Illustrated Weekly*, (March 15, 1879), 17, 22-25, 28; David M. Pletcher, *Rails, Mines and Progress: Seven American Promoters in Mexico, 1867-1911* (Ithaca: Cornell University Press, 1958), ch. I.

[22] Kelley, Remarks of March 6, 1876: *CR*, 4:2:1495-1498; *New York Times*, February 17, 1878, 8; *Bradstreet's*, December 6, 1879, 5.

[23] Douglas conceived his plan in 1861 as the nation was dividing. Apparently, he thought his "Commerical Union" would prevent secession, but he did not clarify how the plan would accomplish this. Douglas did not publish his idea. In 1889, on the eve of the Pan-American conference of 1889-1890, his brother-in-law, J. Madison Cutts published Douglas' proposal. Douglas' commercial union, styled after the German *zollverein*, included the United States, Canada, Central America, and the West Indies and was a *"Union for Commercial Purposes Only."* "Do this," Douglas asserted, "and all the benefits of territorial expansion can and will be secured without incurring its dangers." Douglas, *An American Continental Commercial Union or Alliance*, ed. J. Madison Cutts (Washington: Thomas McGill and Co., 1889), 13-14. In 1911 the Senate reprinted Douglas' proposal. U.S., Senate, *North American Trade, 62nd Cong., 1st Sess., Doc. No. 61, 1911* (Washington: Government Printing Office, 1911).

[24] Howard Schonberger, "The Mississippi Valley Trading Company: The Grange and International Cooperation, 1874-1878," (Unpublished manuscript), 1-2. Professor Schonberger of the University of Maine graciously shared his manuscript.

[25] *The Laws of Wisconsin, Together with the Joint Resolutions and Memorials Passed at the Thirtieth Annual Session of the Wisconsin Legislature, in the Year 1877* (Madison: David Atwood, Printer and Stereotyper, 1877), 635.

[26] *Journal of the Proceedings of the Eleventh Session of the National Grange of the Patrons of Husbandry, Cincinnati, November 21-30, 1877* (Louisville: J. P. Morton Co., 1878), 43.

[27] *Charleston (S. C.) News and Courier*, January 14, 1878; *New York Times*, August 24, 1877, 4; November 9, 5; February 21, 1878, 2, 4; September 6, 1; December 12, 1; December 11, 1879, 1, 4. See Evarts speech to the annual dinner of the New York Chamber of Commerce.

Ibid., May 15, 1877, 2. *New York Tribune*, January 5, 1880, 1; Patrick Joseph Hearden, "Cotton Mills of the New South and American Foreign Policy, 1865-1901," (Unpublished M.A. thesis, University of Wisconsin, 1966), 19.

[28] *Bradstreet's*, October 11, 1879, 4. *Iron Age*, July 19, 1877, 14; August 23, 14.

[29] Lambi, *Free Trade and Protectionism in Germany*, chs. VI-XIII. See David J. Rothman, *Politics and Power, the United States Senate, 1869-1901* (Cambridge: Harvard University Press, 1966).

[30] Richardson, *Messages*, VII, 612.

[31] Compare the platform of the Republican party in 1856 and 1860. Kirk H. Porter and Donald Bruce Johnson (comps.), *National Party Platforms, 1840-1964* (Urbana: University of Illinois Press, 1966), pp. 27-28, 31-33. Stanley Coben, "Northeastern Business and Radical Reconstruction: A Reexamination," *Mississippi Valley Historical Review*, XLVI, No. 1 (June 1959), 67-90; Richard Hofstadter, "The Tariff Issues on the Eve of the Civil War," *American Historical Review*, XLIV, No. 1 (October 1938), 50-55; Thomas Monroe Pitkin, "The Tariff and the Early Republican Party," (Unpublished Ph.D. diss., Western Reserve University, 1935).

[32] Wells, *Report of the Special Commissioner of the Revenue, 1868* (Washington: Government Printing Office, 1868); *Report of the Special Commissioner of the Revenue, 1869* (Washington: Government Printing Office, 1869); Remarks of Justin S. Morrill, May 7, 1866: *Congressional Globe*, 36:3:2434-2438 [hereafter cited as *Globe*, 36:3:2434-2438]; Henry L. Cake, February 23, 1869: *Globe*, 40:3:1477; William D. Kelley and Daniel J. Morrell, January 11, 1870: *Globe*, 42:1:369ff., 617; U.S., House Committee on Manufactures, *Examination of Statements in the Report of the Special Commissioner of Revenue, 41st Cong., 2nd Sess., 1870, House Report No. 72*, (Washington: Government Printing Office, 1870); Henry C. Carey *How Protection, Increase of Public and Private Revenues, and National Independence, March Hand in Hand Together, Reviews of the Report of the Hon. D. A. Wells, Special Commissioner of the Revenue.* (Philadelphia: Collins, 1870); Carey, *Review of the Farmer's Question, as Exhibited in the Recent Report of the Hon. D. A. Wells, Special Commissioner of the Revenue;* (Philadelphia: Collins, 1870); Herbert R. Ferleger, *David A. Wells and the American Revenue System, 1865-1870* (Ann Arbor: Edwards Brothers, Inc., 1942), 267-312;

Fred Bunyan Joyner, *David Ames Wells, Champion of Free Trade* (Cedar Rapids, Iowa: The Torch Press, 1939), 39-94.

[33] *New York Times*, May 5, 1872, 1; May 4, 8; May 7,1; July 24, 7; *New York Tribune*, July 11, 1872, 1.

[34] *New York Tribune*, February 17, 1877, 5; Garfield to [Anonymous], December 15, 1879: James A. Garfield Papers, Library of Congress; Edmund Kirke (ed.), "My Public Life, by President Garfield," *North American Review*, CCCLXVI (May 1887), 460-461; Burke A. Hinsdale (ed.), *The Works of James Abram Garfield* (Boston: James R. Osgood and Co., 1883), II, 782-787; Theodore Clarke Smith, *The Life and Letters of James Abram Garfield* (New Haven: Yale University Press, 1925), I, 591; II, 715-716; Robert Granville Caldwell, *James A. Garfield, Party Chieftain* (New York: Dodd, Mead and Co., 1931), 196-201; Earle Dudley Ross, *The Liberal Republican Movement* (New York: Henry Holt and Co., 1919); Garfield to Burke Hinsdale, n. d.: cited in Caldwell, *Garfield*, 223; Albert V. House, "Republicans and Democrats Search for New Identities, 1870-1890," *Review of Politics* XXXI, No. 4 (October 1969), 470-471.

[35] Kerr to Wells, December 31, 1875, Wells Mss.; *New York Times*, February 2, 1876, 1.

[36] Anson Phelps Stokes to Wells, January 17, 1876; Morrison to Wells, February 20, March 16, 1876; January 14, 1882: Wells Mss. See Tom E. Terrill, "David A. Wells, the Democracy, and Tariff Reduction, 1877-1894," *Journal of American History*, LVI, No. 3 (December 1969), 540-555. J. S. "The Parsee Merchant" Moore also helped draft the bill. Wells to Moore, February 4, [1876]: Wells Mss.

[37] Morrison, Remarks of May 25, 1876: *CR*, 4:4:3312-3322; *CR*, 4:Appendix:594.

[38] *CR*, 7:1:110-118; 7:3:2690; 7:Appendix:473; *New York Times*, February 1, 1878, 2; 10, 1; March 3, 1; 8, 1; 17, 1; 16, 4.

[39] McKinley, Remarks of April 15, 1878: *CR*, 7:3:2541-2546; Kelley, Remarks of May 9, 1878: *CR*, 7:4:3329-3345; *CR*, 7:5:4154-4155. Thirty-six representatives did not vote. *New York Times*, June 6, 1878, 2; *New York Tribune*, June 6, 1878, 1.

[40] *Bradstreet's*, December 31, 1879, 5; January 28, 1880, 4; *New York Times*, January 2, 1879, 5; February 7, 1880, 3.

[41] *CR*, 10:1:136; *New York Times*, December 11, 1879, 4.

[42] *CR*, 10:5:4102-4116. The vote was 31 to 15. Seven of those voting

were members of third parties or had no party affiliation. All 12 Repuliccans who voted suported the bill. Significantly, the Democrats were split on the measure: 12 for, 13 against. *New York Times*, June 4, 1880, 3.

[43] *Bradstreet's*, January 28, 1880, 4; *New York Times*, April 28, 1880, 4.

[44] Elijah A. Morse, Remarks of January 1, 1892: *CR*, 23:1:671; Horace P. Tobey, Trea., Tremont Nail Co., West Waresham, Mass. to Justin S. Morrill, March 12, 1890; June 4, 1890: Nelson Aldrich Papers, Library of Congress; Oscar Lapham to W. C. P. Breckinridge, October 3, 1890; Edward Atkinson to Breckinridge, August 29, 1891; Josiah Quincy to Breckinridge, September 14, 1891: Breckinridge Papers, Library of Congress; Tobey to William E. Russell, March 18, 1892; Tobey to Benton McMillan, March 18, 1892; Russell to William L. Wilson, February 10, 1891; April 20, May 5, 1892; Copy of a letter sent to each member of the Senate Finance Committee by the Executive Committee of the Young Men's Democratic Club of Massachusetts, February 28, 1894; Memorandum by Russell entitled "Massachusetts' Iron Industry . . . ." William E. Russell Papers, Massachusetts Historical Society; Russell, "Significance of the Massachusetts Election," *Forum*, XII, 433-440; Roger Q. Mills, "New England and the New Tariff Bill," *Forum*, IX, 361-370; *New York Times*, September 18, 1890, 1; *Chicago Tribune*, October 12, 1877, 4; Henry J. Brown, "The National Association of Wool Manufacturers," (Cornell University, Unpublished Ph.D. diss., 1949), 403-404; Geoffrey Blodgett, *The Gentle Reformers: Massachusetts Democrats in the Cleveland Era* (Cambridge: Harvard University Press, 1966), 105-106, 133, 176-185, 246. Also see Coben, "Northeastern Business and Radical Reconstruction," *Mississippi Valley Historical Review*, 67-90; Pitkin, "The Tariff and the Early Republican Party," 30-58, 150-151, 155, 166-169. See below, chs. 7, 8; Robert P. Sharkey, *Money, Class, and Party* (Baltimore: Johns Hopkins University Press, 1959), ch. 4.

[45] Hewitt, Remarks of March 20, 1882: *CR*, 13:3:2435-2442. This speech represented an elaborate statement of ideas Hewitt had begun developing in the 1870s.

[46] William R. Morrison, Remarks of May 25, 1876: *CR*, 4:4:3312-3322; Milton J. Durham, Remarks of January 26, 1878: *CR*, 7:2:583; George G. Dibrell, Remarks of March 11, 1878: *CR*, 7:2:1676-1677;

Fernando Wood, Remarks of April 10, 1878: CR 7:3:2393ff.; Roger Q. Mills, Remarks of April 24, 1878: *CR*, 7:3:2792; John R. Tucker Remarks of May 8, 1878: *CR*, 7:Appendix:142.

[47] Manufacturer and Congressman Abram Hewitt corrected David Wells on this point. Hewitt to Wells, March 6, 1878: Wells Mss. Also see *Bradstreet's*, October 11, 1884, 229-230.

[48] See Terrill, "David A. Wells, the Democracy, and the Tariff," *Journal of American History*, 540-555; Harold F. Williamson, *Edward Atkinson, The Biography of an American Liberal, 1827-1905* (Boston: Old Corner Book Store, Inc., 1934), 136, 179-190.

[49] McKinley, Remarks of April 15, 1878: *CR*, 7:3:2541.

[50] Sherman, *Recollections of Forty Years in the House, Senate and Cabinet* (Chicago: The Warner Co., 1895), II, 1805; Bayard, Remarks of February 14, 1883: *CR*, 14:3:2629. Also see E. I. duPont de Nemours Co. to Bayard, February 1, 1878; January 10, 1883: Thomas F. Bayard Papers, Library of Congress.

[51] Williamson, *Atkinson*; Arthur Wallace Dunn, *From Harding to Harrison* (New York: G. P. Putnam's Sons, 1922), I, 44: George Ephriam Hunsberger, "The Development of Tariff Policy in the Republican Party," (Unpublished Ph.D. diss., University of Virginia, 1934), 186. See Brown, "National Association of Wool Manufacturers."

Chapter 2

[1] See ch. 1, footnote 34; *New York Times*, July 13, 1880, 1; Kirk H. Porter and Donald Bruce Johnson (comps.), *National Party Platforms, 1840-1964* (Urbana: University of Illinois Press, 1966), 60-62.

[2] *Journal*, August 10, 30, 1880: James A. Garfield Papers, Library of Congress; Garfield to Sherman, September 25, 1880: John Sherman Papers, Library of Congress [hereafter cited as Sherman Mss.]; Garfield to Whitelaw Reid, September 2, 1880: as quoted in Theodore Clarke Smith, *The Life and Letters of James Abram Garfield* (New Haven: Yale University Press, 1925), II, 1028.

[3] Quoted in William C. Hudson, *Randon Recollections of an Old Political Reporter* (New York: Cupples and Leon, 1911), 112-114; Logan to Sherman, July 19, 1879: Sherman Mss. See H. Wayne Morgan, *From Hayes to McKinley, National Party Politics, 1877-1896* (Syracuse: Syracuse University Press, 1969), 116-118,

[4] Porter and Johnson, *National Party Platforms*, 50, 56.

[5] *New York Times*, August 13, 1880, 4; September 24, 1.

[6] Robert Granville Caldwell, *James A. Garfield, Party Chieftain* (New York: Dodd, Mead and Co., 1931), Ch. XII. Lee Benson, "Research Problems in American Political Historiography," *Common Frontiers of the Social Sciences*, ed. Mirra Komarovsky (Glencoe, Ill.: The Free Press, 1957), 123-146; Paul Kleppner, *The Cross of Culture, A Social Anaylsis of Midwestern Politics, 1850-1900* (New York: The Free Press, 1970), esp. 1-91.

[7] Morrill to Lucius Bigelow, November 7, 1883: The Justin S. Morrill Papers, Library of Congress [hereafter cited as Morrill Mss.] *The American*, I, No. 10 (December 18, 1880), 150; William P. Frye, Remarks of February 10, 1882: *Congressional Record*, 13:1:1051 [hereafter cited as *CR*, 13:1:1051]; William McKinley, Remarks of April 6, 1882: *CR*, 13:3:2659; Stanley P. Hirshson, *Farewell to the Bloody Shirt, Northern Republicans and the Southern Negro, 1877-1893* (Bloomington: Indiana University Press, 1962), 94ff.; Vincent P. DeSantis, *Republicans Face the Southern Question: The New Departure Years, 1877-1897* (Baltimore: Johns Hopkins Press, 1959), 142-150. Whether Garfield made a bargain with Mahone is still not clear, but Arthur did. Hirshson, *Farewell to the Bloody Shirt*, 94-98, 105-115; DeSantis, *Republicans Face the Southern Question*, 142-150, 153-154. U.S., Commerce Department, *Historical Statistics From Colonial Times to 1957* (Washington: Government Printing Office, 1960), 691.

[8] Caldwell, *Garfield*, 313-314.

[9] *Blaine to Garfield*, December 10, 1880: cited in Gail Hamilton [Mary Abigail Dodge] *Biography of James G. Blaine* (Norwich, Conn.: The Henry Bill Publishing Co., 1895), 490.

[10] James D. Richardson (ed.), *Messages and Papers of the Presidents* (Washington: Government Printing Office, 1902), VIII, 11. In 1882, David Wells, the economist and a friend of Garfield, asserted in an address that Garfield had intended to annex Cuba and Puerto Rico by "purchase or otherwise." Wells, *Freer Trade Essential to Future National Prosperity and Development* (New York: William G. Martin's Steam Printing House, 1882), 48-49. Massachusetts' Republican Senator, George F. Hoar, believed the Garfield Administration through its policies would rebuild national confidence in the GOP. These policies included encouraging American exports. Richard E. Welch. *George Frisbie Hoar*

and the Half-Breed Republicans (Cambridge: Harvard University Press, 1971), 103-104.

[11] *Milwaukee Sentinel*, November 6, 1891, 4. Conger gave this interview at a time when Blaine's reciprocity program of the early 1890s was being widely discussed. Blaine to P. H. Morgan, June 16, 1881, No. 137, U.S., Instructions, Mexico, XX, 283-296. Wharton Barker, prominent Philadelphia industrialist, journalist, and Republican gadfly and would-be king-maker, claimed that Garfield favored commerical union for the United States and Latin America as opposed to individual reciprocity treaties. Given the Garfield Administration's action on a treaty with Mexico, Barker's assertion that he and the president "had a clear understanding of this subject" was overblown. Also see *Iron Age*, XXVII (February 17, 1881), 26; William Appleman Williams, *The Roots of the Modern American Empire* (New York: Random House, 1969), 245-246.

[12] Blaine, Remarks of June 5, 1878: *CR*, 7:5:4134.

[13] Blaine, "The Cotton-Goods Trade of the World, and the Share of the United States Therein," *Consular Report No. 12* (June 25, 1881), 1-105, 369-370; *Atlanta Constitution*, February 25, 1882, 4. John T. Morgan to Blaine, December 16, 1881: quoted in Hamilton, *Blaine*, 550; Williams, *The Roots of the Modern American Empire*, 253-254; Patrick Joseph Hearden, "Cotton Mills of the New South and American Foreign Policy," (Unpublished M.S. thesis, University of Wisconsin, 1966), 26-28. Blaine openly appealed to the New South during his campaign for the presidency in 1884. *New York Times*, July 17, 1884, 1-2; H. Wayne Morgan, *From Hayes to McKinley, National Party Politics, 1877-1896* (Syracuse: Syracuse University Press, (1969), 224-225.

[14] Reed, Remarks of February 3, 1883: *CR*, 14:3:2055. Frédéric Bastiat was an influential French political economist and advocate of laissez faire and free trade.

[15] James M. Comly to Blaine, August 29, 1881; Blaine to Comley, November 19, December 1, 1881: U.S., State Department, *Foreign Relations of the United States, 1881* (Washington: Government Printing Office, 1881), 627-628, 633-639.

[16] Blaine to James Russell Lowell, June 4, 1881: U.S., Senate Committee on Foreign Relations, *Correspondence in Relation to an Interoceanic Canal between the Atlantic and Pacific Oceans, the Clayton-Bulwer Treaty and the Monroe Doctrine, and the Treaty between the United States and New Granada of December 12, 1846, 56th Cong.,*

1st Sess., Senate Doc. No. 237 (Washington: Government Printing Office, 1900), 380-383; Blaine, *Political Discussions* (Norwich, Conn.: The Henry Bill Publishing Co., 1887), 411-419; David Saville Muzzey, *James G. Blaine* (New York: Dodd, Mead and Co., 1934), 197; Alice Felt Tyler, *The Foreign Policy of James G. Blaine* (Minneapolis: University of Minnesota Press, 1927), 113, 169, 191; Hamilton, *Blaine*, 704; Herbert Millington, *American Diplomacy and the War of the Pacific* (New York: Columbia University Press, 1948); Blaine to P. H. Morgan, June 16, 1881, Number 137, U.S., Instructions, Mexico, XX, 283-296. For background, also see Walter LaFeber, *The New Empire* (Ithaca: Cornell University Press, 1963) and David M. Pletcher, *The Awkward Years* (Columbia: University of Missouri Press, 1962).

[17] U.S., House Committee on Foreign Affairs, *The Report of the Central and South American Commissioners, 48th Cong., 2nd Sess., 1884, House Ex. Doc. No. 226* (Washington: Government Printing Office, 1884), 83-84

[18] Blaine, *Political Discussions*, 411.

[19] For example, see Richard H. Bastert, "A New Approach to the Origins of Blaine's Pan-American Policy," *Hispanic American Historical Review*, XXXIX, No. 3 (August 1959), 375-412.

[20] Blaine, *Political Discussions*, 411. George Frederick Howe, *Chester A. Arthur, A Quarter-Century of Machine Politics* (New York: Frederick Ungar Publishing Co., 1935), 194-195.

[21] Blaine, *Political Discussions*, 412-414.

[22] Blaine to Elkins, April 11, May 18, November [?], 1881, May 14, 1882, April 4, 1886; Elkins to Blaine, 1892 [?]; undated list of stockholders of the West Virginia Central and Pittsburgh Railway Co.: Stephen B. Elkins Papers, West Virginia University Library; John Hay to Reid, January 26, 1889; W. W. Phelps to Reid, February 12, 1890: Whitelaw Reid Papers, Library of Congress; Muzzey, *Blaine*, 51-52; Tyler, *Foreign Policy of Blaine*, 153; Cleona Lewis, *America's Stake in International Investments* (Washington: Brookings Institution, 1938), 180.

[23] Blaine, *Political Discussions*, 418-419. Also Muzzy, *Blaine*, 219-220.

[24] Harriet S. Blaine Beale (ed.), *Letters of Mrs. James G. Blaine* (New York: Duffield and Co., 1908), II, 31.

[25] Blaine, *Political Discussions*, 415-418.

[26] Hamilton, *Blaine*, 503.

27 Charles E. Russell, *Blaine of Maine, His Life and Times* (New York: Cosmopolitan Book Corp., 1931), 2.

28 Richard H. Bastert, "Diplomatic Reversal: Frelinghuysen's Opposition to Blaine's Pan-Americanism," *Mississippi Valley Historical Review*, XLII, No. 4 (March 1955), 659-661; Davis to Fish, February 4, 1882: as cited in ibid., 660; Richardson, *Messages*, VIII, 97-98; Fish to Davis, December 16, 1881: J. C. Bancroft Davis Papers, Library of Congress.

29 Frelinghuysen to John F. Miller, July 24, 1882: as cited in Lawrence Ollen Burnett, Jr., "The Senate Foreign Relations Committee and the Diplomacy of the Garfield, Arthur and Cleveland Administrations" (Unpublished Ph.D. diss., University of Virginia, 1952), 45-46.

30 Ibid. When the United States issued invitations in 1888 for the International Conference of the American States, it followed Frelinghuysen's advice and offered an explicit agenda of items for the consideration of the conference. There was no mention of an interoceanic canal, an issue the United States considered its own prerogative. U.S., Senate Committee on Foreign Relations, *International American Conference, 51st Cong., 1st Sess., 1890, Senate Ex. Doc. No. 231* (Washington: Government Printing Office, 1890), 1-2.

31 Thomas C. Reeves, "Arthur, Blaine, and the Republican Presidential Nomination of 1884," Southern Historical Association, Miami, November 1972, 14-20.

32 Quoted in ibid., 6.

33 See Howe, *Chester A. Arthur.*

34 Richardson, Messages, VIII, 48-49; *New York Times,* April 8, 1880, 2; September 3, 1881, 1; 14, 2; October 2, 2; November 16, 1, 4; November 17, 1, 4; November 29, 2, 4; November 30, 3, 4; December 1, 3; John A. Kasson, Remarks of March 28, 1882: *CR*, 13:3:2348.

35 Richardson, *Messages*, VIII, 49; *CR*, 13:1:55-63, 71-75, 914, 1051; *CR*, 13:3:2105-2111, 2198, 2200, 2283, 2348, 2389, 2392-2393, 2659-2660, 2712; *CR*, 13:4:3111, 3569; *CR*, 13:Appendix:78-87.

36 *CR*, 13:3:2343; *CR*, 13:4:3686-3687; *New York Times,* June 4, 1880, 3: Bayard to Wells, May 5, 1878: Thomas F. Bayard Papers, Library of Congress [hereafter cited as Bayard Mss.]

37 U.S., Tariff Commission, *Report of the Tariff Commission, 47th Cong., 2nd Sess., 1882, House Miscellaneous Doc. No. 6* (Washington:

Government Printing Office, 1882), I, 217-240; II, 2313-2333. Among
other strong protectionists who supported Hayes' appointment was Joseph
Wharton. Wharton to Justin Morrill, April 21, 1882: Morrill Mss. President Arthur, inexplicably, tried unsuccessfully to get former Secretary
of the Treasury Hugh McCulloch to head the commission. Not only was
McCulloch a member of the New York Free Trade Club, but he was
also a close friend of David Wells. McCulloch to Wells, July 10, 1882:
David A. Wells Papers, Library of Congress [hereafter cited as Wells
Mss.].

[38] There were a few exceptions. Colonel Albert A. Pope, a bicycle
maker, testified that the high cost of raw materials, which he blamed
on the high tariff, kept him out of the foreign market. He told the commission that technological innovations allowed him to pay high wages
without hurting his competitive position, but explained that he could not
compete in the world market if he had to pay high prices for both wages
and raw materials. The commission pointed out that Pope could take
advantage of the drawback proviso, which allowed a 90-percent rebate
of import duties paid on imported materials used in exported manufactures. Pope dismissed this argument, declaring that the drawback system
was too complicated. *Report of the Tariff Commission*, I, 325-328.

[39] Ibid., 5, 7, 49-82; undated clipping from the *New York Herald*,
John Sherman to *Iron Trade Review*, February [?], 1884; E. Ginnett [?]
to Sherman, February 3, 1883; John T. Cameron to Sherman, January
9, 1884; Issac Stafford to Sherman, February 18, 1884: Sherman Mss.;
Nelson Aldrich to Justin Morrill, October 20, 1883: Morrill Mss.; [?]
to Samuel Randall, December 4, 1883: Samuel J. Randall Papers,
University of Pennsylvania; Morrill to Wharton Barker, March 10, 1883:
Wharton Barker Papers, Library of Congress; John Sherman, *Recollec-
tions of Forty Years in the House, Senate and Cabinet* (Chicago: The
Werner Co., 1895), II, 852, 855; Ida M. Tarbell, *The Tariff in Our
Time* (New York: The Macmillan Co., 1911), 131; *Bradstreet's*,
(December 9, 1882), 369; Henry J. Brown, "The National Wool
Manufacturer's Association" (Unpublished diss., Cornell University,
1949), 342-343.

[40] U.S., *Statutes at Large* (Washington: Government Printing Office,
1883), XXII, 508-511; Tarbell, *Tariff in Our Times*, 129. See footnote
39. In 1890, however, William McKinley made certain that this duty
was restored. McKinley, an Ohioan, was particularly sensitive to mid-

western wool producers who were especially strong in Ohio, a state that wavered in its political loyalty. U.S., *Statutes at Large* (Washington: Government Printing Office, 1891), XVI, 594.

⁴¹ *CR*, 14:1:14; John Sherman to Warner Bateman, January 5, 1883: Warner Bateman Papers, Western Reserve Historical Society; Sherman, *Recollections*, II, 855; Tarbell, *Tariff in Our Times*, 119-132.

⁴² This summary and the generalized comments on tariff rhetoric are based upon extensive reading in the tariff debates in the *Congressional Record*. These debates cover approximately 1876 through 1900. For examples of standard presentations of protectionism and of the low tariff position see: William McKinley, Remarks of May 7, 1890: *CR*, 21:5:4247-4257; Roger Q. Mills, Remarks of April 17, 1888: *CR*, 19:4:3048-3063. Also see Robert M. Lively, "The American System: A Review Article," *Business History Review*, XXIX (March 1955), 81-96; Sidney Fine, *Laissez Faire and the General-Welfare State* (Ann Arbor: University of Michigan Press, 1956), 18-23.

⁴³ Kasson, Remarks of January 26, 1883: *CR*, 14:2:1637. Also see Joseph N. Dolph, Remarks of March 12, 1888: *CR*, 9:2:1961; Nathan Goff, April 27, 1888: *CR*, 9:4:3449.

⁴⁴ Margaret Leech, *In the Days of McKinley* (New York: Harper and Bros., 1959); H. Wayne Morgan, *William McKinley and his America* (Syracuse: Syracuse University Press, 1963); Ira V. Brown, "William D. Kelley and Radical Reconstruction," *Pennsylvania Magazine of History and Biography*, LXXXV (July 1961), 316-329; James M. McPherson, *The Struggle for Equality: Abolitionists and the Negro in the Civil War and Reconstruction* (Princeton: Princeton University Press, 1964), 308-309, 319, 323, 350, 378. The protectionists were not the willing tool of a monolithic "big business" which did not then exist and never has. See Alfred D. Chandler, Jr., "The Beginnings of 'Big Business' in American Industry," *Business History Review*, XXXIII, No. 1 (Spring 1959), 1-31.

⁴⁵ Cannon, Remarks of January 8, 1883: *CR*, 14:1:986. See Edward Paul Crapol, "America for the Americans: Economic Nationalism and Anglophobia, 1876-1896," (Unpublished Ph.D. diss. University of Wisconsin, 1969).

⁴⁶ Mills, Remarks of April 17, 1888: *CR*, 19:4:3060-3061.

⁴⁷ Richard B. Bland, Remarks of January 22, 1883: *CR*, 14:2:1677. See U.S., Commerce Department, *Historical Statistics of the United*

States, 537-538; Caroll D. Wright, *First Annual Report of the Commissioner of Labor, 1886* (Washington: Government Printing Office, 1887), 249, 261-262.

[48] William R. Morrison, Remarks of May 26, 1876: *CR,* 4:4:3316: William M. Springer, Remarks of May 2, 1882: *CR,* 13:4:3563. For similar expressions see Sanuel W. Moulton, Remarks of April 11, 1882: *CR,* 13:Appendix:115; John H. Reagan, Remarks of January 8, 1883: *CR,* 14:1:974; Hilary A. Herbert, Remarks of January 27, 1883: *CR,* 14:2:1908-1909; George L. Yaple, Remarks of April 23, 1884: *CR,* 14:4:3307-3319; Frank H. Hurd, Remarks of April 29, 1884: *CR,* 15:5:3552; S. S. Cox, *Free Land and Free Trade* (New York: G. P. Putnam's Sons, 1884); David Lindsey, *"Sunset' Cox: Irrepressible Democrat* (Detroit: Wayne State University Press, 1959), 223.

[49] Wells, *Report of the Special Commissioner of the Revenue, 1868* (Washington: Government Printing Office, 1868), 65-67; Wells, "How Shall the Nation Regain Prosperity? Part III," *North American Review,* CXXV, No. 259 (November-December 1877), 544. Wells, *Freer Trade Essential to Future National Prosperity and Development,* 28-29; Wells, "The Great Depression of Trade, Part I," *Contemporary Review,* III (August 1887), 290-291; Wells, "The Great Depression of Trade, Part II," ibid. LII (September 1887), 385; Wells, *Recent Economic Changes* (New York: D. Appleton and Co., 1890), 25-26, 30-33, 40, 50-61. Some economists at the time noted that Wells' overproduction ideas deviated from orthodoxy. From his observations, Wells found that while technological innovations lowered prices, domestic consumption did not increase enough to sustain continuous employment of labor. Consequently, labor was disturbed, and he wanted to meet the grievances of labor. Moreover, he regarded the problem as too urgent to wait until some natural force harmonized the labor market. Joseph Dorfman, *The Economic Mind in America* (New York: Viking, 1949-1956), III, 135-136.

[50] Morrison to Wells, February 20, 1876, March 16, 1876, January 14, 1882; Bayard to Wells, November 5, 1883, April 16, 1884, February 16, 1887; Hewitt to Wells, October 28, 1876, July 8, 18, 1878, June 3, 1886; A. B. Farquhar to Wells, January 4, 1892; John G. Carlisle to Wells, November 29, 1880; Beck to Wells, December 13, 1884; Manning to Wells, February 25, September 8, 1886; William F. Vilas to Wells, June 8, 24, 1886; Marble to Wells, November 19, 1881: Wells Mss.; Samuel S. Cox to Wells, April 3, 1878; Beck to Wells, December

8, 1881: David A. Wells Papers, New York Public Library; Wells to Bayard, May 21, 1880, July 23, 1883, August 1, 1883, July 19, 1884; Bayard to Wells, July 25, 1884, November 17, 1888; Bayard to Cleveland, February [?], September 24, 1887, February 9, 1888; Bayard to Atkinson, March 11, 1887; Bayard to Secretary of State Gresham, June 28, 1894: Bayard Mss.; Wells to Morrison, January 15, [?], December 10, 1877, January 14, 1880, March 13, February 29, 1884: William R. Morrison Papers, Illinois Historical Society; Wells to Marble, October 30, 1880, September 15, [1884], January 9, [1885], March 28; Marble to Wells, March 6, 1893: Manton Marble Papers, Library of Congress; Wells to W. C. P. Breckinridge, March 23, 1888: Breckinridge Papers, Library of Congress [hereafter cited as Breckinridge Mss.]; Wells to Atkinson, February 25 [?], 1884, March [?], June 21, 1885, [?], 1893, August 1, 1893; Atkinson to Wells, July 23, 1890; Atkinson to Henry Saltonstall, February 12, 1886; Atkinson to Charles D. Owen, April 20, 1886: Edward Atkinson Papers, Massachusetts Historical Society [hereafter cited as Atkinson Mss.]; Wells to R. R. Bowker, October 11, 1885: R. R. Bowker Papers, New York Public Library; Bayard to Cleveland, November 25, 1885: Grover Cleveland Papers; Atkinson to Cleveland, February 11, 1893: *National Archives of the United States of America*, Record Group 233, Records of Congress, House of Representatives File 52A-F452; Atkinson, "Suggestions for Farther [*sic*] Investigation Upon the Tariff Question," ibid.; Cleveland to E. C. Benedict, April 10, 1894: Alan Nevins (ed.), *Letters of Grover Cleveland* (Boston: Houghton Mifflin Co., 1933), 350; Harold F. Williamson, *Edward Atkinson: The Biography of an American Liberal, 1827-1905* (Boston: The Old Corner Book Store, Inc., 1934), 136, 179, 185, 204-207; George T. McJimsey, *Genteel Partisan: Manton Marble, 1834-1917* (Ames: Iowa State University Press, 1971), 218; David Earl Robbins, Jr., "The Congressional Career of William Ralls Morrison" (Unpublished Ph.D. diss., University of Illinois, 1963), 146ff.

51 Jacob D. Cox to Wells, December 17, 1882: Wells Mss; Atkinson to Wells, July 23, 1890; Wells to Atkinson, August 1, 1893: Atkinson Mss.

52 Hewitt, Remarks of March 30, 1882: *CR*, 13:3:2435-2437. See Matthew Simon, "The United States Balance of Payments, 1861-1890," in *Trends in the American Economy in the Nineteenth Century* (Princeton: Princeton University Press, 1960), 711.

53 *CR*, 13:3:2437-2438. The emphasis is Hewitt's; Hewitt to Senator

J. L. McLaurin, June 30, 1897: Abram S. Hewitt Papers, Cooper Union.

[54] *CR*, 13:3:2440-2442. The emphasis is Hewitt's.

[55] Hewitt to Sherman, February 17, 1883; Sherman to Hewitt, February 15, 19, 1883: Sherman Mss. Allan Nevins, *Abram S. Hewitt, With Some Account of Peter Cooper* (New York: Harper and Bros., 1935), 419.

[56] Nevins, *Abram Hewitt*, 412-419.

[57] Edward Atkinson to David A. Wells, November 11, 1875; Wells to Atkinson, June 21, 1885; Wells to Atkinson, December 4, 1884; Atkinson to Henry Saltonstall, February 12, 1886: all in Atkinson Mss. On occasion, Wells lost his patience with the gradual approach to tariff reduction. In July 1886, he told Atkinson that he was "inclining" toward free trade rather than "tariff reform—the whole-thing without compromise," Wells to Atkinson, July 16, 1886: ibid.

[58] Hurd, Remarks of April 29, 1884: *CR*, 14:4:3549-3554. "When it comes to tickling the tariff under the chin, Frank Hurd is generally on hand with an axe handle." *Washington Post*, April 23, 1884, 2.

[59] Morrison to Wells, December 14, 1884: Wells Mss.

[60] Richardson, *Messages*, VIII, 511, 587-588; Arthur T. Lyman, Treasurer of Lowell Manufacturing Company to W. C. P. Breckinridge, February 21, 1888: Breckinridge Mss.

[61] Undated clipping from the *New York Herald*, Sherman to *Iron Trade Review*, February [?], 1884: Sherman Mss.; also see Tarbell, *Tariff in Our Times*, 131; *New York Tribune*, May 20, 1890, 2; L. S. Bent to William McKinley, December 26, 1889: U.S., House Committee on Ways and Means, *Revision of the Tariff, 51st Cong., 1st Sess., 1890 House Misc. Doc. No. 176* (Washington: Government Printing Office, 1890), 39-40. Bent was president of the Pennsylvania Steel Company, which had $3 million invested in Cuban iron mines. In his letter, Bent explained that American ships carried coal to Cuba and returned with iron ore. He suggested that this pattern could be extended to the rest of the West Indies and into South America. Then, the United States could force English coal out of these markets.

[62] Henry Saltonstall to W. C. P. Breckinridge, January 12, 1888: Breckinridge Mss.

[63] Wheeler, Remarks of January 29, 1883: *CR*, 14:2:1749; Clay, Remarks of May 1, 1884, *CR*, 15:4:3667.

[64] For a similar observation see David E. Novack and Matthew Simon, "Commercial Responses to the American Export Invasion, 1871-1914,

An Essay in Attitudinal History,'' *Essays in Entrepreneural History* III, No. 2 (Winter, 1966), 132-133. Also see U.S., House Committee on Foreign Affairs, *Report of the Central and South American Commissioners 49th Cong., 1st Sess., 1885, House Ex. Doc. No. 50* (Washington: Government Printing Office, 1885).

[65] William H. Michael and Pitman Pulsifer (comps.), *Tariff Acts Passed by the Congress of the United States from 1789 to 1895* (Washington: Government Printing Office, 1896), 159, 373. The 90-percent drawback was part of the Tariff Act of 1861, and the Republicans increased it to 99 percent in the McKinley Tariff in 1890.

[66] Morrill, Remarks of January 10, 1883: *CR*, 14:2:1050; Cannon, Remarks of January 8, 1883: *CR*, 14:1:986; McKinley, Remarks of April 30, 1884: *CR*, 15:Appendix:137.

[67] Springer, Remarks of May 2, 1882: *CR*, 13:4:3563.

Chapter 3

[1] James D. Richardson (ed.), *Messages and Papers of the Presidents* (Washington: Government Printing Office, 1902), VIII, 51-52.

[2] *New York Times*, June 24, 1882, 1; January 25, 1883, 3.

[3] J. C. Bancroft Davis to Hamilton Fish, July 9, 1882: Hamilton Fish Papers, Library of Congress.

[4] Richardson, *Messages*, VIII, 244.

[5] U.S., House Committee on Foreign Affairs, *Consular Service, 48th Cong., 1st Sess., 1884, House Ex. Doc. No. 121* (Washington: Government Printing Office, 1884), 2, 6-7.

[6] Carroll D. Wright, *First Annual Report of the Commissioner of Labor, 1886* (Washington: Government Printing Office, 1886), 65.

[7] U.S., Department of Commerce, *Historical Statistics of the United States, Colonial Times to 1957* (Washington: Government Printing Office, 1960), 115, 143, 427.

[8] See Robert V. Bruce, *1877: Year of Violence* (Indianapolis: Bobbs-Merrill, 1959).

[9] *Report of the Secretary of the Interior, 50th Cong., 1st Sess., 1887, House Ex. Doc. No. 1* (Washington: Government Printing Office, 1887), V, 9, 12, 830-831, 902-903. Charles Albro Barker, *Henry George* (New York: Oxford University Press, 1955), ch. XIV; Daniel Bell, ''The Back-

ground and Development of Marxian Socialism in the United States," *Socialism and American Life*, eds. Donald Drew Egbert and Stow Persons (Princeton: Princeton University Press, 1952), I, 241; Samuel Rezneck, "Patterns of Thought and Action in an American Depression, 1882-1886," *American Historical Review*, LXI, No. 2 (January 1956), 289-290, 295, 305-307; John Higham, *Strangers in the Land, Patterns of American Nativism, 1860-1925* (New York: Atheneum, 1963), 35-67.

[10] Henry F. May, *Protestant Churches and Industrial America* (New York: Harper and Bros., 1949), 173-176, 194. Aaron I. Abell, *American Catholicism and Social Action: A Search for Social Justice, 1865-1950* (New York: Doubleday and Co., 1960), Chs. III, IV.

[11] Sidney Fine, *Laissez Faire and the General-Welfare State* (Ann Arbor: University of Michigan Press, 1956), 198ff.

[12] Rezneck, "Patterns of Thought and Action in an American Depression," *American Historical Review* (January 1956), 284-307.

[13] Richardson, *Messages*, VIII, 244.

[14] U.S., House Committee on Foreign Affairs, *Consular Service, 48th Cong., 1st Sess., 1884, House Ex. Doc. No. 121*, 11.

[15] U.S., Department of Commerce, *Historical Statistics*, 540. See *Proceedings of the Sixteenth Annual Meeting of the National Board of Trade, Washington, January, 1886* (Boston: Tolman and White Printers, 1886), 54.

[16] U.S., Department of Commerce, *Historical Statistics*, 540.

[17] *Report of the Secretary of the Interior, 49th Cong., 1st Sess., 1886, House Ex. Doc. No. 1* (Washington: Government Printing Office, 1885), V, 261-262

[18] John L. Gignillat, "Pigs, Politics and Protection: The European Boycott of American Pork, 1879-1891," *Agricultural History*, XXXV, No. 1 (January 1961), 3-12; L. L. Snyder, "The American-German Pork Dispute, 1879-1891," *Journal of Modern History*, XVII, No. 1 (March 1945), 16-28.

[19] U.S., State Department, *Consular Reports*, No. 19 (May 1882), (Washington: Government Printing Office, 1882), 156-157; ibid., No. 22 (August 1882), 672.

[20] *Report of the Secretary of Interior, 1886*, V, 249. See Morton Rothstein, "American Wheat and the British Market, 1860-1905" (Unpublished Ph.D. diss., Cornell University, 1960).

[21] For some examples, see William Appleman Williams, *The Roots*

of the Modern American Empire (New York: Random House, 1969), 292, 301.

22 *Bankers' Magazine* (New York), XXXVIII, No. 10 (April 1884), 733.

23 Ibid., XXXVIII, No. 11 (May 1884), 821-823.

24 David M. Pletcher, *The Awkward Years: American Foreign Relations Under Garfield and Arthur* (Columbia: University of Missouri Press, 1962), 183-185. Formal negotiations began in January 1883.

25 J. Laurence Laughlin and H. Parker Willis, *Reciprocity* (New York: The Baker and Taylor Co., 1903), 7-9, 10-11, 30-69.

26 Frelinghuysen to Miller, December 26, 1884: *New York Tribune*, December 27, 1884, 2; *New York Times*, December 8, 1884, 1; *Iron Age*, August 14, 1884, 16.

27 Frelinghuysen to Miller, March 28, 1884: *National Archives of the United States of America*, Record Group 46, Records of the Congress, House of Representatives File 48-F6.1. U.S., House Committee on Foreign Affairs, *Report of the Central and South American Commissioners, 49th Cong., 1st Sess., 1885, House Ex. Doc. No. 50* (Washington: Government Printing Office, 1885), 6-7.

28 U.S., Senate Committee on Foreign Relations, *Correspondence in Relation to an Interoceanic Canal between the Atlantic and Pacific Oceans, the Clayton-Bulwer Treaty and the Monroe Doctrine, and the Treaty between the United States and New Granada of December 12, 1846, 56th Cong., 1st Sess., 1894, Sen. Ex. Doc. No. 237* (Washington: Government Printing Office, 1900), 409-435.

29 Gerstle Mack, *The Land Divided* (New York: A. A. Knopf, 1944), 215-216.

30 Richardson, *Messages*, VIII, 256; *Iron Age*, December 25, 1884, 1.

31 U.S., Senate, *Executive Journal*, XXIV, 453.

32 Pletcher, *Awkward Years*, 227-233.

33 Frelinghuysen to Senator John T. Morgan, March 13, 1884: Henry Shelton Sanford Papers, The State Historical Society of Wisconsin. Richardson, *Messages*, VIII, 175-176; Tom E. Terrill, "The United States and the Congo, 1883-1885: The Second Liberia" (Unpublished M.A. thesis, University of Wisconsin, 1963); Paul McStallworth, "The United States and the Congo Question, 1884-1914" (Unpublished Ph.D. diss., Ohio State University, 1954); Pletcher, *Awkward Years*, 308-324, 325, 342-345, 347, 350, 352-353.

[34] Sir Lionel Sackville-West to Lord Granville, December 5, 1884; Granville to Sackville-West, February 12, 1885; Great Britain, House of Commons: *Sessional Papers, LXXXI, Commercial, No. 4*, "Correspondence Respecting the Negotiation of a Treaty Regulating Trade between the British West Indies and the United States," 11-18, 20-23. The British also claimed that the United States had offered few benefits for the economic interests of the British West Indies. Lord Edmond Fitzmaurice to Sir R. Herbert, February 12, 1885: ibid., 23-24. Professor David M. Pletcher generously supplied his notes from the British documents. For an example of a conditional most-favored-nation clause, see William M. Malloy (comp.), *Treaties, Conventions, International Acts, Protocols and Agreements Between the United States of America and Other Powers, 61st Cong., 2nd Sess., Sen. Doc. 357* (Washington: Government Printing Office, 1910), I, 1151.

[35] U.S., Department of Commerce, *Historical Statistics*, 550, 552; Pletcher, *Awkward Years*, 288. See Pletcher, *Rails, Mines, and Progress: Seven American Promoters in Mexico, 1867-1911* (Ithaca: Cornell University, Press, 1958).

[36] Justin S. Morrill to Charles Sheldon, November 27, 1884: Justin S. Morrill Papers, Library of Congress [hereafter cited as Morrill Mss.]; Laughlin and Willis, *Reciprocity*, 30-69.

[37] For a detailed history of the treaties, see Pletcher, *Awkward Years*, chs. X, XVI, and pp. 257, 325, 327-328, 333-340.

[38] Malloy, *Treaties*, I, 1147-1150; *Iron Age*, March 20, 1884, 17.

[39] Frelinghuysen to John W. Foster, June 7, July 2, August 29, 1884: Nos. 181, 197, 246, U.S., Instructions, Spain, XIX; Foster to Frelinghuysen, July 17, August 4, 1884: Nos. 225, 237, U.S. Dispatches, Spain, CX. *New York Tribune*, July 9, 1884, 4.

[40] *New York Times*, July 9, 1884, 4.

[41] U.S., Senate Committee on Foreign Relations, *Treaty Between the United States and Spain, 48th Cong., 2nd Sess., 1884, Senate Ex. Doc. No. 10* (Washington: Government Printing Office, 1885).

[42] Foster to Frelinghuysen, January 11, February 28, 1884: Nos. 140, 177, U.S., Dispatches, Spain, CVIII; Frelinghuysen to Foster, March 14, 1884: No. 146, U.S., Instructions, Spain, XIX; Foster to Walter Q. Gresham, October 26, 1884: Walter Q. Gresham Papers, Library of Congress [hereafter cited as Gresham Mss.].

[43] See, for example, Abram S. Hewitt, Remarks of February 27, 1885: *Congressional Record*, Appendix: 169 [hereafter cited as *CR*, Appendix:

169]; Frelinghuysen to Miller, December 26, 1884: *New York Tribune*, December 27, 1884, 2; same to same, December 26, 1884: Senate Foreign Relations Committee Mss., *National Archives* (verbatim transcript of note supplied by Ollen Lawrence Burnette, Jr.); same to same, February 12, 1885: U.S., Senate, *Regarding our Trade Relations with the Several Countries on this Continent (Except British North America), 48th Cong., 2nd Sess., 1885, Senate Misc. Doc. No. 45*, (Washington: Government Printing Office, 1885).

44 *New York Tribune*, March 12, 1884, 1; January 15, 5; January 16, 1; January 17, 2; *Bradstreet's*, January 20, 1883, 37; Pletcher, *Awkward Years*, 190. Also see Harold Baron, "Economic Development and American Foreign Policy, 1865-1892," (Unpublished Ph.D. diss., University of Chicago, 1964), 249-256.

45 Remarks of January 7, 1885, *CR*, 16:1:508. Morrill said these remarks were quite similar to his speech, given in a closed session of the Senate in 1884, against the Mexican Treaty. Ibid, 506. Morrill to Charles Sheldon, November 27, 1884: Morrill Mss.

46 Malloy, *Treaties*, I, 1151. Since none of the treaties was ever implemented, the administration's interpretation of the "most-favored-nation" clause was never tested by other governments.

47 Hewitt, Remarks of February 27, 1885: *CR*, 16: Appendix:169; *Iron Age*, December 18, 1884, 18. See U.S., House Ways and Means Committee, *Convention Between the United States and Mexico, 48th Cong., 1st Sess., 1884, House Report No. 1848* (Washington: Government Printing Office, 1884), 1-5; Perry Belmont, *An American Democrat* (New York: Columbia University Press, 1940), 285-287; Foster, *Diplomatic Memoirs* (Boston: Houghton Mifflin Co., 1909), II, 18; Morrill to Whitelaw Reid, May 15, 1883: Whitelaw Reid Papers, Library of Congress; Morrill to Charles Sheldon, November 27, 1884: Morrill Mss.; Morrill, Remarks of January 7, 1885: *CR*, 16:1:511; *Bulletin of the National Association of Wool Manufacturers*, XIV, No. 4 (December 31, 1884), 311-317; *New York Tribune*, January 15, 1885; interview with Hewitt, *Bradstreet's* May 24, 1890, 327.

48 Pletcher, *Awkward Years*, 183-185.

49 *The American*, IX (December 6, 1884), 135; IX (December 20, 1884), 164; Barker to Morrill, December 8, 1884, in Barker to Cleveland, December 8: Grover Cleveland Papers [hereafter cited as Cleveland Mss.]. *Bradstreet's*, December 6, 1884, 135; *Proceedings . . . National Board of Trade*, 51-63; U.S., House Committee on Foreign Affairs,

Report of the Central and South American Commissioners, . . . House Ex. Doc. No. 50, 27.

[50] Barker to Morrill, January 6, 1885: Morrill Mss; Barker to Morrill, December 8, 1884, in Barker to Cleveland, December 8: Cleveland Mss; Barker to Randall, February 8, 1883, December 8, 1884: Samuel J. Randall Papers, University of Pennsylvania [hereafter cited as Randall Mss.]; Barker to Blaine, December 11, 1884: Wharton Barker Papers, Library of Congress; Barker to Chandler, January 21, 1883: William E. Chandler Papers, Library of Congress [hereafter cited as Chandler Mss.]; Pletcher, *Awkward Years*, 144-145.

[51] Richard W. Townshend, Remarks of May 6, 1884: *CR*, 15:4:3879; Townshend to Cleveland, January 30, 1885: Cleveland Mss. *Washington Post*, June 20, 1890, 4. Also see *Bulletin of the National Association of Wool Manufacturers*, XIV, No. 4 (December 31, 1884), 315.

[52] Samuel Field to Randall, June 7, December 4, 1884; Petition of Philadelphia sugar refiners to Senator John F. Miller, December 16: Randall Mss; B. Silliman to Thomas Bayard, March 7, 1884; Horace N. Fisher to General W. S. Rosecranz, January 7, 1885, in Rosecranz to Bayard, January 10: Thomas F. Bayard Papers, Library of Congress [hereafter cited as Bayard Mss.]; Joseph Wharton to William E. Chandler, February 12, 1883: Chandler Mss.; H. Wittendorf, Pres., and M. Steinberg, Sec., Cigar Packers Union No. 40 of Cincinnati to John Sherman, January 8, 1883; B. F. Brown, President and Walter E. Grigsby, Sec., Cigar Makers Union No. 173, Zanesville, O. to Sherman, January 19; J. Herr to Sherman, February 4, 1884; E. H. Griest to Sherman, January 10, 1883; J. F. Blackburn to Sherman, January 21, 1885: John Sherman Papers, Library of Congress; *CR*, 16:1:299-300, 540, 560, 621, 647, 681, 823; *Iron Age*, January 24, 1884, 26; *Proceedings . . . National Board of Trade*, 52-53, 61, 69; Pletcher, *Awkward Years*, 187-189, 303-307. *Bulletin of the National Association of Wool Manufacturers*, XIV, No. 4 (December 31, 1884), 311, 317.

[53] *New York Tribune*, January 16, 1885, 8; Pletcher, *Awkward Years*, 185-187.

[54] See Foster to Gresham, December 14, 1884: Gresham Mss; Horace White to Bayard, December 19, 1884: Bayard Mss.

[55] Foster, *Memoirs*, I, 259-260.

[56] Pletcher, *Awkward Years*, 278, 297-302.

[57] *The Commercial and Financial Chronicle*, XL, No. 1019 (January 3, 1885), 5-6.

[58] *New York Times*, November 21, 1884, 4; December 13, 4; *New York Tribune*, February 21, 1883, 4; March 16, 4; October 8, 4; November 23, 1884, 6; December 17, 4; For other newspaper responses, see Pletcher, *Awkward Years*, 185-187, 303-307.

[59] *The Commercial and Financial Chronicle*, XLI, No. 1069 (December 19, 1885), 706-707. See Glen Arthur Auble, "The Depression of 1873 and 1882 in the United States," (Unpublished Ph.D. diss., Harvard University, 1949), 224.

[60] *Bradstreet's*, December 6, 1884, 134-135; January 3, 1885, 1; January 24, 1.

[61] *Bankers' Magazine* (New York), XXXIX, No. 6 (December 1884), 401-404; XXXIX, No. 7 (January 1885), 489.

[62] Hugh T. McCulloch, *Annual Report of the Secretary of the Treasury*, 1884 (Washington: Government Printing Office, 1884), xi-xii, xiv-xvii. Despite his pleas for raw materials, President Arthur praised McCulloch's report (Richardson, *Messages*, VII, 244). McCulloch's raw materials stand strongly resembled that of David Wells, a friend he greatly respected. McCulloch, *Men and Measures of Half a Century, Sketches and Comments* (New York: Charles Scribner's Sons, 1889), 240-242, 296, 509.

[63] Richardson, *Messages*, VIII, 244, 250-252.

[64] Ibid., 251-252. Arthur concluded his remarks with an indication that his program could be extended beyond the New World.

[65] Frelinghuysen to Manuel de Jésus Galvan, July 9, October 28, Novermber 20, 1884: U.S., Notes to Foreign Legations, Dominican Republic, I, 47-69, 71-75; Galvan to Frelinghuysen, June 16, July 17, September 11, October 2, November 4, 1884: U.S., Notes from Foreign Legations, Dominican Republic, III. U.S., House Committee on Foreign Affairs, *Report of the Central and South American Commissioners . . . House Ex. Doc. No. 50, 6.*

[66] See footnote 43 above.

[67] Remarks of January 7, 1885: *CR*, 16:1:506-513. See footnote 43 above.

[68] *National Republican*, January 8, 1885, 2; January 10, 4; January 17, 4; January 21, 2; U.S., House Committee on Foreign Affairs, *Report of the Central and South American Commissioners, 48th Cong., 2nd Sess., 1885, House Ex. Doc. No. 226* (Washington: Government Printing Office, 1885). Also see the final report of the commission, cited *supra*, footnote 27.

[69] Foster to Gresham, September 28, 1884: Gresham Mss.

[70] Thomas C. Reeves, "Arthur, Blaine, and the Republican Presidential Nomination of 1884," Southern Historical Association, Miami, November 1972, 14-20; Philip Marshall Brown, "Frederick Theodore Frelinghuysen," *The American Secretaries of State and their Diplomacy*, ed. Samuel Flagg Bemis (New York: Pageant Books, 1958), VIII, 42.

Chapter 4

[1] U.S., Department of Commerce, *Historical Statistics of the United States, Colonial Times to 1957* (Washington: Government Printing Office, 1960), 691.

[2] James D. Richardson (ed.), *Messages and Papers of the Presidents* (Washington: Government Printing Office, 1902), VIII, 327-330.

[3] *New York Tribune*, April 5, 1885, 1; April 6, 1; *New York Times*, April 3, 1885, 1; April 4, 2. They also sent five ships, including the U.S.S. *Tennessee*, flagship of the North Atlantic Station. [?] [Koppel] to Samuel L. M. Barlow, April 7, 1885; Barlow to Bayard, June 23; Secretary to the Navy, William C. Whitney to Admiral James E. Jouett, April 29; William S. Scruggs, U.S. Legation, Bogota, to Bayard, [n.d.]: Thomas F. Bayard Papers, Library of Congress [hereafter cited as Bayard Mss]; Mark D. Hirsch, *William C. Whitney, Modern Warwick* (New York: Dodd, Mead and Co., 1948), 270-271.

[4] Bayard to Wells, May 1, 1885; Bayard Mss.

[5] Weed to Cleveland, April 18, 1885: Grover Cleveland Papers [hereafter cited as Cleveland Mss]; John W. Foster, *Diplomatic Memoirs* (Boston: Houghton Mifflin Co., 1909), II, 296-297; Richardson, *Messages*, VIII, 504.

[6] Bayard to Wilkinson Call, August 29, 1888: Bayard to Cleveland, November 25, 1885: Cleveland Mss.; Williams to Alvey Adee, Second Assistant Secretary of State, March 30, 1889: Richard Olney Papers, Library of Congress.

[7] Samuel Flagg Bemis, *A Diplomatic History of the United States*, 3rd ed. (New York: Henry Holt and Company, 1950), 457-458.

[8] Bayard Memorandum, May 7, 1886: Bayard Mss., as cited in Charles C. Tansill, *The Foreign Policy of Thomas F. Bayard, 1885-1897* (New York: Fordham University Press, 1940), 377.

[9] Ibid., 378.

[10] Ibid., 378-382, 388; Bayard Memorandum, November 30, 1886: Bayard Mss.: as cited in ibid., 379; ibid., 378-382, 388; Sylvester K. Stevens, *American Expansion in Hawaii, 1842-1898* (Harrisburg: Archives Publishing Co. of Pennsylvania, Inc., 1945), 174-175.

[11] Richardson, *Messages*, VIII, 300-301.

[12] *New York Tribune*, January 21, 1887, 1.

[13] Richardson, *Messages*, VIII, 333-334, 500, 783, 785; *Banker's Magazine* (New York) August 1886, 91.

[14] Richardson, *Messages*, VIII, 785.

[15] Bayard to Charles Denby, United States Minister to China, April 18, 1887: Bayard Mss.

[16] Richardson, *Messages*, VIII, 506-507, 785-786.

[17] Ibid., 792. Bayard told the United States Minister to Mexico that the postal agreement with Mexico was integral to increasing trade between the United States and Mexico. Bayard to T. C. Manning, July 1, 1887: Bayard Mss.

[18] Richardson, *Messages*, VIII, 784-785.

[19] Ibid., 589.

[20] *Congressional Record*, 15:1:4-5 [hereafter cited as *CR*, 15:1:4-5].

[21] U.S., Congress, *Congressional Directory*, *1884* (Washington: Government Printing Office, 1884), 103.

[22] U.S., House Committee on Ways and Means, *Hearings on the Morrison Tariff Bill, 48th Cong., 1st Sess., 1884* (Washington: Government Printing Office, 1884), 77. Edward Chase Kirkland, *Industry Comes of Age: Business, Labor and Public Policy 1860-1897* (Chicago: Quadrangle Books, 1967), 188.

[23] U.S., House Committee on Ways and Means, *Hearings on the Morrison Tariff Bill*, 181, 223.

[24] Ibid., 456. Also see U.S., Senate Committee on Education and Labor, *Labor and Capital* (Washington: Government Printing Office, 1885), I, 696-698, 1123, 1125-1128; II, 9, 14-15; 16-18; III, 129-130.

[25] U.S., House Committee on Ways and Means, *Hearings on the Morrison Tariff Bill*, 446; Wells to Bowker, October 11, 1885 as cited in Fred B. Joyner, *David Ames Wells, Champion of Free Trade* (Cedar Rapids: Torch Press, 1949), 167-168. See Edward Chase Kirkland, *Industry Comes of Age*, 187-188.

[26] Thomas Bayard to Wells, April 11, 1884: David A. Wells Papers, Library of Congress [hereafter cited as Wells Mss.].

[27] U.S., House Committee on Ways and Means, *Hearings on the Morrison Tariff Bill*, 493-494.

[28] *New York Tribune*, June 18, 1884, 1.

[29] Kirk H. Porter and Donald Bruce Johnson (comps.) *National Party Platforms, 1840-1964* (Urbana: University of Illinois Press, 1966), 66; Copy of telegram, July 8, 1884: Bayard Mss.; Manton Marble to Daniel Lamont, March 18, 1885: Cleveland Mss.

[30] Remarks of January 23, 1883: *CR*, 14:2:1489.

[31] George L. Miller to Randall, September 10, 1887: Samuel J. Randall Papers, University of Pennsylvania [hereafter cited as Randall Mss.]; Lewis B. Rathberger, "The Democratic Party in Pennsylvania, 1880-1896" (Unpublished Ph.D. diss., University of Pittsburgh, 1955), 139; Sidney I. Pomerantz, "Samuel Jackson Randall" (Unpublished Ph.D. diss., Columbia University, 1932), 145-146, 148-150.

[32] *New York Tribune*, October 4, 1884, 2; October 5, 6; October 6, 4; October 7, 4; October 8, 4; A. L. Conger to John Sherman, January 8, 1884: John Sherman Papers, Library of Congress; John G. Carlisle to David Wells, September 3; W. R. Morrison to Wells, September 7, 1884: Wells Mss.; Wells to Worthington C. Ford, [1884]: Worthington C. Ford Papers, New York Public Library; Wells to R. R. Bowker, August 20, September 8, October 20, 1884: R. R. Bowker Papers, New York Public Library.

[33] W[alter] Dean Burnham, *Presidential Ballots, 1836-1892* (Baltimore: Johns Hopkins University Press, 1955), 246-257. Also see Lee Benson, "Research Problems in American Political Historiography," *Common Frontiers of the Social Sciences*, ed. Mirra Komarovsky (Glencoe, Ill.: The Free Press, 1957), 123-146.

[34] Charles E. Hooker, Remarks of January 29, 1892: *CR*, 23:1:667. For the House debate and action on the rules changes, see *CR*, 17:1:150, 168-169, 171-173, 196-210, 225-241, 278-298, 320; Pomerantz, "Randall," 161-162, 163-165; Morrison to Wells, January 14, 1882: Wells Mss.; William A. Robinson, *Thomas B. Reed* (New York: Dodd, Mead and Co., 1930), 102-103, 114-115. Randall also incurred congressional hostility with his heavy-handed tactics as chairman of the House Appropriations Committee.

[35] U.S., House Committee on Ways and Means, *Reduction of Tariff Taxes and Collection of the Revenue, 49th Cong., 1st Sess., 1886, House Report No. 1620* (Washington: Government Printing Office, 1886), 2, 6.

36 A. K. McClure to Cleveland, April 13, 1886: Cleveland Mss.; Alan Nevins, *Grover Cleveland, A Study in Courage* (New York: Dodd, Mead and Co., 1934), 266-279; George T. McJimsey, *Genteel Partisan: Manton Marble, 1834-1917* (Ames: Iowa State University Press, 1971), 224-231, 246, 250.

37 U.S., House Committee on Ways and Means, *Reduction of Tariff Taxes and Collection of Revenues*, 17-19.

38 U.S., House Committee on Ways and Means, *Reduction of Tariff Taxes and Collection of Revenues*, 17-19; *New York Tribune*, June 18, 1886, 1, 4; *Philadelphia Press*, June 18; *Galveston News*, June 18; *Philadelphia Ledger*, June 21; *Birmingham Age*, June 18: *Public Opinion*, (June 26, 1886), 201, 204.

39 *Philadelphia Press*, June 18, 1886: *Public Opinion*, I, No. 11 (June 26, 1886), 201; *New York Tribune*, June 16, 1886, 4; *Philadelphia Record*, August 3, 6, 1886.

40 *Public Opinion*, II, No. 31 (November 13, 1886), 81; *Louisville Courier-Journal*, November 4, *New York Staats Zeitung*, November 5, *Florida Times-Union*, November 7, *Detroit Free Press*, November 6, *St. Louis Republican*, November 5, Interviews with Morrison, Carlisle, and Hurd on November 4, 5, 6: *Public Opinion*, November 13, 1886, 82-85.

41 Ibid.; U.S., Department of Commerce, *Historical Statistics*, 691.

42 Richardson, *Messages*, VIII, 509-511. See John Higham, *Strangers in the Land, Patterns of American Nativism, 1860-1925* (New York: Atheneum, 1963), 35-67.

43 *New York Tribune*, December 19, 1886, 2; December 20, 1; *Louisville Courier-Journal*, December 20, *St. Louis Globe-Democrat*, December 19, *National Republican*, December 20, *Albany Journal*, December 20, *Pittsburgh Times* [n.d.]: *Public Opinion*, December 25, 1886, 201-205; D. H. Perry, "Notes and Memoranda: Proposed Tariff Legislation since 1883," *Quarterly Journal of Economics*, II (October 1887), 69-79.

44 Rathberger, "The Democratic Party in Pennsylvania," 174, 176-177; Nevins, *Cleveland*, 371; Singerly to Daniel Lamont, June 29, 1885; Scott to Lamont, August 27, 1887: Cleveland Mss.; *New York Tribune*, September 2, 13, 1887, 4.

45 Rathberger, "The Democratic Party in Pennsylvania," 170-171; *Chicago Times*, June 21, 1886: *Public Opinion*, (June 26, 1886), 201.

46 *New York Tribune*, August 5, 1886, 1; December 25, 1887, 9.

[47] Richardson, *Messages*, VIII, 549-557; Nevins, *Cleveland*, 371; Rathberger, "The Democratic Party in Pennsylvania," 174.

[48] *Pittsburgh Commercial Gazette* [n.d.], *Ohio State Journal* [n.d.]: *Public Opinion*, May 28, 1887, 145; October 1, 1887, 522; Rathberger, "The Democratic Party in Pennsylvania," 173; [Randall] to [?], [n.d.]: Randall Mss.

[49] Richardson, *Messages*, VIII, 581-582. The administration made another, smaller step toward easing the monetary strain upon the national banks. It sometimes gave national banks early notice of bond purchases, and allowed them to issue currency in anticipation of the purchases. Ibid.

[50] *New York Times*, September 1, 1877, 1; September 2, 5; *Washington Post*, September 1, 1887, 1; September 2, 2. Nevins, *Cleveland*, 371. See *New York Times* and *New York Herald*, August 30-September 2, 1887; September 13.

[51] Reed. to Henry Cabot Lodge, September 19, 1887: Henry Cabot Lodge Papers, Massachusetts Historical Society.

Chapter 5

[1] McClure to Cleveland, April 15, 1886; Hoadly to Cleveland, November 22, 1887: Grover Cleveland Papers [hereafter cited as Cleveland Mss.].

[2] Warner to Cleveland, November 19, 1884: ibid. Also see H. E. Smith to Cleveland, November 13; L. Best, Jr., to Cleveland, November 18; H. H. Warner to Cleveland, November 19; B. F. Smith to Cleveland, November 22; J. Schoenof to Cleveland, December 1; A. M. Gibson to Daniel Lamont, December 3; W. P. Herring to Cleveland, December 31; D. M. Richardson to Cleveland, November 5, 1885; Henry T. Niles to Cleveland, December 28; George Hoadly to Cleveland, November 22, 1887: ibid.

[3] Remarks of Bayard, May 6, 1885: *Congressional Record*, 15:4:3867 [hereafter cited as *CR*, 15:4:3867]; Bayard to Wells, July 10, 1883; November 5, April 16, 1884; July 25, August 22, 1885; February 16, 1886; November 17, 1888; Wells to Bayard, March 29, 1880, May 21, July 19, 1883; August 1, December 20, April 28, 1885; August 1, December 10, Bayard to Cleveland, February, 1887; February 11, September 24, April 9, 1888; Bayard to Secretary of State Walter Q. Gresham, June 28, 1894: Thomas F. Bayard Papers, Library of Congress

[hereafter cited as Bayard Mss.]; Bayard to Cleveland, November 25, 1885: Cleveland Mss.; Daniel Manning, *Annual Report of the Secretary of the Treasury, 1885* (Washington: Government Printing Office, 1885), I, xxxv; ibid., *1886* (Washington: Government Printing Office, 1886), I, xix-lviii; Manning to the National Association of Wool Manufacturers, October, 1885: as cited in R. R. Bowker (ed.), *The President's Message, 1887* (New York: G. P. Putnam's Sons, 1888), 31-32; David Harpster to William Whitman, August 13, 1887: *Bulletin of the National Association of Wool Manufacturers,* XVII (1887), 290-292; Manning to Wells, September 8, 1886: David A. Wells Papers, Library of Congress [hereafter cited as Wells Mss.]; George T. McJimsey, *Genteel Partisan: Manton Marble, 1834-1917* (Ames: The Iowa State University press, 1971), 242-245.

⁴ *Selected Addresses and Orations of William F..Vilas* (Madison, Wis.: Privately published, 1912), 147-148; Vilas to Wells, August 2, 1886: as cited in Horace Samuel Merrill, *William Freeman Vilas* (Madison: The State Historical Society of Wisconsin, 1954), 53; Vilas to Wells December 15, 1886: Wells Mss.; Carlisle, Remarks of March 3, 1883: *CR,* 14:4:3724-3727; Carlisle to Wells, March 20, 1883; William Walter Phelps to Wells, December 7: Wells Mss.; Mills, Remarks of April 17, 1888; May 7, 1890: *CR,* 19:4:3058; 21:5:4257-4268; A. B. Farquhar to Wells, January 4, 1890: Wells Mss.; Scott, Remarks of July 3, 1888, CR. 19:4 and 5:3999-4010; Hewitt, Remarks of March 30, 1882: *CR,* 13:3:2435-2438; Hewitt to Wells, June 3, 1886; Morrison to Wells, February 20, 1876; January 14, March 16, 1882; February 14, July 15, 1883; March 2, 1884; February 10, December 14, 1887: Wells Mss.; Wells to Morrison, February 29, 1884: as cited in James A. Barnes, *John G. Carlisle* (New York: Dodd, Mead and Co., 1931), 80; Edward Atkinson to Henry Saltonstall, February 12, 1886; Atkinson to Charles D. Owen, April 20, 1886; Wells to Atkinson, February 25 [?], 1884, March 3 [?], June 21, 1885; August 1, 1893; [?], 1893; Atkinson to Wells, July 23, 1890; Edward Atkinson Papers, Massachusetts Historical Society; Wells to R. R. Bowker, October 11, 1885: as cited in Fred B. Joyner, *David Ames Wells, Champion of Free Trade* (Cedar Rapids: Torch Press, 1939), 167-168; Wells to Manton Marble, October 30, 1880; September 15, [1884]; September 28, [1884]; January [1885]; March 28, [1885]; March 6, 1893: Manton Marble Papers, Library of Congress. Tom E. Terrill, "David A. Wells, the Tariff, and the Democracy, 1877-1894," *Journal of American History,* LVI, No. 3 (December

1969), 540-555; McJimsey, *Genteel Partisan: Manton Marble*, 244-245.

5 Lamb to Lamont, April 17, 1886; A. B. Farquhar to Cleveland, December 7, 1887; M. D. Harter to Cleveland, December 7; Collier White Lead Company to Cleveland, December 7; Cleveland Mss.; *New York Times*, January 1, 1886, 5; January 11, 5; May 24, 5; June 7, 5; June 26, 5.

6 Vilas to Wells, December 15, 1886: Wells Mss. See Robert Kelley, "Presbyterianism, Jacksonianism and Grover Cleveland," *American Quarterly*, XVIII (Winter 1966), 615-636.

7 *New York Times*, November 9, 1887, 1; November 13, 11; S. Fairchild to James B. Beck, February 13, 1888: Cited in C. Joseph Bernardo, "The Presidential Election of 1888" (Unpublished Ph.D. diss., Georgetown University, 1949), 45-46: *New York Tribune*, December 8, 1887, 3; Allan Nevins, *Grover Cleveland, A Study in Courage* (New York: Dodd, Mead and Co., 1934), 369-370.

8 Nevins, *Cleveland*, 5, 234-235, 327-333, 426; John L. Gignilliat, "Pigs, Politics and Protection," *Agricultural History*, XXXV, No. 1 (January 1961), 3-12; L. L. Snyder, "The American-German Pork Dispute, 1879-1891," *Journal of Modern History*, XVII, No. 1 (March 1945), 16-28.

9 Nevins, *Cleveland*, 372; Sidney I. Pomerantz, "Samuel Jackson Randall" (Unpublished Ph.D. diss., Columbia University, 1932), 197; Carlisle to W. C. P. Breckinridge, September 12, 1887: Breckinridge Papers, Library of Congress [hereafter cited as Breckinridge Mss.]; J. J. Dull to Randall, September 7, 1887; George L. Miller to Randall, September 10, 1887: Samuel P. Randall Papers, University of Pennsylvania [hereafter cited as Randall Mss.].

10 Scott to Cleveland, September 16, 1887: Cleveland Mss.

11 The *New York Tribune* covered most of the tour. In particular, see *New York Tribune*, October 1, 1887, 1; October 2, 1-2; October 11, 2. Also see *Public Opinion*, October 15, 1887, 1-3.

12 Merrill, *Vilas*, 52-54, 78-79, 124-131, 203-204. Also see *Atlanta Constitution*, December 10, 1887, 4.

13 *New York Tribune*, June 18, 1886, 1; December 19, 2. See Nelson, Remarks of March 29, 1888: *CR*, 19:3:2504-2509. *Chicago Tribune*, December 7, 1887, 4; December 9, 4; *New York Times*, July 4, 1886, 1; *Public Opinion*, December 17, 1887, 217-219; Joseph Medill to Shelby M. Cullom, January 18, 1888: Shelby M. Cullom Papers, Illinois State Historical Library.

[14] Merrill, *Vilas*, 227-232; Kirk H. Porter and Donald Bruce Johnson (comps.), *National Party Platforms, 1840-1956* (Urbana: University of Illinois, 1956), 89-91.

[15] Hoadly to Cleveland, November 22, 1884: Cleveland Mss.

[16] Quoted in Nevins, *Cleveland*, 376-377. Don M. Dickinson, prominent Michigan Democrat also got a preview of the message. Dickinson to Col. Daniel Lamont, November 4, 1887; Cleveland Mss.

[17] *New York Times*, November 9, 1887, 1; November 13, 11. Mark D. Hirsch, *William C. Whitney, Modern Warwick* (New York: Dodd, Mead and Co., 1948), 362; Bayard to E. J. Phelps, November 21, 1887: Bayard Mss.; Robert McElroy, *Grover Cleveland, The Man and the Statesman* (New York: Harper and Brothers, 1903) I, 271.

[18] James D. Richardson (ed.), *Messages and Papers of the Presidents* (Washington: Government Printing Office, 1902), VIII, 581-590. The Government Printing Office distributed 50,000 copies of the message in early 1888. Later, R. R. Bowker worked with Cleveland to publish an annotated copy of the message. The latter included Secretary Manning's letter to the National Association of Wool Manufacturers. T. E. Benedict to Lamont, December 8, 1887: Cleveland Mss.; see Bowker, *The President's Message*.

[19] Richardson, *Messages*, VIII, 589; Nevins, *Cleveland*, 380.

[20] Farquhar to Cleveland, December 7, 1887; M. D. Harter to Cleveland, December 7: Cleveland Mss; H. C. Payne to Harter, October 30, 1889: Breckinridge Mss.; Farquhar to Abram Hewitt, February 13, 1888: Abram S. Hewitt Papers, Cooper Union. By February 13, Farquhar had visited several cities, including New Orleans, Chattanooga, and Birmingham. After his interview with Hewitt, he planned to call on Andrew Carnegie.

[21] Cleveland to Tammany Hall, June 29, 1888: George F. Parker (ed.), *The Writings and Speeches of Grover Cleveland* (New York: Cassell Publishing Co., 1892), 22-23, 88.

[22] Smith M. Weed to Lamont, April 7, 1888: Cleveland Mss; Pomerantz, "Randall," 148; Nevins, *Cleveland*, 386, 416-419. Henry B. Payne and Smith M. Weed, prominent Democrats from Ohio and New York respectively, also joined the disaffected. Charles Foster to John Sherman, December 23, 1887: John Sherman Papers, Library of Congress [hereafter cited as Sherman Mss.].

[23] Elkins to Davis, October 28, 1889: Stephen B. Elkins Papers, West Virginia University Library; Harry J. Sievers, *Benjamin Harrison*,

Hoosier Stateman, From the Civil War to the White House, 1865-1888 (New York: University Publishers, Inc., 1959), 310-312; John Alexander Williams, "Davis and Elkins of West Virginia, Businessmen in Politics," (Unpublished Ph.D. diss., Yale University, 1967), 112-113, 324.

[24] Quoted in Nevins, *Cleveland,* 384-385. Also see *New York World,* December 9, 10, 1887 for a survey of congressional reactions to the message.

[25] Calvin Brice to Randall, October 6, 1888; Phil B. Thompson to Randall, September 22; A. J. Warner to Randall, September 3, 12; Charles A. Dana to Randall, October 18; Smith M. Weed to Randall, November 8, Randall Mss.; Lewis B. Rathbeger, "The Democratic Party in Pennsylvania, 1880-1896," (Unpublished Ph.D. diss., University of Pittsburgh, 1955), 194-195; Nevins, *Cleveland,* 386. In February, Gorman tried unsuccessfully at a private dinner party to get Randall, Scott, and William L. Wilson to compromise their differences. Festus P. Summers, *William L. Wilson and Tariff Reform* (New Brunswick: Rutgers University Press, 1953), 81-82; Randall to "Dear Sir," December 15, 1887; George T. Oliver to James Atwell, December 28, 1888; A. J. Warner to Randall, February 24; James M. Swank to Randall, March 1; Randall to George C. Tichenor, March 22: Randall Mss. See George F. Baer to F. L. Stetson, April 15, 1887 which was enclosed in Stetson to Cleveland, April 18: Cleveland Mss.

[26] *Chicago Tribune,* March 20, 1887, 7; Brown, Remarks of January 23, 1883: *CR,* 14:2:1490; *Public Opinion,* June 26, 1886, 204; June 11, 1887, 189, 192; October 1, 1887, 524; December 10, 1887, 195; February 4, 1888, 396, 398; February 11, 1888, 421; Hanson to Randall, February 1, December 10, 1888; Grady to Randall, September 23, December 21, 1887; January 9, 1888; Skaggs to Randall, December 29, 1887; Lee to Randall, December 16, 1884; Noble to Randall, December 23; Caldwell to [?] Forney, June 7; West to Randall, December 23; Frank G. Ruffin to Randall, December 30, 1887; Randall Mss.; *Bulletin of the American Iron and Steel Association,* XXI (March 30, 1887), 82; XXIII (February 15, 1888), 49; Stanley P. Hirshon, *Farewell to the Bloody Shirt, Northern Republicans and the Southern Negro, 1877-1893* (Bloomington: Indiana University Press, 1962), 160-161. For other expressions of southern fears about the tariff dividing the white vote, see *Mobile Register* quotation in *Public Opinion,* December 17, 1887, 218; and the comment by Wade Hampton of South Carolina in the *New*

York World, August 2, 1889, 1; C. Vann Woodward, *Origins of the New South, 1877-1913*, Vol. IX of *A History of the South*, eds. Wendell Holmes Stephenson and E. Merton Coulter (Baton Rouge: Louisiana State University Press, 1951), 16-17; Nevins, *Cleveland*, 385.

27 Collier White Lead Company to Cleveland, December 7, 1887; H. H. Hart to Cleveland, December 6; C. R. Breckinridge to Cleveland, December 6; George to Cleveland, December 7; Burt to Cleveland, December 8; Peckham to Cleveland, December 7; Samuel Pellatier to Cleveland, December 7: Cleveland Mss.; *Public Opinion*, February 4, 1888, 395; Nevins, *Cleveland*, 387-388. *New York Times*, December 7, 1887, 4, *Public Opinion*, December 10, 1887, 193-196; December 17, 217-221; January 14, 1888, 317-320.

28 Manuscript, dated December 7, 1887: James G. Blaine Papers, Library of Congress.

29 *Official Proceedings of the Republican National Convention, Chicago, June 19-25, 1888* (Minneapolis: Charles W. Johnson, 1903), 8.

30 *New York World*, December 8-10, 1887; *Public Opinion*, December 10, 1887, 193-196; December 17, 217-221; January 14, 1888, 317-320; John R. Rhodes to Randall, December 7, 1887; George L. Converse to Randall, December 12: Randall Mss. Nevins, *Cleveland*, 386-387.

31 John R. Reagan to Chauncy F. Black, July 7, 1888: Jeremy S. Black Papers, Library of Congress; Nevins, *Cleveland*, 389, 415-416; McJimsey, *Genteel Partisan: Manton Marble*, 428-429. Brice, however, did restrict Democratic protectionists on the stump. George L. Converse to Randall, October 4, 1888: Randall Mss.

32 Myrtle Roberts, "Roger Q. Mills," (Unpublished M.A. thesis, University of Texas, 1929), 77.

33 U.S., Senate Committee on Finances, *Customs, Tariffs: Senate and House Reports, 60th Congress, 2nd Session, 1908, Senate Doc. No. 547* (Washington: Government Printing Office, 1909), 15, 16-20.

34 Ibid., 30-31, 34.

35 Ibid., 43-44, 46.

36 Mills, Remarks of April 17, 1888: *CR*, 19:4:3058.

37 Ibid., 3058-3062.

38 U.S., Commerce Department, *Historical Statistics of the United States, From Colonial Times to 1957* (Washington: Government Printing Office, 1960), 537-538. See U.S. , House Committee on Foreign Affairs,

Report of the Central and South American Commissioners, 49th Congress, 1st Session, 1885, House Ex. Doc. 50 (Washington: Government Printing Office, 1885).

[39] McMillin, Remarks of April 24, 1888: *CR*, 19:4:3297-3304; George F. Parker, *Recollections of Grover Cleveland* (New York: The Century Co., 1909), 182; William D. Bynum, Remarks of April 25, 1888: *CR*, 19:4:3349-3355. For similar comments, see P. T. Glass, Remarks of April 25, 1888: ibid., 3377-3380; Thomas Wilson, Remarks of May 2, 1888; ibid., 3640-3643; L. F. McKinney, Remarks of May 3, 1888: ibid., 3703-3707; William L. Wilson, Remarks of May 5, 1888: ibid., 19:Appendix:55.

[40] William D. Kelley, Remarks of April 17, 1888: *CR*, 19:4:3064-3069. Despite their protestations, most of the Republicans in Congress supported the calling of the First International Conference of the American States. William Walter Phelps, Remarks of March 1, 1888: *CR*, 19:2:1657. J. C. Burrows, Remarks of April 28, 1888: *CR*, 19:4:3306-3314. One Democrat, Representative Perry Belmont of New York, favored the conference because Congress was prepared to reduce the tariff, "the first necessary step for the establishment and extension of foreign markets." Belmont, Remarks of March 1, 1885: ibid., 1655.

[41] Thomas B. Reed, Remarks of May 19, 1888: *CR*, 19:5:4445.

[42] Nelson Dingley, Remarks of May 3, 1888: *CR*, 19:4:3696.

[43] Ibid., 3696.

[44] Ibid., 3697; Edward Nelson Dingley, *The Life and Times of Nelson Dingley, Jr.* (Kalamazoo, Michigan: Ihling Bros. and Everard, 1902), 232ff., 357.

[45] U.S., House Committee on Ways and Means, *Reduction of Tariff Taxes and Collection of the Revenue, 49th Cong., 1st. Sess., 1886, House Report No. 1620* (Washington: Government Printing Office, 1886), 5: E. Greenfield's Sons and Co. to William McKinley, February 13, 1890: U.S., House Committee on Ways and Means, *To Reduce the Revenue and Equalize Duties on Imports, and For Other Purposes, 51st Cong., 1st Sess., 1890, House Report No. 1466* (Washington: Government Printing Office, 1890), 1391-1392.

[46] Kirk H. Porter and Donald Bruce Johnson (comps.), *National Party Platforms, 1840-1960* (Urbana: University of Illinois Press, 1961), 77; "1888— Draft of the National Platform for St. Louis Convention, June 5th, 88," Manton Marble Papers, New York Historical Society. Gorman took care to note on the draft that it had been written by Marble and

"Agreed to by Presdt. Cleveland, Secty. [William C.] Whitney, Speaker Carlisle and myself at 5 p.m. May 31st, 88." Then, Cleveland added the final touches to the draft, and it was dispatched to St. Louis. *New York Times,* June 6, 1888, 1, 4; June 7, 1; June 8, 1; Horace Samuel Merrill, *Bourbon Leader: Grover Cleveland and the Democratic Party* (Boston: Little, Brown and Co., 1957), 123-125; McJimsey, *Genteel Partisan: Manton Marble,* 248-249.

47 Porter and Johnson, *National Party Platforms,* 76-78; "Draft of the National Platform." In one place the draft did exceed the emotionalism of the final platform. The Republicans in the Senate, according to the draft, had reduced the Senate "from a useful opposition to a factious cabal. . . . [The Senate's] financial schemes are a daily menace to the commonwealth. Senators are actual beneficiaries and open advocates of taxes promoting a privileged class."

48 Porter and Johnson, *National Party Platforms,* 81-82.

49 Sievers, *Benjamin Harrison, Hoosier Statesman,* Ch. 20; *Official Proceedings of the Republican National Convention, 1888, 108-112. Charles Hedges (comp.), Speeches of Benjamin Harrison* (New York: United States Book Co., 1892), 68, 114. The emphasis is Harrison's.

50 *New York Tribune,* July 22, 1888, 9. There were eight strays. Three Republicans, one from New York, one from North Carolina, and Knute Nelson of Minnesota, voted for the bill. One representative, who called himself an Independent Republican, joined them. There were four Democratic defectors, three from New York and one from Pennsylvania. Congressman Randall was absent because of illness. He was paired against the bill. Ibid. Cleveland to Wilson S. Bissell, July 22, 1888: Allan Nevins (ed.), *Letters of Cleveland, 1850-1908* (Boston: Houghton, Mifflin Co., 1933), 187-188.

51 Frank Hiscock to Whitelaw Reid, January 6, 19, 1888; William E. Chandler to Reid, July 23; Hiscock to Reid, July 26: Whitelaw Reid Papers, Library of Congress [hereafter cited as Reid Mss.]; James M. Swank to Allison, June 9, 1888: William B. Allison Papers, Iowa State Department of History and Archives [hereafter cited as Allison Mss.]; Leland L. Sage, *William Boyd Allison* (Iowa City: State Historical Society of Iowa, 1956), 232-233.

52 W. W. Phelps to Reid, September 22, 1888, Reid Mss.; George Edmunds to Allison, September 14, 1888; Charles Beardsley to Allison, September 22: Allison Mss.; John C. Spooner to J. M. Rusk, October 10, 1888: J. M. Rusk Papers, The State Historical Society of Wisconsin;

New York Herald, August 18, 1888, 2; Edward A. White, "The Republican Party in National Politics, 1888-1891," (Unpublished Ph.D. diss., University of Wisconsin, 1941), 218-219, 230-231.

[53] U.S., Senate, *Customs, Tariffs,* 48-49.

[54] Ibid., 122-131, 132-134, 146, 159, 198-199.

[55] Ibid.

[56] Ibid., 50-51; Sage, *Allison,* 232-233; White, "The Republican Party in National Politics," 231.

[57] Joseph Wharton to William B. Allison, July 7, 1888; James M. Swank to Allison, August 16, September 13, September 26; Flyer entitled "1,101,887 Tariff Tracts Distributed!" and marked "confidential," Allison Mss.; Clark to John Sherman, December 7, 1887: Sherman Mss.; Henry J. Brown, "National Association of Wool Manufacturers," (Unpublished Ph.D. diss., Cornell University, 1949), 392; Robert D. Marcus, *The Grand Old Party, Political Structure in the Gilded Age, 1880-1896* (New York: Oxford University Press, 1971), 129-138.

[58] See Richard Joseph Jensen, "The Winning of the Midwest: A Social History of Midwestern Elections, 1888-1896," (Unpublished Ph.D. diss., Yale University, 1967); Paul Kleppner, *The Cross of Culture, A Social Analysis of Midwestern Politics, 1850-1890* (New York: The Free Press, 1970).

[59] See footnote 28 above. *New York Tribune,* July 19, 1884, 1-2; Swank to Morrill, December 1, 1886: Justine S. Morrill Papers, Library of Congress. Harrison, however, refused to avoid the issue of the black vote during the campaign. Whitelaw Reid to Harrison, September 25, 1888; Harrison to Reid, September 27: Benjamin Harrison Papers; Sievers, *Benjamin Harrison, Hoosier Statesman,* 361.

[60] See footnote 28 above. *Atlanta Constitution,* December 7, 1887, 2; December 10, 4; December 13, 4; November 5, 1888, 4; November 6, 4; November 7, 4; Hirshson, *Farewell to the Bloody Shirt,* Ch. 7.

[61] See footnote 58 above.

[62] *New York Times,* November 9, 1888, 1. Cleveland's popular vote was, however, somewhat misleading. He won only one northern state, Connecticut, and his margin there was less than 500 votes. Texas gave him a 140,000 vote margin. Ibid; W[alter] Dean Burnham, *Presidential Ballots, 1836-1892* (Baltimore: Johns Hopkins University Press, 1955), 246-257; Nevins, *Cleveland,* 426-427, 439. John Boyle to Randall, November 8, 1888; James O'Brien to Randall, November 8; A. J. Warner to Randall, November 17: Randall Mss.; Shelby M. Cullom,

Fifty Years of Public Service (Chicago: A. C. McClurg and Co., 1911), 246.

⁶³ Richardson, *Messages,* VIII, 773-777.

Chapter 6

¹ Edward A. White, "The Republican Party in National Politics, 1888-1891," (Unpublished Ph.D. diss., University of Wisconsin, 1941), 354ff.

² Harrison to Howard Cale, November 17, 1890: Benjamin Harrison Papers. Also see John Caldenwood to John Sherman, July 2, 1890: John Sherman Papers, Library of Congress; L. T. Michener to William B. Allison, February 15, 1890: William B. Allison Papers, Iowa State Department of History and Archives; Whitelaw Reid to W. W. Phelps, May 3, 1890: Whitelaw Reid Papers, Library of Congress [hereafter cited as Reid Mss.]. See Norbert R. Mahnken, "The Congressmen of the Grain Belt States and Tariff Legislation," (Unpublished Ph.D. diss., University of Nebraska, 1941); Duane Marshall Leach, "The Tariff and The Western Farmer," (Unpublished Ph.D. diss., University of Oklahoma, 1964); Clarence Lee Miller, *The States of the Old Northwest and the Tariff* (Emporia, Kan.: *Emporia Gazette,* 1929). For more on Western farm pressure on the Harrison Administration, see William Appleman Williams, *The Roots of the Modern American Empire* (New York: Random House, 1969), 323-327, 332-333.

³ U.S., Bureau of the Census, *Historical Statistics, From Colonial Times to 1957* (Washington: Government Printing Office, 1960), 99; Gerald N. Grob, *Workers and Utopia* (Evanston: Northwestern University Press, 1961); Lewis L. Lorwin, *The American Federation of Labor: History, Policies and Prospects* (Washington: The Brookings Institution, 1933), ch. 2.

⁴ James D. Richardson (ed.), *Messages and Papers of the Presidents* (Washington: Government Printing Office, 1902), VIII, 774.

⁵ Charles Hedges (comp.), *Speeches of Benjamin Harrison* (New York: United States Book Co., 1892), 68, 114.

⁶ Harrison to Blaine, January 17, 1889: Albert T. Volwiler (ed.), *Correspondence between Benjamin Harrison and James G. Blaine, 1882-1893* (Philadelphia: The American Philosophical Society, 1940), 44-45. As early as 1887, Blaine visualized Harrison as president, and himself

as secretary of state. Gail Hamilton [Mary Abagail Dodge], *Biography of James G. Blaine* (Norwich, Conn.: The Henry Bill Publishing Co., 1895), 651.

[7] Blaine to Harrison, January 21, 1889: Volwiler, *Correspondence Between Benjamin Harrison and James G. Blaine*, 49.

[8] Richardson, *Messages,* IX, 200-201. Secretary Tracy declared in 1891 that "The rapid extension of commercial relations has doubled the importance of our interests, especially in the Pacific. It was said a few years ago by a foreign observer: 'Some day or other there will be a great rivalry of three or four nations in the Pacific for the commerce of those seas, and the country which has cultivated its strength with a view to that contingency will carry off a chief part of the prize.' The rivalry has already begun." Benjamin Tracy, *Report of the Secretary of the Navy, 1891* (Washington: Government Printing Office, 1892), 30. Edward C. Kirkland, *Industry Comes of Age, Business, Labor and Public Policy, 1860-1897* (Chicago: Quadrangle Books, 1967), 30.

[9] Richardson, *Messages,* IX, 10, 35-36, 189, 317. See Frederick Douglass, "Haiti and the United States." "Inside History of the Negotiations for the Mole St. Nicolas, Part I," *North American Review,* CCCCXVIII (September 1891), 337-345; ibid. "Part II," CCCCXIX (October 1891), 450-459.

[10] Jeremiah M. Rusk, *Report of the Secretary of Agriculture, 1890* (Washington: Government Printing Office, 1891), 9-14, 54-55; *Report of the Secretary of Agriculture, 1892* (Washington: Government Printing Office, 1893), 23-24; P. D. Armour to Rusk, March 27, 1891; March 26, 1892; G. H. Swift to Rusk, September 14, 1891: Jeremiah M. Rusk Papers, The State Historical Society of Wisconsin; *New York Tribune,* April 23, 1890, 4; James Erlenborn, "The American Meat and Livestock Industry and American Foreign Policy, 1880-1896," (Unpublished M.S. thesis, University of Wisconsin, 1966), 83-109; also see Bingham Duncan, "Protectionism and Pork: Whitelaw Reid as Diplomat: 1889-1891," *Agricultural History,* XXXIII, No. 4 (October 1959), 190-195; John L. Gignilliat, "Pigs, Politics and Protection: the European Boycott of American Pork, 1879-1891," *Agricultural History,* XXXV, No. 1 (January 1961), 3-12; L. L. Snyder, "The American-German Pork Dispute, 1879-1891," *Journal of Modern History,* XVII, No. 1 (March 1945), 16-28.

[11] Richardson, *Messages,* IX, 122-124; Rusk, *Report of the Secretary of Agriculture, 1891* (Washington: Government Printing Office, 1892),

10-16, 21-24; Rusk to B. F. Tillinghast, February 2, 1892: *National Archives of the United States of America* Record Group 16, Records of the Department of Agriculture: Domestic Letters of the Secretary, Vol. 130, 263: *New York Herald,* March 23, 1892, 2; *Milwaukee Sentinel,* October 24, 1891, 6; Circular Letter of Charles J. Murphy, March 22, 1892: Abram S. Hewitt Papers, Cooper Union; Allen Burton Spetter, "Harrison, and Blaine: Foreign Policy 1889-1893," (Unpublished Ph.D. diss., Rutgers University, 1967), 187-188.

¹² Harrison to Blaine, August 3, 1891; Blaine to Harrison, August 10: Volwiler, *The Correspondence Between Benjamin Harrison and James G. Blaine,* 170, 173-174. Whitelaw Reid to Blaine, June 13, 1891; Reid to Harrison, October 9; Harrison to Reid, October 21: Reid Mss.; Harrison to John T. Morgan, February 8, 1892: John T. Morgan Papers, Library of Congress; Spetter, "Harrison and Blaine," 164-165; William A. Williams, *The Roots of the Modern American Empire* (New York: Random House, 1969), 327. Fred Harvey Harrington, *God, Mammon, and the Japanese: Dr. Horace N. Allen and Korean-American Relations, 1884-1905* (Madison: University of Wisconsin Press, 1944), 134-135, 146.

¹³ Harrison's dominance in the foreign policy of his administration is clearly demonstrated by Professor Spetter in "Harrison and Blaine."

¹⁴ The countries represented were Argentina, Bolivia, Brazil, Chile, Colombia, Costa Rica, Ecuador, Guatemala, Haiti, Honduras, Mexico, Nicaragua, Paraguay, Peru, Salvador, Uraguay, Venezuela, and the United States. U.S., Senate, *Minutes of the International American Conference, 51st Cong., 1st Sess., 1890, Sen. Ex. Doc. No. 231* (Washington: Government Printing Office, 1890), 2-3.

¹⁵ Ibid., 9-18; Thomas F. McGann, *Argentina, the United States, and the Inter-American System, 1880-1914* (Cambridge: Harvard University Press, 1957), 132-134.

¹⁶ Ibid., 9, 17-18; M. Romero, "The Pan-American Conference Part I," *North American Review,* CCCCVI (September 1890), 364. But Fernando Cruz, Guatemalan Minister to the United States, expressed the belief that most Latin Americans were unaware of the variety and quality of American products. Spetter, "Harrison and Blaine," 196-197.

¹⁷ For example, see *New York Tribune,* March 25, 1890, 4; April 2, 4; *National Archives of the United States of America,* Record Group 43, Records of the International Conference of American States, 1889-1890, Box No. 4, Entry 13 [hereafter cited as *ICAS*]; Anonymous, Special

Agent to William H. Trescott, August 2, 1889: *ICAS*, Box unnumbered, Entry 18. The *Tribune* just happened to send a correspondent on an extended Latin American tour in 1890. A long series of articles on the economic potential of the region followed.

[18] *ICAS*, Box unnumbered, Entry 21; E. E. Perry to William E. Curtis, [n.d.]: *ICAS*, Box No. 4, Entry 12; *Report of the Ninth Annual National Farmers' Congress, Montgomery, Alabama, November 13-15, 1889* (Macedonia, Indiana: Blue Grass Blade Job Office, 1890), 17.

[19] *ICAS*, Box No. 4, Entry 13; Box unnumbered, Entry 19; Box unnumbered, Entry 21; William I. Martin to Blaine, September 24, 1889: *ICAS*, Box No. 4, Entry 13; Andrew Carnegie to Blaine, July 22, 1889: Andrew Carnegie Papers, Library of Congress.

[20] G. Montague, Chairman of Committee to Visit Tampa, Florida to President of the Board of Directors of the Chicago Board of Trade, July 9, 1889: *ICAS*, Box unnumbered, Entry 18; B. L. Goulding, Secretary of the Chattanooga Chamber of Commerce to State Department, September 24, 1889: *ICAS*, Box No. 5, Entry 13; City Council of Brunswick, Georgia to James G. Blaine, March 13, 1890: *ICAS*, Box unnumbered, Entry 19; Committee on Commerce, Committee on Outward Trade to President and Board of Richmond Chamber of Commerce, September 27, 1889: *ICAS*, Box unnumbered, Entry 18.

[21] F. G. Peirra, Secretary of the Spanish-American Commercial Union to William E. Curtis, August 29, 1889: *ICAS*, Box unnumbered, Entry 19; *Proceedings at the Banquet of the Spanish-American Commercial Union, New York, May 1, 1889* (New York: Hispana-Americano Publishing Co., 1889), 10-14; *Iron Age*, April 4, 1889, 516; Williams, *Roots of the Modern American Empire*, 328-329.

[22] Nobel, Remarks of May 1, 1889: *Proceedings at the Banquet of the Spanish-American Commercial Union*, 8-12.

[23] Foster, Remarks of May 1, 1889: ibid., 17-19.

[24] Ibid., 3-4; Charles R. Flint to Benjamin F. Tracy, March 24, 1889: Benjamin F. Tracy Papers, Library of Congress; Charles R. Flint, *Memories of an Active Life* (New York: G. P. Putnam's Sons, 1923), 9, 21, 73-114, 150ff., 175-176. Flint later organized the United States Rubber Company trust. Ibid., 298; McGann, *Argentina*, 130-131; J. F. Hanson to Blaine (copy), July 30, 1889: *ICAS*, Box unnumbered, Entry 21. Also see Patrick Joseph Hearden, "The Cotton Mills of the New South and American Foreign Policy," (Unpublished M.S. thesis, University of Wisconsin, 1966). The remainder of the American delegation

included other leading businessmen and politicians and an experienced diplomat. Along with Flint, John B. Henderson dominated the American delegation. He was a former United States Senator, Washington lawyer, and a very influential figure in Republican circles. Another former senator, Henry G. Davis, attended; he enjoyed considerable wealth from railroads and mining. Andrew Carnegie, an enthusiast for a customs union and peace through arbitration, and Clement Studebaker also represented major industries. Morris Estee, California lawyer and Republican leader, spoke for the Far West. T. Jefferson Coolidge, New England merchant and financier, had direct economic interests in South America. Coolidge and several partners from Boston and New York had, by 1894 at the latest, invested $3 million in wharves, a coaling station, and railroads in Colombia. Coolidge later helped to organize the United Fruit Company. William Henry Trescot, an early prototype of the career diplomat, brought his experience in foreign affairs to the conference. He was the only member of the American delegation who spoke Spanish fluently. McGann, *Argentina*, 130-133; T. Jefferson Coolidge to Richard Olney, October 25, 1894; Olney to Hilary A. Herbert, May 6, 1893: Richard Olney Papers, Library of Congress.

25 *Minutes of International American Conference*, 1-2, 17.

26 McGann, *Argentina*, 7, 67, 71, 80-88, 90-97, 100-190.

27 *Minutes of International American Conference*, 106-108; U.S., Senate, *International American Conference, Reports of the Committees and Discussions Thereon, 51st Cong., 1st Sess., 1890, Senate Ex. Doc. No. 232* (Washington: Government Printing Office, 1890), Part 1, 105-261; Part 2, 961-964, 972-986, 1011, 1037, 1040-1042, 1056-1059, 1068, 1135-1137. McGann, *Argentina*, 154-157.

28 *New York Tribune*, March 27, 1890, 2; March 28, 3; *New York Times*, March 25, 1890, 1; March 26, 4; March 28, 4; Henry J. Brown "The National Association of Wool Manufacturers," (Unpublished Ph.D. diss., Cornell University, 1949), 393-397.

29 *Bradstreet's*, October 5, 1889, 631.

30 Reid to Blaine, December 2, 1889: *Reid Mss., New York Tribune*, April 21, 1890, 1; *New York Times*, April 23, 1890, 4.

31 *International American Conference, Reports*, Pt. 1, 93-95, 103-105, 265-267, 277 403-411; Pt. 2, 875; *Congressional Record*, 24:3: 1893, 2495 [hereafter cited as *CR*, 24:3:1893].

32 American merchants who were active in Latin America complained about the lack of adequate, routine banking facilities. They claimed Euro-

pean merchants using European credit institutions had a clear advantage over them. Moreover, they believed they had to have long term credits to meet European competition. The Central and South American Commission had found great interest during its investigations in 1884 in the creation of an American bank to meet these needs, and the concern had increased since then. Prodded by Charles R. Flint, the banking committee of the Pan-American congress reported favorably on an inter-American bank. The United States government then acted to establish the institution. On May 22, 1890, Secretary of State Blaine forwarded the committee report to President Harrison, and at the same time offered a draft for a message to the Congress supporting the bank. The president reacted favorably on May 27.

The next day, Congressman Robert R. Hitt introduced a bill for the establishment of the bank. The Harrison Administration asked for a bank under federal charter in New York with Latin American branches. Predictably, the *Tribune* favored it. So did a number of chambers of commerce, boards of trade, and other commercial associations. Even before Congress had acted, the banking committee of the Pan-American conference authorized Andrew Carnegie, Cornelius N. Bliss, Henry G. Davis, Clement Studebaker, and T. Jefferson Coolidge to take subscriptions. J. Edward Simmons, president of the Fourth National Bank of New York, W. H. T. Hughes, manager of Ward Steamship Company, and William M. Ivins, formerly with the W. R. Grace Company and a lawyer for American merchants involved in Latin American trade, encouraged the creation of the bank.

The House Committee on Banking and Currency took charge of Hitt's bill and held hearings on the proposal. While a majority of the committee favored the plan, a stubborn minority blocked it. The minority claimed that the bank "would have not merely the business of this country but a monopoly of commerce of all these countries, and it would practically regulate competition." After this proposal died, American bankers resorted to improvisation. They used foreign banks as their correspondents for overseas facilities. Several large New York banks and trust companies also opened foreign departments within their own institutions.

The plan for an inter-American railroad evoked a more positive reaction. Congress appropriated $65,000 for a commission for the railway and an initial survey. Henry G. Davis, Richard C. Kerens, and Alexander Cassett formed the commission, and they expended ten years of effort publicizing the project. The commission hired a few engineers who made preliminary surveys in Central America. Ultimately, however, the project expired from apathy, lack of funds, and tropical disease and heat. U.S., House Committee on Foreign Affairs, *Report of the Central and South American Commissioners, 49th Cong., 1st Sess., 1885, House Ex. Doc. No. 50* (Washington: Government Printing Office, 1886) 1-56; *International American Conference, Reports,* Pt. 2, 829-837; U.S., House Committee on Banking and Currency, *International American Bank, 54th Cong., 2nd Sess., 1897, House Report No. 3054* (Washington: Government Printing Office, 1897), 1-20; Blaine to Harrison, May 22, 1890; Volwiler, *Correspondence,* 101; Richardson, *Messages* (1902 ed.), IX, 70-71; *New York Tribune,* May 29, 1890, 6; June 13, 1890, 5; *New York Times,* May 20, 1890, 9; Paul Abrahams, "The Foreign Expansion of American Banks" (Unpublished manuscript), 4-5. Mr. Abrahams graciously shared his manuscript. John Anthony Caruso, "The Pan-American Railway," *Hispanic American Historical Review,* XXXI, No. 4 (November 1951), 613. Later, Congress passed two more appropriations of $65,000 each for a railway survey. Ibid., 616-617.

³³ Julius W. Pratt, *A History of United States Foreign Policy* (Englewood Cliffs, N. J.: Prentice-Hall, Inc., 1955), 346; McGann, *Argentina,* 121, 169, 182; Charles R. Flint to William E. Curtis, September 3, 1890: Nelson Aldrich Papers, Library of Congress [hereafter cited as Aldrich Mss.]; Will Clyde to Hamilton Fish, March 15, 1889: Hamilton Fish Papers, Library of Congress.

³⁴ McGann, *Argentina,* 169; U.S., House, *Report of the Central and South American Commissioners*; Flint to Curtis, September 3, 1890: Aldrich Mss. Also see William E. Curtis, *Trade and Transportation between the United States and Latin America, 51st Cong., 1st Sess., 1890, Senate Ex. Doc. No. 54* (Washington: Government Printing Office, 1890).

Chapter 7

¹ Harrison to Blaine, October 1, 1891: Albert T. Volwiler (ed.), *The Correspondence Between Benjamin Harrison and James G. Blaine, 1882-1893* (Philadelphia: American Philosophical Society, 1940), 202; for their basic assumptions about expansion, see *New York Tribune,* September 1, 1890, 6; James D. Richardson (ed.), *Messages and Papers of the Presidents* (Washington: Government Printing Office, 1902), IX,

35-36, 122-125, 189, 309-312; J. S. Shriver (comp.), *Through the South and West with the President* (New York: *The Mail and Express,* 1891).

² William Appleman Williams, *The Roots of the Modern American Empire* (New York: Random House, 1969), ch. XII.

³ U.S., Senate, Committee on Finance, *Customs Tariffs: Senate and House Reports, 1888, 1890, 1894, 1897, 60th Cong., 2nd Sess., 1908, Senate Doc. No. 547* (Washington: Government Printing Office, 1909), 242-265; McKinley, Remarks of May 7, 1890: *Congressional Record,* 21:5:4247-4248 [hereafter cited as *CR,* 21:5:4247-4248]; *New York Tribune,* March 28, 1890, 6; *New York Times,* March 29, 1890, 5.

⁴ *New York Tribune,* April 16, 1890, 1; *New York Times,* March 25, 1890, 1; March 26, 1.

⁵ Robert M. Lafollette, *Autobiography* (Madison: University of Wisconsin Press, 1960), 49-50; Blaine to McKinley, April 10, 1890: quoted in Gail Hamilton [Mary Abigail Dodge], *Biography of James G. Blaine* (Norwich, Conn.: The Henry Bill Publishing Co., 1895), 683.

⁶ U.S., House Committee on Ways and Means, *To Reduce the Revenue and Equalize Duties on Imports, and for Other Purposes, 51st Cong., 1st Sess., 1890, House Report No. 1466* (Washington: Government Printing Office, 1890), 8-10, 14-15, 17; *New York Tribune,* March 28, 1890, 6; *New York Times,* March 29, 1890, 5; Memorandum to Harrison, June 4, 1890. The *New York Tribune* reproduced the substance of the memorandum. *New York Tribune,* June 19, 1890, 1-2. Blaine to Senator William P. Frye, July 11, 1890; as cited in *New York Tribune,* July 17, 1890, 2. *New York Times,* July 15, 1890, 4; July 16, 4; July 18, 4; *Bradstreet's,* July 19, 1890, 456.

⁷ *CR,* 21:4:3368.

⁸ The State Department version of the episode was reproduced in the *New York Tribune,* June 23, 1890, 1.

⁹ Margaret Leech, *In the Days of McKinley* (New York: Harper and Bros., 1959), 46; Remarks of May 7, 1890: *CR,* 21:5:4250; Remarks of September 27, 1890: *CR,* 21:11:10577. Miss Leech incorrectly asserts that the May attack upon Blaine was the only time that McKinley ever publicly derided a fellow Republican. Leech, *McKinley,* 46. *New York Tribune,* May 22, 1890, 1; *CR,* 21:6:5112-5113; Fred Wellborn, "The Influence of the Silver Republican Senators, 1889-91," *Mississippi Valley Historical Review,* XIV, No. 4 (March 1928), 471-472.

¹⁰ James D. Richardson (ed.), *Messages and Papers of the Presidents* (Washington: Government Printing Office, 1917), XIII, 6620-6622;

U.S., House Committee on Ways and Means, *Report of the Committee on Ways and Means Concerning Reciprocity and Commercial Treaties, 54th Cong., 1st Sess., 1896, House Report No. 2263* (Washington: Government Printing Office, 1896). A large number of newspapers, commercial associations, boards of trade, chambers of commerce, farmers' groups, and political conventions gave support to Blaine's reciprocity plan. Some of these included Democratic party state conventions. Even before Blaine made reciprocity a major public issue, some people expressed a strong interest in it in 1889. For sources, see *New York Tribune*, April 18, June 24, July 25, 26, 28, August 8, 15, 16, 28, 30, 31, September 5, 7, 9, 10, 18, 1890; *Chicago Tribune*, August 1, 1890, 1; August 7, 4; August 9, 4; *Bulletin of the American Iron and Steel Association*, August 20, 1890, 236; *Bradstreet's*, September 6, 1890, 566-567; *Iron Age*, August 7, 1890, 217. *National Archives of the United States of America*: Record Group 43, Records of the International Conference of American States, 1889-1890, Box No. 4, Entry 12; Box No. 8, Entry 17, [hereafter cited as *ICAS*]; Farmers' Union, Summit, Kansas, to John H. Anderson, M. C., December 21, 1889: *National Archives*, Record Group 233, Records of Congress, House File 51A-F15.9; Kansas City Commercial Club to Congress, May 6, 1890: ibid., Record Group 46, Records of Congress, Senate File 51A-J10; *Journal of the Proceedings of the Twenty-fourth Session of National Grange of the Patrons of Husbandry, Atlanta, 1890* (Philadelphia: J. A. Wagenseller, 1890), 47; *Indiana Farmer* XXV, No. 25 (April 26, 1890), 103; *Pacific Rural Press*, XXXVIII, No. 18 (November 1889), 517. For Cuban support of reciprocity, see *New York Tribune*, September 10, 1890, 7.

[11] *CR*, 21:7:6207; *New York Tribune*, June 19, 1890, 1-2; Richardson, *Messages* (1902 ed.), IX, 74.

[12] See footnote 6 above.

[13] *CR*, 21:7:6259; Hale, Remarks of September 2, 1890: *CR*, 21:10:9541.

[14] Blaine to Morrill, June 20, 1890: Justin S. Morrill Papers, Library of Congress; Andrew Carnegie to Gladstone, March 28, 1891: Andrew Carnegie Papers, Library of Congress [hereafter cited as Carnegie Mss.]; Hale, Remarks of September 2, 3, 1890: *CR*, 21:10:9541, 9601; *CR*, 30:2:2228-2229; *CR*, 21:10:9908; Harrison to Blaine, October 1, 1891: Volwiler, *Correspondence*, 202.

[15] *New York Tribune*, July 19, 1890, 4, July 26, 1; *CR*, 21:8:7733-7734; George Gray, Remarks of September 3, 1890: *CR*, 21:10:9600-

9611; Hilary Herbert, Remarks of September 27, 1890: *CR,* 21:11:10587-10589; George Vest, Remarks of July 2, 28, 1890: *CR,* 21:7:6916; 21:8:7803-7811; *Public Opinion,* June 28, 1890, 264-266; *Iron Age,* October 9, 1890, 599; Platt to Lynde Harrison, August 23, 1890: quoted in Louis A. Coolidge, *An Old-Fashioned Senator: Orville H. Platt of Connecticut* (New York: G. P. Putnam's Sons, 1910), 238. Also see *ibid.,* 235-238. Also see Franklin MacVeagh, "Foreign Trade and Reciprocity," *Bedford's Magazine* (June 1891), reprinted in *Literary Digest,* June 13, 1891, 172; Roger Q. Mills, "Reciprocity—Why Southward Only?" *Forum,* XI (May 1891), 268-275. The vote on the Hale Amendment when Senator Gray reintroduced it was 19 yeas, 38 nays, 27 absent. Two Democrats, both from Texas, voted no. *CR,* 21:10:9908-9909.

[16] *New York Tribune,* June 23, 1890, 1: Reed to McKinley, January 30, 1892: William McKinley Papers. See footnote 10 above.

[17] Blaine to Frye, July 11, 1890: as cited in *New York Tribune,* July 15, 1890, 2; also see *New York Times,* July 18, 1890, 4; Blaine to Louis A. Dent [July 23, 1890]: Louis A. Dent Papers, Southern Historical Collection, University of North Carolina Library [hereafter cited as Dent Mss.]. Dent was Blaine's personal secretary.

[18] Frye to Blaine, July 16, 1890; Blaine to Frye, July 22: as cited in *New York Tribune,* July 26, 1890, 1; also see *New York Times,* July 22, 1890, 4; July 23, 4.

[19] Blaine to W. W. Clapp, editor of the *Boston Journal,* September 15, 1890: as cited in *New York Tribune,* September 17, 1890, 1.

[20] *New York Tribune,* July 27, 1890, 6; the *Tribune* faithfully gave a detailed account of the fight for the reciprocity section of the McKinley Tariff. It consistently pictured Blaine as the noble leader battling the forces of ignorance. Still, the factual presentation of the *Tribune* was generally accurate. Subject to these qualifications, the *Tribune* is excellent source for the reciprocity fight. It published letters from Blaine's campaign for reciprocity and evidences of public support of the reciprocity program. The *New York Times* presented a less favorable account. It, however, concentrated its sarcasm on the high duties of the McKinley Bill and usually ignored reciprocity. Also consult J. Laurence Laughlin and H. Parker Willis, *Reciprocity* (New York: The Baker and Taylor Co., 1903), 183-206.

[21] J. F. Imbs to Blaine, June 19, 1890; Blaine to Imbs, June 19: as cited in the *New York Tribune,* June 20, 1890, 2. Imbs to Ferdinand

Schumacker, July 18, 1890 in Schumacher to John Sherman, [n.d.]; Wellington Milling Co. to Sherman, July 31, 1890: John Sherman Papers, Library of Congress.

[22] Louis A. Dent to Franklin D. Roosevelt, October 26, 1932: *Dent Mss.*

[23] Volwiler, *Correspondence,* 109-113; P. C. Cheney to Louis Michener, March 23, 1893: Louis Michener Papers, Library of Congress; Harrison to Blaine, July 23, 1890: Dent Mss.

[24] *CR* 18:1:273; Harrison to Blaine, July 17, 23, 1890: Volwiler, *Correspondence,* 109, 112; *New York Tribune,* August 29, 1890, 2.

[25] *New York Tribune,* August 29, 1890, 2.

[26] Ibid., August 31, 1890, 6.

[27] Ibid.; *Public Opinion,* September 6, 1890, 495-498; *Milwaukee Journal,* August 30, 1890, 1; *DesMoines Leader*, August 30, 1890, 1; *Burlington* (Iowa) *Hawkeye,* August 30, 1; *The Iowa State Register* (Des Moines), August 30, 1890, 1; *New Orleans Picayune,* August 30, 1890, 2.

[28] Harrison to Blaine, September 1 [?], 1890: Volwiler, *Correspondence,* 122; *New York Tribune,* August 31, 1890, 6; *New York Times,* September 2, 1890, 4; *New York World,* August 31, 1890, 4. Also see footnote 15 above.

[29] Quoted in *New York Tribune,* September 27, 1890, 5.

[30] Ibid., September 1, 1890, 6.

[31] Hamilton, *Blaine,* 687; David S. Muzzey, *James G. Blaine* (New York: Dodd, Mead and Co., 1934), 447; Charles R. Flint to William E. Curtis, August 8, September 2, 1890: *ICAS,* Box No. 4, Entry 12; John W. Foster to Aldrich, September 4, 1890; Flint to Curtis, August 21, 1890: Nelson Aldrich Papers, Library of Congress; Thomas F. McGann, *Argentina, the United States, and the Inter-American System, 1880-1914* (Cambridge: Harvard University Press, 1957), 169; *Bradstreet's* XVIII, No. 636 (September 6, 1890), 566-567. See Flint, "The United States and South America," *The South American Journal,* April 13, 20, 1889, 458-459, 502-504.

[32] See footnote 10 above.

[33] *CR,* 21:10:9943, 21:11:10641; McKinley, Remarks of September 27, 1890: *CR,* 21:11:10577. Republican Senators George F. Edmunds of Vermont and William M. Evarts of New York opposed the reciprocity section as unconstitutional and unworkable, but they did vote for the amended McKinley Bill, which included the reciprocity provision.

Evarts, Remarks of September 8, 1890: *CR,* 21:10:9882-9883; *CR,* 21:10:9909; *CR,* 21:11:10740; *New York Times,* September 1, 1890, 1. Because most of the votes were along party lines, it is very difficult to determine specifically the congressional support and opposition to reciprocity. Many House Republicans were more opposed to Blaine's lobbying tactics than to the reciprocity amendment. Congressman Robert R. Hitt, of course, was in favor of the plan. In the Senate, A. S. Paddock of Nebraska, Henry W. Blaire of New Hampshire, Shelby Cullom of Illinois, John C. Spooner of Wisconsin, Pierce, Frye, Hale, and Aldrich backed the administration. Senator John Sherman of Ohio doubted the feasibility of the program, but he voted for the amendment. *CR,* 21:4:3368; Paddock, Remarks of September 1, 1890; Frye, Remarks of September 2; Pierce, Remarks of September 3; Cullom, Remarks of September 8; Spooner, Remarks of September 8; Sherman, Remarks of September 2; *CR,* 21:10:9457, 9516, 9540-9544, 9605-9613, 9880; *New York Times,* September 13, 1890, 1. Speaker Reed caustically asked, "What is reciprocity?" Quoted in *New York Times,* September 13, 1890, 1; Vincent P. De Santis, *Republicans Face the Southern Question: The New Departure Years, 1877-1897* (Baltimore: Johns Hopkins University Press, 1959), 208; Stanley P. Hirshson, *Farewell to the Bloody Shirt, Northern Republicans and the Southern Negro, 1877-1893* (Bloomington: Indiana University Press, 1962), ch. VII.

³⁴ Kirk H. Porter and Donald Bruce Johnson (comps.), *National Party Platforms, 1840-1956* (Urbana: University of Illinois Press, 1956), 93, 107-108; Richardson, *Messages* (1902 ed.), IX, 122-123, 141-142, 180-181; Richardson, *Messages* (1917 ed.), XIII, 6620-6622.

³⁵ John C. Spooner to Henry C. Payne, September 11, 1890: John C. Spooner Papers, Library of Congress; Whitelaw Reid to William Walter Phelps, May 3, 1890: Whitelaw Reid Papers, Library of Congress [hereafter cited as Reid Mss.]; [?] Metcalf to W. C. P. Breckinridge, September 3, 1890: Breckinridge Family Papers, Library of Congress; Edward A. White, "The Republican Party in National Politics, 1888-1891," (Unpublished Ph.D. diss., University of Wisconsin 1941), 325, 430, 440-444, 451-57.

³⁶ See footnote 10 above. L. A. Levorsen to William E. Curtis, October 6, 1890: *ICAS,* Box Number 4, Entry 12; White, "The Republican Party," 451, 457-458; Richard Jensen, "The Winning of the Midwest: A Social History of Midwestern Elections, 1888-1896," (Unpublished Ph.D. diss., Yale University, 1967), Ch. VI; Paul Kleppner, *The*

Cross of Culture, A Social Analysis of Midwestern Elections, 1850-1900 (New York: The Free Press, 1970), Ch. IV. Also see Kleppner, "The Tariff as a Political Issue: The Democratic Case," Organization of American Historians, Los Angeles, April 1970.

[37] Edward Stanwood, *American Tariff Controversies in the Nineteenth Century* (New York: Houghton Mifflin Co., 1903), 308-311; Ida M. Tarbell, *The Tariff in Our Times* (New York: The Macmillan Co., 1911), 212-213.

[38] John W. Foster, *Diplomatic Memoirs* (Boston: Houghton Mifflin Co., 1909), II, 7; U.S., Senate Commitee on Finance *Commercial Arrangement with Brazil, 51st Cong., 2nd Sess., 1890, Senate Executive Document No. 66* (Washington: Government Printing Office, 1891), 1-4.

[39] U.S., House Committee on Ways and Means, *Report Concerning Reciprocity and Commercial Treaties, 9. Bradstreet's* XVIII, No. 621 (May 24, 1890), 327; *New York Tribune,* September 15, 1891, 6; *New York Times,* February 13, 1892, 1.

[40] U.S., Department of Commerce, *Historical Statistics of the United States, From Colonial Times to the Present* (Washington: Government Printing Office, 1960), 552, 554; Richardson, *Messages* (1902 ed.), IX, 312; Harold U. Faulkner, *Politics, Reform and Expansion, 1890-1900* (New York: Harper and Brothers, 1959), 109.

[41] *National Archives*: Record Group 59, Report Book 18, U.S., Department of State, 162-165, 167-171: cited in Allen Burton Spetter, "Harrison and Blaine: Foreign Policy, 1889-1893," (Unpublished Ph.D. diss., Rutgers University, 1967), 79-81.

[42] Blaine to Harrison, October 14, 1891: Volwiler, *Correspondence,* 187, 187 fn.

[43] Julius W. Pratt, *Expansionists of 1898* (Gloucester, Mass.: Peter Smith, 1959), chs. II, III.

[44] Harrison to Blaine, October 1, 1891: Volwiler, *Correspondence,* 202.

[45] Charles C. Tansill, *Canadian-American Relations, 1875-1911* (New Haven: Yale University Press, 1943), 435-437, and generally. See footnote 14 above.

[46] L. L. Snyder, "The American-German Pork Dispute, 1879-1891," *Journal of Modern History,* XVII No. 1 (March 1945), 16-28; John L. Gignilliat, "Pigs, Politics and Protection: the European Boycott of American Pork, 1879-1891," *Agricultural History,* XXXV, No. 1 (January 1961), 3-12; James Louis Erlenborn, "The American Meat and

Livestock Industry and American Foreign Policy, 1880-1896,'' (Unpublished M.S. thesis, University of Wisconsin, 1966), 16-17. Germany alone in 1880 imported $100,799,414 worth of pork and pork products from the United States.

[47] See footnote 46; Jeremiah M. Rusk, *Report of the Secretary of Agriculture, 1891* (Washington: Government Printing Office, 1892), 108; W. W. Phelps to Blaine, January 24, 1891; William F. Wharton to Phelps, June 6; Wharton to Count von Arco Valley, June 6; Phelps to Wharton, September 3; Wharton to Whitelaw Reid, June 15; Reid to Blaine, July 23; October 29, 30; November 16: all in U.S., State Department, *Foreign Relations of the United States, 1891* (Washington: Government Printing Office, 1891), Pt. I, 489-490, 493, 495, 501-502, 511-512, 517-518, 527-528; Harrison to Blaine, August 3, 1891; Blaine to Harrison, August 10; Reid to Harrison, October 9: Volwiler, *Correspondence,* 170, 170 fn, 173; Reid to Blaine, June 13, 1891; Reid to Harrison, October 9; Harrison to Reid, October 21: Reid Mss. Also see ch. VI. Erlenborn, "The American Meat and Livestock Industry and American Foreign Policy," ch. IV; Royal Cortissoz, *The Life of Whitelaw Reid* (New York: Charles Scribner's Sons, 1921), II, 151.

[48] Richardson, *Messages* (1902 ed.), IX, 308, 311-312, 329-330.

[49] Blaine, "The Presidential Election of 1892," *North American Review,* CLV, No. 432 (November 1892), 520-523.

[50] Manuscript entitled "The McKinley Bill" and dated "1890": Andrew Carnegie Mss. See Carnegie, "The McKinley Bill," *Nineteenth Century,* XXIX (June 1891), 1027-1036.

[51] *Bradstreet's,* April 12, 1890, 231.

[52] Donald M. Dozer, "Benjamin Harrison and the Presidential Campaign of 1892," *American Historical Review,* LIV, No. 1 (October 1948), 49-77; Jensen, "Winning the Midwest," ch. VI; Kleppner, *The Cross of Culture,* ch. IV.

[53] J. S. Clarkson to William B. Allison, September 11, 1890: William B. Allison Papers, Iowa State Department of History and Archives; U.S., House, Committee on Ways and Means, *Reciprocity and Commercial Treaties,* 147-545. Supporters of the reciprocity program included the National Board of Trade, the National Livestock Exchange, the National Association of Wool Manufacturers, the Southwestern Winter Wheat Millers' Association, the Winter Wheat Millers' League, the American Paper Makers' Association, the Louisville, and Nashville Railroad Company, the Baldwin Locomotive Works, B. F. Goodrich Company,

National Cash Register, the New York Board of Trade and Transportation, Associated Manufacturers, an association of agricultural implements makers for foreign sales, the Baltimore Board of Trade, the New Jersey State Board of Trade, the National Association of Manufacturers, the Armour and Cudahy meat packing companies, Parke-Davis Company, and Charles Pillsbury. The W. R. Grace Company was one of the few who were hostile or indifferent to the reciprocity program. *Ibid.* Also see Williams, *Roots of the Modern American Empire*, 393-396.

54 U.S., House, Committee on Ways and Means, *Reciprocity and Commercial Treaties*, 178.

55 Porter and Johnson, *National Party Platforms*, 107-108; *New York Times*, September 6, 1892, 1-2.

56 William McKinley, *The Tariff* (New York: Henry Clay Publishing Co., 1896), 161-165; McKinley, *Speeches and Addresses* (New York: Doubleday and McClure, 1900), 7; Richardson, *Messages* (1917 ed.), XIII, 6620-6622. Also see David Arganian, "McKinley and Commercial Reciprocity," (Unpublished M.A. thesis, University of Wisconsin, 1958).

Chapter 8

1 *Iron Age*, October 9, 1890, 599.

2 For example, see Edward Stanwood, *American Tariff Controversies in the Nineteenth Century*, II (Reissue; New York: Russell and Russell, 1967), ch. XVII; F. W. Taussig, *The Tariff History of the United States*, Introduction by David M. Chalmers (8th ed. red.; New York: G. P. Putnam's Sons, 1931), Pt. IV, Ch. VI; John R. Lambert, *Arthur Pue Gorman* (Baton Rouge: Louisiana State University Press, 1953), ch. X; Festus P. Summers, *William L. Wilson and Tariff Reform* (New Brunswick: Rutgers University Press, 1953), XIII; H. Wayne Morgan, *From Hayes to McKinley, National Party Politics, 1877-1896* (Syracuse: Syracuse University Press, 1969), 460-476; Allan Nevins, *Grover Cleveland, A Study in Courage* (New York: Dodd, Mead and Co., 1934), ch. XXXI; J. Laurence Laughlin and H. Parker Willis, *Reciprocity* (New York: The Baker and Taylor Co., 1903), ch. VIII.

3 See James Morrison Russell, "Business and the Sherman Act, 1890-

1914," (Unpublished Ph.D. diss., University of Iowa, 1966), 184-185.

⁴ U.S., House Committee on Ways and Means, *To Reduce Taxation, To Provide Revenue for the Government, and for other Purposes, 53rd Cong., 2nd Session, 1894, House Report No. 234* (Washington: Government Printing Office, 1894), 1-14; James D. Richardson (ed.) *Messages and Papers of the President,* (Washington: Government Printing Office, 1902), IX, 459, 552, 626, 741; Edward Atkinson to Charles Nordhoff, March 19, 1894: Edward Atkinson Papers, Massachusetts Historical Society [hereafter cited as Atkinson Mss.].

⁵ *Bradstreet's*, October 5, 1889, 631; May 16, 1896, 308-309; Cleveland to Vilas, July 25, 1894; Cleveland to Thomas C. Catchings, August 27; Allan Nevins (ed.), *Letters of Grover Cleveland, 1850-1908* (Boston: Houghton, Mifflin Co., 1933), 363-366. On the consensus see Charles S. Campbell, *Special Business Interests and the Open Door Policy* (New Haven: Yale University Press, 1951), chs. I, II; Ray Ginger, *Age of Excess: The United States from 1877 to 1914* (New York: The Macmillan Co., 1965), 53-55, 159, 185-187; Thomas J. McCormick, *China Market, America's Quest for Informal Empire, 1893-1901* (Chicago: Quandrangle Books, 1967), ch. I; Walter La Feber, *The New Empire* (Ithaca: Cornell University Press, 1963), ch. IV; Julius W. Pratt, *Expansionists of 1898* (Baltimore: Johns Hopkins University Press, 1936), 252-253; William Appleman Williams, *The Roots of the Modern American Empire* (New York: Random House, 1969), 293 ff. The phrase "conservative consensus" is taken from McCormick.

⁶ David A. Wells to William M. Springer, February 1, 1892: William M. Springer, *Tariff Reform the Paramount Issue* (New York: Charles L. Webster and Co., 1892), 319-322; Stanwood, *American Tariff Controversies*, II, 307-311; Henry J. Brown, "The National Association of Wool Manufacturers," (Unpublished Ph.D. diss., Cornell University, 1949), 403-405.

⁷ William E. Russell, "The Significance of the Massachusetts Election," *Forum*, XII (December 1891), 433-440; John E. Russell to W. C. P. Breckinridge, July 14, 1889; Oscar Lapham to Breckinridge, October 3, 1890: Breckinridge Manuscripts, Library of Congress [hereafter cited as Breckinridge Mss.]; Horace P. Tobey, Treasurer, Tremont Nail Co., West Wareham, Mass. to "Dear Sir"; Tobey to Benton McMillin; Tobey to William E. Russell, March 18, March 26, April 15, 1892; Russell to William L. Wilson, March 26, April 20, 1892; Wilson to Russell, May 5, 1892; Tobey to Edward Atkinson, April 15, 25, 1892;

Memorandum dated 1892 and entitled "Massachusetts' Iron Industry
. . . ."; Minutes of the Executive Committee of the Young Men's Demo-
cratic Club of Massachusetts, February 28, 1894; Address before Young
Men's Democratic Club of Massachusetts, March 14, 1894: all in Wil-
liam E. Russell Papers, Massachusetts Historical Society; *New York
Times*, September 19, 1890, 2; *Bradstreets'*, October 5, 1889, 630; U.S.,
Senate Committee on Education and Labor, *Relations between Labor and
Capital*, (Washington: Government Printing Office, 1885), I, 1079; *Con-
gressional Record*, 26:6:5165 [hereafter cited as *CR*, 26:6:5165]; Brown,
"National Association of Wool Manufacturers," 403-405; Geoffrey
Blodgett, *The Gentle Reformers: Massachusetts Democrats in the Cleve-
land Era* (Cambridge: Harvard University Press, 1966), viii-ix, 73-82,
94-98, 172; Summers, *Wilson*, 174. See Richard Hofstadter, "The Tariff
Issue on the Eve of the Civil War," *American Historical Review*, XLIV,
No. 1 (October 1938), 50-55; Stanley Coben, "Northeastern Business
and Radical Reconstruction: A Re-examination," *Mississippi Valley His-
torical Review*, XLVI, No. 1 (June 1959), 67-90; Thomas Monroe Pitkin,
"The Tariff and the Early Republican Party," (Unpublished Ph.D. diss.,
Western Reserve University, 187-201.

    [8] Summers, *Wilson*, 168-169, 174.

    [9] See supra, footnote 7; Roger Q. Mills, "New England and the Tariff
Bill," *Forum*, IX (June 1890), 361-370; John R. Russell to W. C. P.
Breckinridge, July 14, 1889; Edward Atkinson to Breckinridge, August
29, 1891: Breckinridge Mss.; William E. Russell to Richard Olney,
March 15, 1894: Grover Cleveland Papers; William E. Endicott, Jr. to
Olney, March 16, 1894; H. L. Higginson to Olney, November 18:
Richard Olney Papers, Library of Congress; Atkinson to William L. Wil-
son, August 3, 7, 1891; Clifton R. Breckinridge to Atkinson, March
15, 1892; November 8, 1893: Atkinson Mss.; William E. Russell to Wil-
son, February 10, 1891: William L. Wilson Papers, West Virginia
University Library [hereafter cited as Wilson Mss.]; Blodgett, *Mas-
sachusetts Democrats*, 172-175, 177-184; Harold F. Williamson, *Edward
Atkinson, the Biography of an American Liberal, 1827-1905* (Boston: Old
Corner Book Store, Inc., 1934), 147, 150-153, 160, 166-176, 179-190;
Horace Samuel Merrill, *William Freeman Vilas* (Madison: The State His-
torical Society of Wisconsin, 1954), ch. VI; Henry Watterson, *"Marse
Henry": An Autobiography* (New York: George H. Doran Co., 1919),
II, 138; Tom E. Terrill, "David A. Wells, the Democracy, and Tariff
Reduction, 1877-1894," *Journal of American History*, LVI, No. 3

(December 1969), 551. John A. Pickler, Remarks of January 13, 1894: *CR*, 26:1:796-799. Atkinson claimed to be nonpartisan, but he usually worked more closely with Democrats than with Republicans.

[10] Stege and Coldewey to W. C. P. Breckinridge, January 27, 1894; Richard H. Edmonds to Breckinridge, January 27, 1894: Breckinridge Mss.; *Manufacturers' Record*, December 15, 1893, 329-330; December 22, 350; December 29, 363-364; January 5, 1894, 377-379; January 26, 425.

[11] Blodgett, *Gentle Reformers*, 12, 188-189. See Brown, "National Association of Wool Manufacturers"; Pitkin "The Tariff and the Early Republican Party," 30-58, 150-151, 166-169.

[12] *Bradstreets'*, October 12, 1889, 647; E. Morris, Treasurer of Ottaquechee Woolen Company to Justin S. Morrill, May 22, 1894: Justin S. Morrill Papers, Library of Congress; Blodgett, *Gentle Reformers*, 193; Williamson, *Atkinson*, 188; Summers, *Wilson*, 168, 173-174; Brown, "National Association of Wool Manufacturers" 411ff.

[13] Paul Kleppner, *The Cross of Culture, A Social Analysis of Midwestern Elections, 1850-1900* (New York: The Free Press, 1970), ch. IV; Horace Samuel Merrill, *Bourbon Leader: Grover Cleveland and the Democratic Party* (Boston: Little, Brown, and Co., 1957), 146; Edward A. White, "The Republican Party in National Politics, 1888-1891," (Unpublished Ph.D. diss., University of Wisconsin, 1941), 441-444; Richard Joseph Jensen, "The Winning of the Midwest: A Social History of Midwestern Elections, 1888-1896," (Unpublished Ph.D. diss., Yale University, 1967), chs. VI, VIII. J. S. Clarkson to William B. Allison, November 15, 1894: William B. Allison Papers, Iowa State Department of History and Archives [hereafter cited as Allison Mss.].

[14] Cleveland to Wilson S. Bissell, March 1, 1892: Nevins, *Letters of Grover Cleveland*, 279.

[15] Cleveland to L. Clarke Davis, December 17, 1891; Cleveland to William L. Wilson, July 2, 1894: Nevins, *Letters of Cleveland*, 274, 354-357; *New York Times*, January 9, 1892, 1-2; Cleveland's annual messages, especially the 1887 annual message; Summers, *Wilson*, 165-167, 169.

[16] Richardson, *Messages*, IX, 396; *New York Times*, January 9, 1892, 1-2. Also see Robert Kelley, "Presbyterianism, Jacksonianism and Grover Cleveland," *American Quarterly*, XVIII, No. 4 (Winter 1966), 615-636.

[17] Jeanette P. Nichols, "The Politics and Personalities of Silver Repeal

in the United States Senate," *American Historical Review*, XLI, No. 1 (October 1935), 33-34, 52.

[18] Milton Friedman and Jacobson Schwartz, *A Monetary History of the United States, 1867-1960* (Princeton: Princeton University Press, 1963), ch. III, esp. pp. 331-334.

[19] Charles H. Jones, Editor of the *St. Louis Republic* to William L. Wilson, February 17, 1893: Wilson Mss.

[20] *CR*, 26:2:1796-1797.

[21] Nevins, *Cleveland*, 569-572; Stephen B. Elkins to Henry G. Davis, February 10, 15, 1894; S. G. Neale to Elkins, July 17, 20, 28; J. H. Manley to Elkins, August 29: Stephen B. Elkins Papers, West Virginia University; William E. Chandler to Whitelaw Reid, January 20, 1894: Whitelaw Reid Papers, Library of Congress [hereafter cited as Reid Mss.]; Matthew C. Butler to Henry Watterson, October 14, 1903: cited in James A. Barnes, *John G. Carlisle, Financial Statesman* (New York: Dodd, Mead and Co., 1931), 341-342; Lambert, *Gorman*, 207-214, 219-220, 224-226; John Alexander Williams, "Davis and Elkins of West Virginia: Business in Politics," (Unpublished Ph.D. dissertation, Yale University, 1967), 177-198. See U.S., Senate Special Committee to Investigate, *Attempts at Bribery, etc., Senate Reports Nos. 436, 457, 477, 485, 486, 487, 624, 1894* (Washington: Government Printing Office, 1895). A duty may be either *ad valorem* or specific. The former is geared to the price of an article, the latter to the quantity of an article. In an era of falling prices like the late nineteenth century, if duties were specific, tariffs automatically rose as prices fell. Understandably protectionists favored specific duties, tariff reductionists *ad valorem* duties.

[22] Cleveland to William L. Wilson, July 2, 1894: Nevins, *Letters of Cleveland*, 354-357.

[23] Watterson, *"Marse Henry,"* II, 134-139; Arthur Krock (ed.), *The Editorials of Henry Watterson* (New York: George H. Doran Co., 1923), 72-74; *Official Proceedings of the National Democratic Convention* (Chicago: Cameron, Amberg and Co., 1892), 82-92; Grober Cleveland to William C. Whitney, July 9, 1892: William C. Whitney Papers, Library of Congress: John Hay to Whitelaw Reid, [n.d.], quoted in Royal Cortissoz, *The Life of Whitelaw Reid* (New York: Charles Scribner's Sons, 1921), II, 181.

[24] *Washington Post*, July 27, 1894, 1-2; William L. Wilson to Editor, *New York World*, August 14, 1894; Diary, February 6, 1897: Wilson Mss.

[25] Henry Cabot Lodge to P. Richards, Jr., July 2, 1894: Henry Cabot Lodge Papers, Massachusetts Historical Society [hereafter cited as Lodge Mss.].

[26] *Public Opinion*, August 16, 1894, 461-462; August 23, 485-489; August 30, 511-513.

[27] Cleveland to Thomas C. Catchings, August 27, 1894: Nevins, *Letters of Cleveland*, 364-366; Richardson, *Messages*, IX, 552, 626, 741.

[28] Walter Q. Gresham to C. E. Byer, May 2, 1894: Walter Q. Gresham Papers, Library of Congress [hereafter cited as Gresham Mss.]. Roger Q. Mills, "The Wilson Bill," *North American Review*, CLVIII, No. 447 (February 1894), 242-243; William L. Wilson, "The Principle and Method of the New Tariff Bill," *Forum*, XVI (January 1894), 545.

[29] William L. Wilson to Editor, *New York World*, August 14, 1894; Diary, February 2, 1897; Wilson Mss.; Cleveland to Wilson, July 2, 1894: Nevins, *Letters of Cleveland*, 354-357; James A. Tawney, Remarks of January 25, 1894: *CR*, 26:2:1417-1419; *CR* 26:4:3936; Remarks of William D. Washburn, April 23, 1894: *CR* 3962-3993; *CR*, 26:4:3962-3963; *CR*, 26:5:4309, 4438; *CR*, 26:7:6058-6060; Frank Barny, Secretary, Millers' National Association to William B. Allison, June 15, 1894: Allison Mss.; Summers, *Wilson*, 201-202; Williams, *The Roots of the Modern American Empire*, 39, 367-370; Laughlin and Willis, *Reciprocity*, 237-239; James Louis Erlenborn, "The American Meat and Livestock Industry and American Foreign Policy, 1880-1896," (Unpublished M.S. thesis, University of Wisconsin, 1966), ch. V.

[30] Richardson, *Messages*, IX, 442, 639-640, 732-734; William Rockefeller, Pres., Standard Oil Company of New York to Secretary of State Walter Q. Gresham, January 4, 1894: *National Archives of the United States of America* [hereafter cited as *National Archives*], Record Group 59; Gresham to Isidor Straus, January 6, 1894: Gresham Mss.; *Bradstreet's*, February 3, 1894, 66. Richard Graham, *Britain and the Onset of Modernization in Brazil, 1850-1914*, IV of *Cambridge Latin American Studies*, eds. David Joslin and John Street (Cambridge: The University Press, 1968), 306-310; LaFeber, *The New Empire*, 197-300; Thomas J. McCormick, *China Market*, ch. II.

[31] U.S., Department of Agriculture, *Yearbook of the U.S. Department of Agriculture, 1894* (Washington: Government Printing Office, 1895), 9; Morton, "Farmers, Fallacies, and Furrows," *Forum*, XVII (June 1894), 385-393; Morton quoted in Horace Samuel Merrill, *Bourbon Leader: Grover Cleveland and the Democratic Party* (Boston: Little,

Brown and Co., 1957), 170; *Manufacturers' Record*, April 28, 1893, 231; Williams, *The Roots of the Modern American Empire*, 39, 358-359, 367-370.

[32] U.S., House Ways and Means Committee, *Reciprocity and Commercial Treaties; 54th Cong., 1st Sess., 1896, House Report No. 2263* (Washington: Government Printing Office, 1896); *Bradstreet's*, April 4, 1896, 209. Also ibid., July 3, 1897, 424; August 7, 498-499; National Board of Trade to [U.S., House of Representatives], February 13, 1896: *National Archives*, Record Group 233, H. R. 54A-H11.6); *Manufacturers' Record*, November 9, 1894, 221; Williams, *Roots of the Modern American Empire*, 393-396; Paul W. Glad, *McKinley, Bryan, and the People* (New York: J. B. Lippincott Company, 1964), 97.

[33] *Bradstreet's*, January 12, 1895, 24; W. P. Wilson, "The Philadelphia Commercial Museum," *Forum*, XXVII (October 1899), 113-118; *Bradstreet's*, June 20, 1896, 387; McKinley's speech as quoted in Albert K. Steigerwalt, Jr., *The National Association of Manufacturers, 1895-1914: A Study in Business Leadership*, Michigan Business Studies, XVI, No. 2 (Ann Arbor: University of Michigan Business Research, 1964), 21. Also see McKinley's remarks at the Lincoln Banquet of the Marquette Club, *Chicago Tribune*, February 13, 1896, 1-2.

[34] *New York Tribune*, August 27, 1896, 1-2; Thomas C. Platt to Wharton Barker, June 7, 1895: Wharton Barker Papers, Library of Congress [hereafter cited as Barker Mss.]; James S. Clarkson to Samuel Fessenden, October 15, 1896: James S. Clarkson Papers, Library of Congress; Whitelaw Reid to Stephen B. Elkins, March 17, 1896; John Hay to Reid, August 31: Reid Mss.; Wm. McKinley to C. A. Boutelle, August 1, 1896; Wm. M. Osborne to McKinley, September 1: William McKinley Papers; Warner P. Sutton to Wm. E. Chandler, June 25, 1896: William E. Chandler Papers, Library of Congress; *Review of Reviews* XIV, No. 5 (November 1896), 548; H. Wayne Morgan, *From Hayes to McKinley, National Party Politics, 1877-1896* (Syracuse: Syracuse University Press, 1969), 489; Margaret Leech, *In the Days of McKinley* (New York: Harper and Bros. 1959), 142; Shelby M. Cullom, *Fifty Years of Public Service* (Chicago: A. C. McClurg and Co., 1911), 274; Glad, *McKinley, Bryan and the People*, 108-109, 179, 182; Stanley L. Jones, *The Presidential Elections of 1896* (Madison: The University of Wisconsin Press, 1964), 93.

[35] Henry Cabot Lodge to Theodore Roosevelt, December 2, 1896: Henry Cabot Lodge (ed.), *Selections from the Correspondence of Theo-*

dore Roosevelt and Henry Cabot Lodge, 1884-1918 (New York: Charles Scribner's Sons, 1925) I, 241; *Memoirs of Lyman J. Gage* (New York, House of Field, Inc., 1937), 122; *Review of Reviews,* XV, No. 1 (January 1897), 15; XV, No. 6 (June, 1897), 648-649; XVII, No. 1 (January 1898), 10; Laughlin and Willis, *Reciprocity,* 568.

[36] U.S., Senate Committee on Finance, *Customs Tariffs, Senate and House Reports, 1888, 1890, 1894, 1897, 60th Cong., 2nd Sess., 1908, Doc. No. 547* (Washington: Government Printing Office, 1909), 423-425; Statement of John A. Kasson, January 10, 1900 in U.S., Senate Committee on Foreign Relations, *Reciprocity Convention with France, 56th Cong., 1st Sess., 1899, Senate Doc. No. 225* (Washington: Government Printing Office, 1900), 69; Nathaniel Wright Stephenson, *Nelson W. Aldrich, A Leader in American Politics* (New York: Charles Scribner's Sons, 1930), 139-148. Also see Laughlin and Willis, *Reciprocity,* chs. IX, X. On allegations that the rates of the Dingley Tariff were raised in anticipation of reciprocal trade agreements, see Lewis L. Gould, "New Perspectives on the Republican Party, 1877-1913," *American Historical Review,* LXXVII, No. 4 (October 1972), 1079-1080 fn.

[37] Charles Hoffmann, *The Depression of the Nineties, An Economic History* (Westport, Conn.: Greenwood Publishing Corp., 1970), 279-280; Taussig, *Tariff History,* 331-333; Charles S. Olcott, *The Life of William McKinley* (Boston: Houghton Mifflin Co., 1916), I, 351; Stephenson, *Aldrich,* 139-148.

[38] *Washington Post,* October 15, 1897, 4; *Bradstreet's,* October 16, 1897, 657. Neither the *Post* nor *Bradstreet's* specified the source of this pressure. Edward Younger, *John A. Kasson, Politics and Diplomacy from Lincoln to McKinley* (Iowa City: State Historical Society of Iowa, 1955).

[39] Younger, *Kasson,* ch. XIX; Tom Edward Terrill, "An Economic Aspect of the Spanish-American War," *Ohio History,* LXXVI, Nos. 2 and 3 (Winter and Spring 1967), 73-75, 100.

[40] U.S., Senate Committee on Foreign Relations, *Reciprocity Convention with France,* 63-81, 94-162; John Ball Osborne, "Expansion through Reciprocity," *The Atlantic Monthly,* LXXXVIII, No. 80 (December 1901), 726-730; *New York Times,* February 27, 1900, 6; George W. Wells, President and Treasurer, American Optical Co. to William B. Allison, January 1, 1900; Theodore C. Search, President, National Association of Manufacturers to Allison, January 7; W. H. Bower to Allison, January 3; Justice, Bateman and Co. to Allison,

January 23; same to same, February 2; Bradner W. Lee, Chairman, Republican Party Central Committee, California to Allison, February 2; Ontario-Cucamonga Fruit Exchange to Allison, February 5; The Iowa Farming Tool Co. to Allison, February 6; Hervey Lindley to Allison, February 6; Stephen T. Gage to Allison, February 7; James A. Carr, Vice President, Hoosier Drill Co. to Allison, February 8; Chandler and Taylor Co. to Allison, February 10; George S. Hensel, President, Hensel Colladay Co. to Allison, February 10; M. Austin, Treasurer, The Plano Manufacturing Co. to Allison, March 10; Robert Mather, Second Vice President, Chicago, Rock Island and Pacific Railway Co. to Allison, March 12; F. S. Kretsinger, President, The Iowa Farming Tool Co. to Allison, April 18; Russell W. Knight, President, New England Butt Co. to Allison, February 13: The Kursheedt Manufacturing Co. to Allison, March 13; James Leffel and Co. to Allison, February 8; Newark Embroidering Works to Allison, March 29; National Braid Co. to Allison, February 8; Charles F. Quincy to Allison, February 6; David C. Beaman, The Colorado Fuel and Iron Co. to Allison, November 30, 1901; Austin A. Burnham, General Secretary, National Business League, October 9: all in Allison Mss; E. J. Gibson, "Reciprocity and Foreign Trade," *Forum*, XXXII (December 1901), 470-471; *Manufacturer's Record*, January 25, 1900, 2-3; February 8, 37-38; *Review of Reviews*, XXIV, No. 6 (December 1901), 647-648; Shelby M. Cullom, *Fifty Years of Public Service* 374-375; Younger, *Kasson*, 375-376; Lilyan Sydenham, "McKinley Reciprocity, 1897-1903," (Unpublished M.A. thesis, University of Virginia, 1953), 149-150. On Allison's change see Allison to Theodore Roosevelt, November 2, 1901: Allison Mss.

[41] U.S., Senate Committee on Foreign Relations, *Reciprocity Convention with France*, 63-64, 66-81, 135; *Protectionist*: quoted in Laughlin and Willis, *Reciprocity*, 336. Also see Kasson to William B. Allison, October 18, 1898: Allison Mss.; Kasson's remarks to the Illinois Manufacturers' Association, *New York Times*, October 25, 1901, 8; *Chicago Tribune*, October 25, 3. This speech was reprinted as "Information Respecting Reciprocity and the Existing Treaties" (Washington: Government Printing Office, 1901).

[42] *New York Times*, March 10, 1901, 1; *Washington Post*, January 31, 1900, 4; Olcott, *Life of McKinley*, II, 296; James D. Richardson (ed.), *Messages and Papers of the Presidents* (Washington: Government Printing Office, 1917), XIII, 6435, 6465; Henry Cabot Lodge to Paul Dana, December 7, 1889: Lodge Mss.; Lodge to Nelson W. Aldrich,

June 20, 1901: Nelson W. Aldrich Papers, Library of Congress; Stephenson, *Aldrich,* 171, 450 footnote 10. John A. Kasson, "Impressions of President McKinley, with Especial Reference to his Opinions on Reciprocity," *Century,* LXIII, Old Series (December, 1901), 275; H. Wayne Morgan, *William McKinley and His America* (Syracuse: Syracuse University Press, 1963), 462-466.

[43] *New York Tribune,* April 30, 1901, 1-2; May 1, 4; May 2, 1-2; May 4, 3; Leech, *In the Days of McKinley,* 576-579; H. Wayne Morgan, *William McKinley and His America,* 512-520; Olcott, *Life of McKinley,* I, 126.

[44] Richardson, *Messages* (1917 ed.), XIII, 6620-6622.

[45] Ibid.: Olcott, *Life of McKinley,* II, 300; Walter Wellman, "The Last Days of William McKinley," *Review of Reviews,* XXIV, No. 4 (October 1901), 417.

[46] Robert M. Lafollette, *Lafollette's Autobiography: A Personal Narrative of Political Experiences* (Madison, Wis.: The Robert M. LaFollete Co., 1913), 115.

[47] U.S., Tariff Commission, *Reciprocity and Commercial Treaties* (Washington: Government Printing Office, 1919), 33-34, 36-38, 317-322, 361-381.

[48] Henry Cabot Lodge to William B. Allison, May 11, 18, 1904; Theodore Roosevelt to Allison, May 5: Allison Mss.; Roosevelt to Nicholas Murray Butler, August 12, 1902; Roosevelt to Joseph B. Bishop, April 27, 1903; Roosevelt to Lodge, May 11, 23, June 2, 1904; Roosevelt to Elihu Root, June 2, 14: Elting E. Morison et al. (eds.), *The Letters of Theodore Roosevelt* (Cambridge: Harvard University Press, 1951-1954), III, 313, 471-472; IV, 796, 803, 812-813, 833; Stephenson, *Aldrich,* 179-180; Kirk H. Porter and Donald Bruce Johnson (comps.) *National Party Platforms, 1840-1964* (Urbana: University of Illinois Press, 1966), 138-139; Henry F. Pringle, *Theodore Roosevelt* (New York: Harcourt, Brace and World, Inc., 1956), 241, 291-292; James Ford Rhodes, *The McKinley and Roosevelt Administrations, 1897-1909* (Port Washington, N. Y.: Kennikat Press, 1965), 220, 292; George E. Mowry, *The Era of Theodore Roosevelt, and the Birth of Modern America, 1900-1912* (New York: Harper and Row, 1958), 127-129; U.S., Tariff Commission, *Reciprocity and Commercial Treaties,* 209-215, 227-261.

[49] *Bradstreet's,* September 7, 1901, 561; October 26, 674; December 21, 805; *Proceedings of the National Reciprocity Convention Held under*

the Auspices of the National Association of Manufacturers, November 19-20, 1901 (Washington: n.p., 1901); Nath. French, Corresponding Secretary, Tri-City Reciprocity League, Davenport, Iowa to William B. Allison, February 10, 1904; William I. Buchanan to Allison, September 27, 1905; C. N. Stoddard to Allison, November 22; L. G. Krumm to Allison, November 25; Alvin H. Sanders, Chairman, American Reciprocal Tariff League, December 14: Allison Mss.; Younger, *Kasson,* 379; *Review of Reviews,* XXV, No. 1 (January 1902), 8, 18. Also see U.S., Industrial Commission, *Report of the Industrial Commission* (Washington: Government Printing Office, 1901), XIV, 235, 587-588, 592; Sydenham, "McKinley Reciprocity," 132-134.

⁵⁰ U.S., Department of Commerce, *Historical Statistics of the United States, Colonial Times to 1957* (Washington: Government Printing Office, 1960), 550; *Bradstreet's,* June 8, 1901, 354-355; *New York Times,* February 22, 1898, 6; *Review of Reviews,* XIX, No. 2 (February 1899), 147; *Literary Digest,* XXIII (July 27, 1901), 96-97; *New York Tribune,* May 8, 1901, 3; *Bradstreet's,* August 7, 1897, 498-499; January 1, 28, 1898, 1, 66-67; Statement of W. P. Wilson, Director of the Philadelphia Commercial Museum, *Report of the Industrial Commission,* XIV, 440; David E. Novack and Matthew Simon, "Commercial Responses to the American Export Invasion, 1871-1914, An Essay in Attitudinal History," *Explorations in Entrepreneural History,* III, No. 2, Second series (Winter, 1966), 121-147; Cleona Lewis, *America's Stake in International Investments* (Washington: Brookings Institution, 1938), 578 ff; *Report of Industrial Commission,* XIV, 231, 235, 343-344, 456, 473, 475, 508, 661, 702; Augustos O. Bacon, *Discrimination in Prices between Domestic and Foreign Consumers of Our Protected Goods* (Washington: 1904), 4-5: cited in McCormick, *China Market,* 28-29; Matthew Simon, "The United States Balance of Payments, 1876-1896" in *Trends in the American Economy in the Nineteenth Century* (Princeton: Princeton University Press, 1960) 711; Alfred D. Chandler, Jr., "The Beginnings of 'Big Business' in American Industry," *Business History Review,* XXXIII, No. 1 (Spring 1959), 1-31.

⁵¹ Richard C. Edwards, "Economic Sophistication in Nineteenth Century Congressional Tariff Debates," *The Journal of Economic History,* XXX, No. 4 (December 1970), 829-838.

⁵² Finley Peter Dunne, *Mr. Dooley: Now and Forever,* ed. Louis Filler (Stanford: Academic Reprints, 1954), 269.

⁵³ Platt to Wharton Barker, November 15, 1892: Barker Mss.

[54] William F. Draper, Remarks of January 13, 1894: *CR*, 26:1:802.

[55] Hurd, Remarks of April 29, 1884: *CR*, 15:4:3549.

[56] *New York Tribune*, October 8, 1892, 1; Richardson, *Messages and Papers of the Presidents* (1917 ed.), XIV, 6620-6621.

[57] Brooks Adams, "Reciprocity or the Alternative," *The Atlantic Monthly*, LXXXVIII (August 1901), 145-155.

[58] R. A. Rempel and Tom E. Terrill, "Conflict in the Atlantic Community: The Tariff Controversy, Great Britain and the United States, 1880-1914," Organization of American Historians, April 1972. See Rempel, *Unionists Divided: Arthur Balfour, Joseph Chamberlain and the Unionist Free Traders* (Newton Abbot, England: David and Charles, 1972.

[59] Watterson, *"Marse Henry,"* II, 205.

Bibliographical Essay

Government documents were the single most important source of material for this study, especially the *Congressional Globe* and the *Congressional Record*. Congressional hearings, *Messages and Papers of the Presidents, Foreign Relations of the United States,* and government reports provided valuable insights. A candid expression of American foreign policy toward Hawaii, which was articulated as early as the 1870s, is recorded in U.S., House Committee on Ways and Means, *Hawaiian Treaty, 44th Cong., 1st Sess., 1876, House Report No. 116* (Washington: Government Printing Office, 1876). The issues raised and debated here bear striking resemblance to the issues involved in American expansion after 1895. Two convenient references were U.S., Senate Committee on Finance, *Customs, Tariffs: Senate and House Reports, 1888, 1890, 1894, 1897, 60th Cong., 2nd Sess., 1909, Sen. Doc. No. 547* (Washington: Government Printing Office, 1909), and U.S., Tariff Commission, *Reciprocity and Commercial Treaties* (Washington: Government Printing Office, 1919). The contents of reciprocity treaties, ratified or not, reflect the tactics of the American expansionist strategy developed by the protectionists in the Gilded Age. A comparison of U.S., Senate Committee on Foreign Relations, *Treaty between the United States and Mexico, 47th Cong., 2nd Sess., 1884, Sen. Ex. Doc. No. 75* (Washington: Government Printing Office, 1884) and U.S., Senate Committee on Foreign Relations, *Reci-*

procity Convention with France, 56th Cong., 1st Sess., 1899, Sen. Doc. 225 (Washington: Government Printing Office, 1900) shows how the McKinley Administration elaborated upon and altered earlier Republican reciprocity treaties to develop a more comprehensive reciprocity treaty with France. This shift reflected the confidence that emerged in the 1890s in the ability of American manufacturers to compete with European manufacturers. The shift may also indicate that American leaders had come to doubt the capacity of Latin America to absorb enough of what was believed to be the excess production of American factories. Finally, McKinley may have genuinely feared a tariff war with Europe.

The Republican-controlled Congress of 1895-1896 found considerable popularity among various interest groups for reciprocal trade agreements. The report, U.S., House Committee on Ways and Means, *Reciprocity and Commercial Treaties, 54th Cong., 1st Sess., 1895* (Washington: Government Printing Office, 1898), was released the same year that McKinley appointed the Reciprocity Commission. The reports of two commissions proved very valuable: U.S., House Committee on Foreign Affairs, *Report of the Central and South American Commissioners, 48th Cong., 2nd Sess., 1885, House Ex. Doc. No. 226* (Washington: Government Printing Office, 1885); ibid., *49th Cong., 1st Sess., 1886, House Ex. Doc. No. 50* (Washington: Government Printing Office, 1886); and U.S., House Committee on Ways and Means, *Report of the Tariff Commission, 47th Cong., 2nd Sess., 1882, House Misc. Doc. No. 6* (2 vols.: Washington: Government Printing Office, 1882).

Tariff hearings had limited value since the focus of this study was on the political elite, not interest groups. Of these hearings, I found the most interesting recorded in U.S., House Committee on Ways and Means, *Revision of the Tariff, 51st Cong., 1st Sess., 1890* (Washington: Government Printing Office, 1890) and, from the same committee *Import Duties and War Tariff Taxes, 48th Cong., 1st Sess., 1884, House Report No. 792* (Washington: Government Printing Office, 1884). The former preceded the drafting of the McKinley Tariff Bill, and the latter, the Morrison Tariff Bill of 1884. I frequently turned to U.S., Department of Commerce, *Historical Statistics, From Colonial Times to 1957* (Washington: Government Printing Office, 1961). And, of course, I found David A. Wells' reports as Special Commissioner of Revenue very useful, especially the *Report of the Special Commissioner of Revenue, 1868* (Washington: Government Printing Office, 1868) and ibid., *1869* (Washington: Government Printing Office, 1869).

Wells developed his ideas about tariff reduction and trade expansion more thoroughly after 1870. Of his voluminous publications, the best are a three-part article, "How Shall the Nation Regain Prosperity?" that appeared in the *North American Review* in 1877 (No. 125, pp. 110-132, 283-308, 544-556); a two-part article in the August and September 1887 issues of *Contemporary Review* (pp. 275-293, 381-400); and his book, *Recent Economic Changes* (New York: D. Appleton and Co., 1890) that has implications beyond the limits of my study. Wells' writing and thinking also graphically demonstrated the failure of most American expansionists to grasp the contradictions inherent in their logic. They assumed the United States could rise to preeminence in world markets without risking serious disruptions in the international order. This contradiction and his anglophilism, for instance, allowed Wells to launch a vigorous attack upon President Cleveland's policy during the 1895 Venezuelan boundary crisis in his *The United States and Great Britain in America and Europe* (New York: G. P. Putnam's Sons, 1896). Brooks Adams had a more realistic, if somewhat overdrawn analysis: "Reciprocity or the Alternative," *The Atlantic Monthly*, LXXXVII (August 1901), 145-155. Lloyd C. Cardner has reproduced this essay in *A Different Frontier, Selected Readings in the Foundations of American Economic Expansion* (Chicago: Quandrangle Books, 1966).

In addition to the Wells' and Adams' articles, other important articles and items appeared in the periodicals of the day. Of these the most helpful were the *Forum* and *North American Review*. Prominent political, business, and, occasionally, labor organization figures wrote essays for both. In their attempts to present a wide range of views, these periodicals differed significantly from E. L. Godkin's *Nation*. More scholarly essays usually appeared in such journals as the *Journal of Political Economy* and the *Quarterly Journal of Economics*. Some trade journals and bulletins of a more limited range provided some needed details and important insights. Among these were *Bradstreet's*, *Commercial and Financial Chronicle*, *Iron Age*, the *Bulletin of the National Association of Wool Manufacturers*, the *Bulletin of the American Iron and Steel Association*, and the publications of the American Protective Tariff League and the tariff reduction groups. The *Manufacturers' Record* left a significant record of strong southern protectionist sentiment. *Public Opinion, Review of Reviews*, and *Literary Digest* furnished useful surveys of a broad spectrum of newspaper opinion and periodicals.

Generally, newspapers only supplied useful details and perspectives.

Beyond this the *New York Tribune* performed a very significant function. In consistently presenting its ideas on the tariff, it also reported many of the major activities of James Blaine and his faithful following. In view of the extremely limited Blaine Papers (Library of Congress), the *Tribune* was essential, but it had to be carefully balanced by other sources. Too often the *Tribune* equated Washington with Blaine. For instance, it seriously underestimated the role of President Harrison in the struggle to secure the reciprocity amendment to the McKinley Tariff and Harrison's central role in the development of the reciprocal trade program of his administration. An excellent example of Blaine's thinking about reciprocity and his persuasive skills can be found in U.S., Senate, *Reciprocity Treaties with the Latin American States, 51st Cong., 1st Sess., 1890* (Washington: Government Printing Office, 1890).

The *Chicago Tribune* presented the more moderate tariff views of a large body of midwestern Republicans. The *New York Evening Post* did the same for the more extreme tariff reductionists. The *New York Times,* the *New York Herald,* and the *New York Tribune* published articulate, differing editorials on the tariff. The difficulties of being both inclined to protectionism and a loyal southern Democratic newspaper were reflected in some of the ambivalent editorials of the *Atlanta Constitution.*

Although published materials supplied most of the material for this study, manuscript collections had an important place. The David A. Wells Papers (Library of Congress) and the Edward Atkinson Papers (Massachusetts Historical Society) revealed much about the thinking, activities, and frustrations of the tariff reductionists. So did the Thomas F. Bayard Papers (Library of Congress). Bayard often engaged in reflective and interesting correspondence, rather than the cryptic type found in many collections of political leaders. Festus P. Summers graciously shared his notes and some photocopies of the William L. Wilson Papers, which reflected Wilson's intellectual inclinations and the struggles of this low tariff congressman from the late 1880s through the 1894 fight over the Wilson-Gorman Tariff Act. The Samuel J. Randall Papers (University of Pennsylvania) furnished important insights into the assumptions, reasoning, and labors of the Democratic protectionists. The Randall Papers also contain a virtual catalogue of southern Democrats who supported high tariffs and an industrial South. The Blaine Republicans were followed in the extensive, valuable Whitelaw Reid Papers (Library of Congress). The John Sherman Papers (Library of Congress) and the William B. Allison Papers (Iowa State Department of History and Archives) are large, usually dull collections, but they reflect the difficulties of two ambitious senators who tried to reconcile tariff conflicts within Republican ranks, to resolve patronage disputes among the party faithful in their respective states, and to bolster their chances for higher office.

Among the presidential papers, the most helpful collections were those of Cleveland and Harrison. Both presidents sent and received a number of thoughtful letters. In both cases, too, scholars have made very useful editions of these papers. See Allan Nevins (ed.), *Letters of Grover Cleveland, 1850-1908* (Boston: Houghton Mifflin Co., 1933) and Albert T. Volwiler (ed.), *The Correspondence of Benjamin Harrison and James G. Blaine, 1882-1893* (Philadelphia: The American Philosophical Society, 1940). The latter contains some interesting material on the elusive Blaine. Also of considerable importance were *The Messages and Papers of the Presidents,* edited by James D. Richardson.

Every student of the tariff in nineteenth-century America should review two standard texts: Frank W. Taussig, *The Tariff History of the United States,* Introduction by David M. Chamlers (Eighth rev. ed.; New York: Capricorn Books, 1964) and Edward Stanwood, *American Tariff Controversies in the Nineteenth Century* (Boston: Houghton Mifflin, 1903). Both, however, are biased. Taussig's free trade inclinations show throughout. His main purpose was to determine the actual economic impact of American tariffs. The data and the model available to him precluded his making an adequate answer. Yet, his work has had considerable influence on subsequent interpretations of American tariff history, and his book is still useful. Stanwood was related by marriage to Blaine, and they were good friends, as is reflected in Stanwood's biased account. Still, Stanwood presents a reliable descriptive narrative of the politics of the tariff, the main intent of his book. To these two, James L. Laughlin and J. Parker Willis, *Reciprocity* (New York: Baker and Taylor, 1903), should be added. Laughlin and Willis shared Taussig's biases. They also thought that Republican reciprocity was a sham and that Blaine was either a knave or a buffoon. They almost completely miss the political significance of the Republican drive to implement reciprocity treaties in the 1890s. Still, Laughlin and Willis made a good detailed analysis of reciprocity sections in the McKinley and Dingley Tariff Acts and of the contents of the resulting treaties.

I owe substantial debts to other scholars. William Appleman Williams, *Tragedy of American Diplomacy* (Rev. ed.; New York: Dell Publishing Co., 1962) gave me some crucial insights, particularly into the close ties between domestic and foreign policy. In attempting to make sense of the diplomacy of the Gilded Age, I found two books invaluable: Walter LaFeber, *The New Empire, An Interpretation of American Expansionism 1860-1898* (Ithaca: Cornell University Press, 1963), and David M. Pletcher, *The Awkward Years: American Foreign Relations under Garfield and Arthur* (Columbia: University of Missouri Press, 1962). Charles Callan Tansill's *The Foreign Policy of Thomas F. Bayard, 1885-1897* (New York: Fordham University Press, 1940) is too uncritical, but it is thorough and reproduces some important correspondence at length.

In their very different ways, Geoffrey Blodgett in *The Gentle Reformers: Massachusetts Democrats in the Cleveland Era* (Cambridge: Harvard University Press, 1966) and Horace Samuel Merrill in his *Bourbon Democracy in the Middle West, 1865-1896* (Baton Rouge: Louisiana State University Press, 1953) and *Bourbon Leader: Grover Cleveland and the Democratic Party* (Boston: Little, Brown and Co., 1957) taught me a good deal about the Cleveland Democrats and their efforts to remain dominant in the Democratic party. Blodgett's analysis of the mentality of the Cleveland Democrats greatly clarified one of the political enigmas of the Gilded Age. Thomas F. McGann's *Argentina, the United States, and the Inter-American System, 1880-1914* (Cambridge: Harvard University Press, 1957) greatly simplified the task of analyzing the Pan-American Conference of 1889-1890. Of the numerous documentations and descriptions of the social disruption and discontent of the Gilded Age, John Higham's *Strangers in the Land, Patterns of American Nativism, 1860-1925* (New York: Atheneum, 1963) and Robert H. Weibe's *The Search for Order, 1877-1920* (New York: Hill and Wang, 1967) were the most satisfying and helpful of the generalized studies.

Recently, significant efforts to understand the Gilded Age as it expressed itself politically have been made, based on the concepts and methods of political science. Walter Dean Burnham found important fluctuations in the size of voter turnout during the nineteenth and twentieth centuries ("The Changing Shape of the American Political Universe," *American Political Science Review*, LIX, No. 1 [March 1965], 7-28). Burnham has also written a good, succinct essay about the constituencies of the major parties in American history. See Burnham, "Party Systems and the Political Process," in *The American Party Systems, Stages of Political Development*, eds. William Nisbet Chambers and Walter Dean Burnham (New York: Oxford University Press, 1967), Ch. X. The same volume contains a striking essay by Samuel P. Hays: "Political Parties and the Community-Society Continuum," Ch. VI. Also see Hays' "The Social Analysis of American Political History, 1880-1920," *Political Science Quarterly*, LXXX, No. 3 (1965), 373-394. Nineteenth-century voter behavior has been intensively examined in three other good, though uneven, studies: Paul Kleppner, *The Cross of Culture, A Social Analysis of Midwestern Elections, 1850-1900* (New York: Free Press, 1970); Richard Joseph Jensen, "The Winning of the Midwest: A Social History of Midwestern Elections, 1880-1896" (Unpublished Ph.D. dissertation, Yale University, 1967); and Samuel Thompson McSeveny, "The Politics of Depression: Voting Behavior in Connecticut, New York, and New Jersey, 1893-1896" (Unpublished Ph.D. dissertation, University of Iowa, 1965). These have eased my task and, hopefully, made it more rewarding.

Biographies figured significantly in the research for this volume. Only those most important for my purposes will be cited. Allan Nevins wrote two of these: *Grover Cleveland: A Study in Courage, 1850-1908* (New York: Dodd, Mead and Co., 1932) and *Abram Hewitt, With Some Account of Peter Cooper* (New York: Harper and Bros., 1935). Both are solid works, although Nevins was too sympathetic to Cleveland and Hewitt. More seriously, his use of only one of Cleveland's character traits as his central frame of reference made understanding Cleveland difficult, if not impossible. But the thoroughness of Nevins' work, including excellent indices, has put Gilded Age scholars lastingly in his debt. Merrill's biography of Cleveland, cited above, is a better interpretation of the Democratic leader. Other useful biographies include Leland L. Sage, *William Boyd Allison: A Study in Practical Politics* (Iowa City: State Historical Society of Iowa, 1956); George F. Howe, *Chester A. Arthur: A Quarter-Century of Machine Politics* (New York: F. Ungar Publishing Co., 1935); Harold F. Williams, *Edward Atkinson: The Biography of an American Liberal* (Boston: The Old Corner Book Store, Inc., 1934); David Saville Muzzey, *James G. Blaine, a Political Idol of Other Days* (New York: Dodd, Mead and Co., 1934); John R. Lambert, *Arthur Pue Gorman, 1839-1906* (Baton Rouge: Louisiana State University Press, 1953); Edward L. Younger, *John A. Kasson: Politics and Diplomacy from Lincoln to McKinley* (Iowa City: State Historical Society of Iowa, 1955); Margaret Leech, *In the Days of McKinley* (New York: Harper and Bros., 1959); H. Wayne Morgan, *William McKinley and his America*

(Syracuse: Syracuse University Press, 1963); and Summers, *William L. Wilson and Tariff Reform* (New Brunswick: Rutgers University Press, 1953). Gail Hamilton [Mary Abagail Dodge], *Biography of James G. Blaine* (Norwich, Conn.: The Henry Bill Publishing Co., 1895) is uncritical, but it reproduces some important correspondence and has some interesting first-hand impressions. To help me clarify the eastern Democrats' attempts to contain the silverites by emphasizing tariff reduction, George McJimsey kindly let me read the typescript of his *The Gentile Partisan: Manton Marble, 1836-1917* (Ames: Iowa State University Press, 1971).

The early evolution of Republican protectionism has received some able treatment that supplied needed background. See Stanley Coben, "Northeastern Business and Radical Reconstruction: A Re-examination," *Mississippi Valley Historical Review,* XLVI, No. 1 (June 1959), 67-90; Richard Hofstadter, "The Tariff on the Eve of the Civil War," *American Historical Review,* XLIV, No. 1 (October 1938), 50-55; and Thomas M. Pitkin, "Western Republicans and the Tariff in 1860," *Mississippi Valley Historical Review,* XXVII, No. 3 (December 1940), 401-420. The last is taken from a good dissertation: Pitkin, "The Tariff and the Early Republican Party," (Unpublished Ph.D. dissertation, Western Reserve University, 1935). Other specialized studies used included David Arganian, "McKinley and Commercial Reciprocity," (Unpublished M.A. thesis, University of Wisconsin, 1958); Duan Marshall Leach, "The Tariff and the Western Farmer," (Unpublished Ph.D. dissertation, University of Oklahoma, 1964); and Clarence Lee Miller, *The States of the Old Northwest and the Tariff* (Emporia, Kan.: *Emporia Gazette* Press, 1929). Another valuable dissertation is an excellent study of the wool manufacturers' highly successful lobby: Henry J. Brown, "The National Association of Wool Manufacturers," (Unpublished Ph.D. dissertation, Cornell University, 1949). For a suggestive view of William D. "Pig Iron" Kelley, see Ira V. Brown, "W. D. Kelley and Radical Reconstruction," *Pennsylvania Magazine of History and Biography,* LXXXV (July 1961), 316-329.

Finally, the vital importance of farm exports in the Gilded Age is illustrated in John L. Gignillat, "Pigs, Politics and Protection: The European Boycott of American Pork, 1879-1891," *Agricultural History,* XXXV, No. 1 (January 1961), 3-12; Morton Rothstein, "America in the International Rivalry for the British Wheat Market, 1860-1914," *Mississippi Valley Historical Review,* XLVII, No. 3 (December 1960), 401-418; and

L. L. Snyder, "The American-German Pork Dispute, 1879-1891," *Journal of Modern History*, XVII, No. 1 (March 1945), 16-28. These have been greatly amplified and are given a much broader interpretive framework in William Appleman Williams, *The Roots of the Modern American Empire, A Study of the Growth and Shaping of Social Consciousness in a Marketplace Society* (New York: Random House, 1969).

Index

295